TRIGGERED

Triggered

JOE R
MEYER

CONTENTS

Dedicated to those who often go misunderstood, where ones thoughts can only truly be expressed by written word, the beauty of a blog, unfiltered, raw and myself. Thank you to my loved ones, wife, daughter, sister, father for letting me be me, this is the truest expression of myself.

FOREWORD

Writing is in my blood; it's the place that gives a voice to the world and what better place to do that in in a blog. For years I have kept my voice to myself, I have kept silence in my opinions, my thoughts. Having heard of blogging and journaling. It was until I began my blog that I truly felt free to write what I thought, unencumbered and unafraid to speak my mind. Blogging has been so free to my voice and my writing as I continue to write weekly on topics such as celebrations, social issues, politics, mental health and anything I truly feel too.

It was not until I began writing novels that I came to realize that I should put my blogs into a book, realizing that what if my blogs suddenly disappeared, never to be seen again as my voice is locked into each of my blogs. Its also acts as a small time capsule to the times , the adversity, the happiness that I experienced during the years writing my blogs which began in June 2019. I can truly say now, I was going through a transition of happiness and anxiety as I was in a role that I enjoyed but had been under great stress since the winter of 2018, afraid of my job security. This was also a time when Mikaylah was starting kindergarten and we had moved so life seemed to be going well, until it didn't, which is the story of my life for the most part. This was also a time when I had a great loss, the loss of my teaching role which I loved, due to the college being insolvent, out of business for financial reasons, a truly painful time as I was teaching college since 2011.

Since 2019 I have struggled greatly with work, in the forms of being laid off and fired along with financial, mental health struggles, raising a family and just trying to be financially secure. Wrapped into this blog is my pain, happiness, emotions, anger, hate, love and all the emotions one can experience, as I often wrote about all moments in my life. I want to give you the reader to share with me this point in time. Since beginning my blog I have written hundreds of pieces, which I will placing in multiple volumes, as you the reader will see the change in me over time as I my voice has grown, become more impassioned I will continue to write for one main reason, its my form of therapy, its my outlet to what I go through each day, its my madness within a few blocks of text. In addition, I write these blogs as a form of history for my daughter and family to have if I am no longer here. It is my hope you enjoy my pieces as much as I enjoyed writing them. Happy reading!

PART 1 -MENTAL HEALTH

| 1 |

Mental Illness, The Struggle and Being Victorious!

July 9, 2019

Mental Illness is Not a dirty word

Mental illness, a word that many will hear and associate with many different things, some look at mental illness as a taboo when it comes to talking about the subject. Although it seems like society is adjusting to the subject being blasted across the news, the news doesn't truly display the damage Mental illness does. The reason I know is because I used to suffer from mental illness, but it took a lot of work to get where I am today.

Growing up Mental illness wasn't really a subject I spoke about and it definitely wasn't spoken to me, but I suffered. It is my belief it started when I was in my teens, but it was created by events that affected my life. I can only speak for me, but maybe what I have to resonates with those who read this. Growing up I had a Mother, a Father, Grandparents, Aunts,

Uncles, Cousins like most, but the factor that stood out for me was the involvement those in my life had, especially during the most critical stages in my life.

This may go in a little into my story, so I apologize, but this will provide some context to hopefully examine how I may have developed mental illness in the first place. This is not to cry about my story or play victim, as many those who read this may say well I have had it a lot worse than you, so let me tell you. I know those who suffer from mental illness have probably had worse situations that caused mental illness.

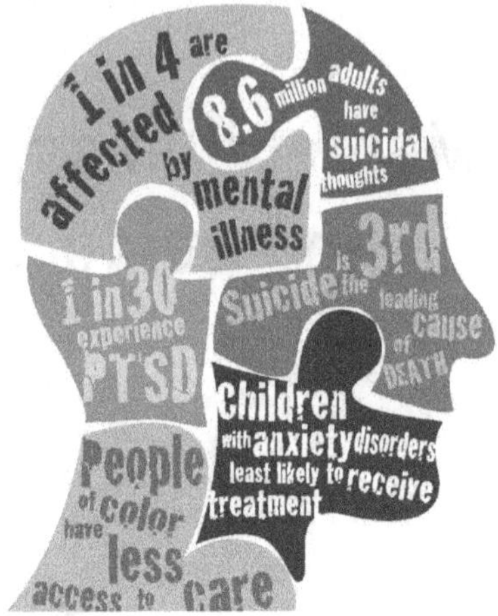

The Story of My Struggle

Growing up like I mentioned I grew up fairly average upbringing, like I mentioned I had a Mother, Father, who were divorced at a young age, but has been in life until now. When Mom and Dad divorced, we were not equipped to live on our own, so at the time my Mother searched for her long lost father, who she found, a man who hadn't been in her life for decades, but she felt the need to find him, a decision I wish I could have advised her not too. Due to the divorce, we went to go live with him in a tiny 1 bedroom apartment for me and my sister.

Growing up this man began what would be considered abuse that would affect me for the rest of my life, nothing physical all verbal and emotional as a strict disciplinarian who would act as my father, make in stand in the corner when I misbehaved, yell at me, call me names, use profanity when ever he had the chance. The point in my life is kind of blurb except those things, I don't remember the happy moments, but I am sure there were some or many. My mother was our defender, but at the same time she was helpless unable to support herself, probably due to her own mental , physical and emotional abuse she suffered growing up. My mom pretty much did everything she could to keep it going for me and my sister , she did work, but it was never enough to get out of poverty, as we continued to depend on my grandfather.

This cycle went on until the day she died in 2015, free at last as she depended on him, during the years of dependence she develop sicknesses, probably due to the amount of stress he imposed on her and all of us, but as Kids and Teens, it affects us differently until we get old enough to understand and process the evil affect evil people have on you. Through my teens, it progressed even worse with the verbal abuse at times I was pushed around, as he bullied his way into subjecting me manual labor, not chores, physical manual labor because he had no one else to do it. Again I can't say I remember those years, it's amazing how it's all blocked out if and when I had fun as a child and a teen, but there are instances.

Every day growing up, the same routine, called stupid for the most part growing up, told I wouldn't amount to anything and for the most part I believe it, which I feel has affected me to this day. The other side of the coin many may ask is where was your father, like I mentioned he was in our lives on a weekend basis, but even that seemed like a getaway to not being told how stupid or worthless I was. Spending time with my father, I can say I feel he does love me, but was never a man to show it, maybe that was one of the reasons my mother and father didn't last. I understand that all men are different, some are and many are not emotional , but I really did look for that in my father. I looked for someone to talk to me, hug me, tell me he was proud of me, I don't remember that ever happening growing up, but I am sure it happened.

Those Who Were Supposed to Be There

Combined with the two men in my life who were supposed to offer the support I needed, I didn't get. Mom was there, but when it comes to a boy and his father, those relationships I believe have an effect over a boy who one day turns into a man mental stability and just overall stability . In high school around the age of 17/18 that's when my mental health really started to decline, slowly at first.

Like many experienced sadness, some hopefulness, fear of the future, and of course all the emotions a teen is going through trying to figure out who I was, I can say maybe my feelings where not A-typical but it was A-typical for me, because I didn't feel in control anymore, on top of that I was bullied by high school staff. After high school, went off to college, mental heath quickly spiraled out of control as I not only homesick, but I didn't have a grasp on what was happening to me, I did seek help in High school and college seeing the psychologist, but that's all it was no meds at this point.

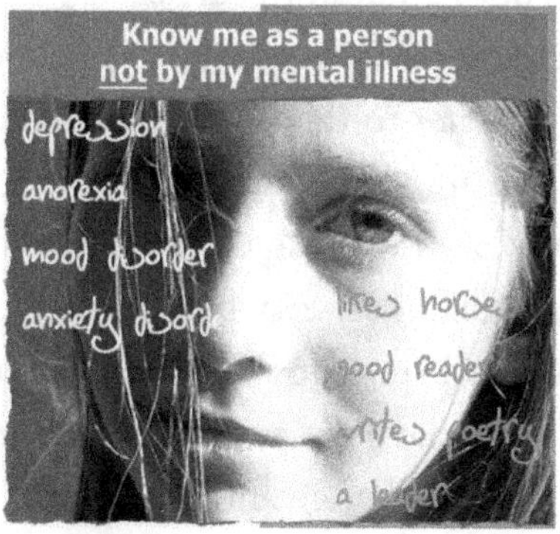

I quickly left college and went back home, as my mental health was spiraling out of control, I was an emotional wreak, now living back home about to be emotional abused again, this time I was older, my grandfather felt it necessary to be even harder on me, making my life a daily hell to live under his roof, i quickly move in Dad. Moving in with dad allowed to have some freedom, but it will refer to that Blog entitled : Saying Goodbye to the House of Evil .

If you have gotten to this point, then you must want to know how I overcame my mental illness, first I was not easy, from 1997 - 2008 those were probably the toughest years of my life, years that I am sorry to say I caused a lot of damage to myself mental, emotionally and even professionally. I was on medications for a number of years, went to to see psychologist and psychiatrists , especially after a every hard time in February 2007 when I was hospitalized. I share this with you because there is a light at the end of tunnel, I may seen hopeless and at times you do feel like giving up, up don't give up, I can say that if I had, I would not have what I have to day which is my wife and daughter who I love dearly.

Where It Has Lead Me

Mental illness many times does go unnoticed, because from many like myself who suffered we were told and felt it's best not to say anything and be a downer to those around us. I understand its hard subject to talk about, because in many cases you do talk about it and it really is a down subject, but it doesn't have to be, it can be an open dialogue to what is going on with a person and it's best just to listen, don't be afraid to ask question and learn to understand, have patience because mental illness can cause an individual to change and act differently which is nothing to do with you in most cases, we are just trying to cope the best way we can. We know its hard on family and friends to see us like that and you may feel helpless, but a listening ear and a shoulder to cry on is sometimes what we need, we don't need others trying to solve the issues of our life for us.

Other ways I have been able to cope is exercise, eating right, putting aside the little things that don't matter, live in the now, spend time with those you love, try to enjoy life and know tomorrow will be better and know in the long run you are stronger then you think, I know I am. I think the Joseph from 2007 would have cracked by know will all the pressure I have now taking care of a family, jobs, money stresses, but at the end of day my life is better here on earth with them and those around you feel the same way.

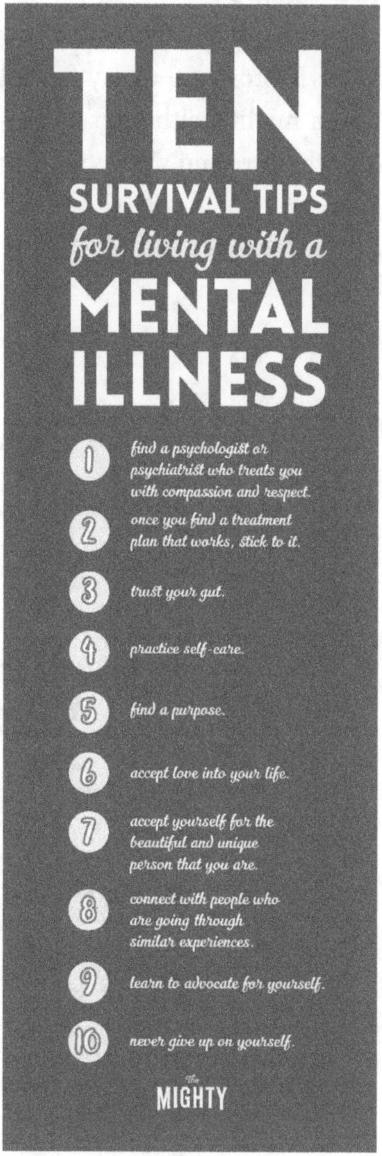

Invest in yourself, as for myself, that is why writing is one of passions, that allows me to express myself each day, something no one can take a way.

Be strong, Your are strong!

If you do feel like you can't cope please speak with someone like a as Pastor, due to my faith, has strengthen me in having peace in my life, although life will never be perfect, there are those who care and who will listen.

| 2 |

Dealing with Stress, Depression During Holidays

December 4, 2021

The holidays can be one of the most difficult times to get through lasting two long months of November to December starting as early as October for some as the reminders start to come earlier each year. Thanksgiving and especially Christmas can lead to many to fall into depression and even many leading to suicide. One can wonder but understands the holidays are stressful, lonely and for many a huge financial cost of being merry.

As someone who has struggled with depression and anxiety, I know the pressures many face during these times. Over years the pressure has not led up to those hard times, but I feel them always around the corner. Growing up in Los Angeles, south central Los Angeles to be exact, a place know for high crime, violence and gangs.

Part of what led to my depression during those times was the fact that I had a grandfather who verbally abused me from childhood and the holidays were a stressful time and not a time of joy , even on Christmas day, but mom tried. The happiest moments were filled with the delicious smells of moms cooking, where a turkey, a ham or roast and of course got to drink soda pop and eat sweets, a tradition I carry on today.

To me the holidays are one of the most important times to spend with family, putting aside the gift giving, but just time to connect with each other. Some may not always have those individuals in their life especially a good friend which makes these times particularly difficult. Even for someone who now has my personal life in a much better place then years past it can still be stressful with everywhere you go, stores filled, covid, and always money never being enough.

Its amazing how many of equate money to happiness especially during these times, but there are some practical ways to minimize the stress that accompany the holidays.

Look on the Bright side and be positive is a good start but not reflecting on the things you think are more valuable than your mental health like material things. Self-care is really what gets you through these times, whether its exercising, eating right and working to relax.

What can be especially stressful is family themselves, especially around the dinner table and lets not forget the discussions whether its politics and religion which can make many uneasy and even angry. Setting boundaries can help everyone involved know what is expected and what will not be tolerated "Whether it be making your own schedule, telling someone how things will be different this year or simply saying "No", setting boundaries and being your own boss can hep you with stress and guilt."

As mentioned, money issues can overwhelm individuals and families during this time of the year as we want to give to our families and children but trying to do that when making ends meet which can be daunting for many. Make a budget for all you will need for the holidays and try your best to stick to it. It may not be worth it to overextend yourself and then having to pay for it later.

Dealing with the loss of a loved one

The year was 2015, December 9th to be exact when my mother unexpectedly passed away as myself, my wife, daughter and sister were at the happiest place on earth Disneyland. I will never forget that year which despite my family being there was lonely and incredibly sad. Feelings of grief and loss often compound around the holidays. Remember its ok to take time to cry and express your feelings, and you can not force yourself to be happy during the holiday season.

Its so important to reach out if your feeling lonely and isolated, which can be easy during these COVID times. Local groups, churches or other community organization have support groups to engage either by phone, in person or by web and social media. If you are feeling stress during the holidays talk to a friend, or family about your concerns, try reaching out with a text, a call or video chat.

For some, COVID is the first thing that comes to mind when thinking of holiday stressors. Many continue to weigh the pros and cons of celebrating with family this year. It's a very difficult choice to make when you or someone close to you is high risk. When you have family members who aren't particularly impacted or concerned about COVID, it can create additional complications, they are less likely to take safety precautions during a gathering and more likely to pressure you to attend.

Reach out to a counselor or professional if you are struggling and your ability to cope is unsuccessful, don't go at it alone.

Let's all try to enjoy these times, take a deep breath as you step into the malls, but if malls overwhelm you, shop online and let the professionals deliver to you. Kick up, relax, enjoy a tall glass of eggnog (Yum) , a hearty meal and don't forget to watch your holiday classics, mine are Christmas Vacation and It's a wonderful Life.

If you do need to talk to someone reach out to :

National Suicide Prevention Lifeline: 800-273-8255

| 3 |

Living In Regret and How to Overcome It

September 11, 2021

Regret can be something that eats away at you if you don't rectify it quickly and gain some perspective. Many of you may agree with this statement as I have come to reflect on regret a lot in my life and I think many of us do at times. To put this in perspective, recently I started a new job which also includes new incredible people. These new colleagues are so incredible it caused me to reflect on my own regrets in my life especially since graduating Uni.

My new colleagues in many different age groups from mid-twenties to fifties and older have opened my eyes to how little I have lived in life. One of the common themes I soon realized is how little I have really traveled in my life, something I have yearned to do since college but never did. Many of my co-workers have been all over the United States and abroad listing many great places they have been.

In a way I am envious of their life although I know we should not feel envy for others because we all live our lives differently. One thing is for sure from age of twenty I have truly been asleep to seeing the world and what it has to offer. I would have loved to travel abroad when younger, live in different states and take control of my independence at an earlier age.

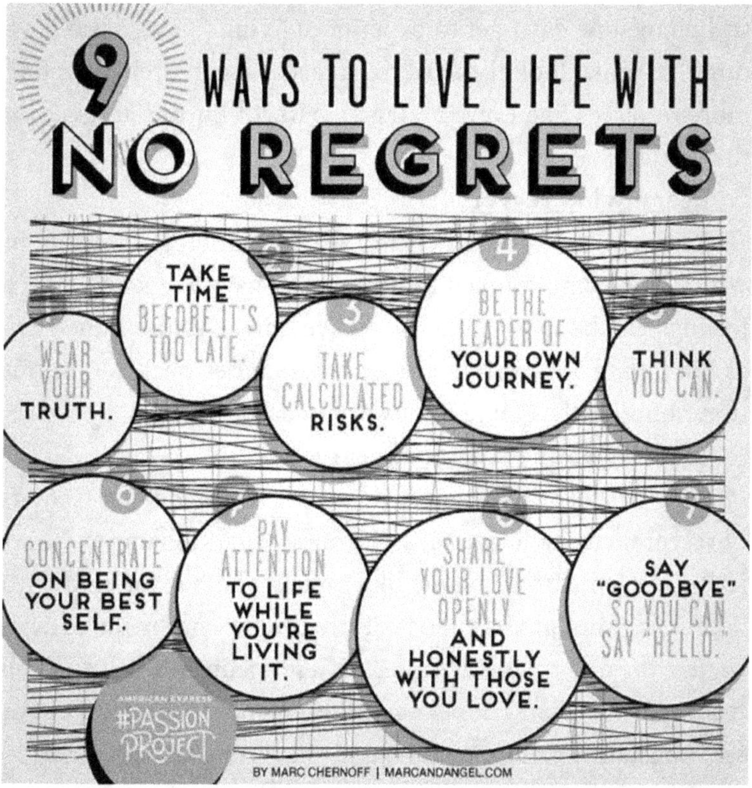

Even it seems many who are young such as right out of college appear to have more eye opening experience then I have. It could be they had a different upbringing of those who encourage them to travel, live life different and experience life before settling down. Not to say you can not do those things later in life with a family but its just more difficult.

For example there has always been one place I yearn to live in Oregon, a place although I don't have a lot of connections to loved from the moment I traveled there. The trees, the smell of pine, the calmness of the state and just everything there and I truly hope one day I get to experience living there. I also have other dreams I look forward to experience definitely traveling more to places like London, Japan, parts of Europe and within the United States.

Learn what regret is

Regret is considered a critical way of thinking or feeling in which you blame yourself for things that have happened. These feelings can be over things you have done and not done such as not taking a job offered, not saving money or it can even it something really simple in our day to day lives.

Identify your feelings of regret

This will all be different from person to person, but feelings of regret include: sadness, loss, remorse, anger, shame and anxiety. Coupled with someone like myself who has suffered with depression and anxiety most of my life this has made it even harder on my psyche at times. These feelings can leave you feeling defeated and hopeless, thinking about what you did or said constantly thinking you are in the wrong all the time.

Consider where the regret comes from

I know many of us are not psychologist but feelings of regret can from many different areas in our life such as :

- **Lifestyle**
- **Work**
- **Family**
- **Children**
- **Marriage**

All of these areas have very impactful parts in our life especially family, where many can feel regret for having a family or not having one, getting married and not getting married and even having children. Some of you reading may feel you have lived your life exactly how you have wanted although life is never perfect you have not allowed regret to stop your life plan. For others who live in constant regret here are some ways to over come those feelings.

Get therapy

Talking to someone, a professional may be the answer to really dig deep into your mind on where and why these feelings affect you so much.

Write down your regrets

I am definitely someone who encourages everyone to write out there thoughts, get them on paper or in a blog somewhere where you can release those feelings. That is truly one of reasons I write on this blog so that others can see what I go through and attempt to help each other. With regret, people often wonder "Why" they acted or didn't act, and this is often where people become stuck. List your regrets and any questions you keep asking yourself.

Learn your lesson

Once you deal with regret and write down or talk to someone about your regrets, maybe now would be the time to correct those regrets if possible. Try to look for lessons learned and recognize the life lessons and go from there. We all have the ability to restart so if there are regrets and you can accomplish them now, go out and do it.

Apply what you have learned

Once you have learned your lesson go out and change those behaviors and never look back. Know you have the ability to change, making sure to apply the wisdom you've gained.

Control how regrets influence your future and life

While you can not change what has happened in the past, you can choose how past effects your present and future. All too often we continue to live in the past, could of , should of , would of. Taking control and know tomorrow is another day to make a new goal, a new accomplishment and move on from regret.

Your Journey is your own, don't live it in regret

Once we get past understanding regret, living with it and moving on from it then maybe we can start to breath again and no we will not let regret determine our future. Give yourself a break, cut yourself some slack in beating yourself up over past regrets and practice a new mindset. Continue to write out your thoughts and feelings releasing any future regrets and practice self-forgiveness which I feel makes all the difference. Know that we all make mistakes in life, errors in judgment but some of us have an easier time moving on others do not , but we can all change that.

Lastly I think it so important we are around the right people, many times we are around those who affirm our regrets making us feel worse, but in reality we need to have empathy and understanding. Continue to learn and grow from how we think so we can all learn to be healthier minded people, it will make our world and the world a better place.

| 4 |

The Loss of Enjoyment in These Times and How to Ge

September 18, 2021

We are times many of us have never experienced before due to COVID-19 pandemic with so much loss of life and being forced to stay home for our protection and the protection of others. We are all going through this situation differently. For someone like myself who has a family, a wife and daughter to support has had the privilege to work from home which includes my full-time job and teach in the evenings.

Life appeared to be going great in January when I finally getting back to work from losing my job in October and I was very excited until this pandemic completely turned our lives inside out in a flash. Living in the United States and more specifically California we are in a very populated state which went into lock down very quickly.

We all have our Story

My employer immediately put the employee's health first by allowing us to work from home, in addition to the college I teach out be allowed to teach in an online format. Employers have had to adjust the way we are allowed to work which hopefully has opened the eyes of employers on how we can all work from home and still be successful.

I have been home since March 16th with wife and child on lock down as my daughters' school is now part of the stay a home order which I am now also home schooling while working. Some of you may be saying ok get to the point.

The point is that due to being locked down the loss of enjoyment is in reach and for many it has arrived as there is literally nowhere to go and even those places we are able to go is typically the market or fast food we must hurry back home once again. Yes we do have parks which are still open and if those were closed I feel many of us would not be able to handle this situation.

I am someone who has experienced deep depression and still do from time to time, so being locked down has caused me to lose enjoyment in my life at this time. That doesn't mean I don't love my family and want to support them, but it means mentally and physically I am being affected on a different level. I will feel angry at times, I feel tired, I feel frustrated, I feel on the edge and I will withdrawn at times as I try to work out still a way to cope with these changes.

The Hardest Part

The hardest part of this situation is being home all the time, as I am someone who has to be out and about. Although I get to have a nice stroll in the park regularly, I no longer feel the need to be around people during this time and many of us have this fear of the people we are around especially strangers who may pass the virus to us causing us to take it home and infect our families a fear we should all have.

I know it's easy to say don't live in fear, but that is exactly what is happening now as many I see do not following proper protocols of covering up, washing hands and just staying home increasing the chances the virus spreading. I get that we will have a vaccine at some point, but I will not be right now. In addition, the addition of the News and Media really amplify what is happening with COVID-19. I get the media has a job to do, which is based on ratings which equals money.

Being the United States we have every form of news one can imagine from CNN to Fox to Local to Specialty the list goes on which adds to the voices of confusion which in my view adds to playing on peoples fears especially when imagery is used to suck the viewer in. This in affect causes panic which leads for many like myself into depression and fear, not something we should be striving for.

Loss of enjoyment is real and its happening now but there are ways to control our reaction and limit how we feel. Here are some ways we can get back our enjoyment and be more positive in these times:

Focus on what you can control

Fear and depression can make us feel powerless. Additionally, add in anxiousness of what is going on today limiting your view to such areas of "I can't see my friends", " The stock market taking a dive" and "The fear of getting sick".

While you cannot control your feelings or the actions of others, you are not powerless. Shifting your attention to those things you can control can restore your sense of urgency and self-confidence.

Things you can control such as what you eat , your daily routine such as exercise and self care. All of these things matter on focusing our energy on the positive.

Limit Your Media Intake

As mentioned earlier media intake can really play to our fears, in my cases it actually has caused me to grow angrier. Of course, we want information on the pandemic, but really limit how much you watch and from whom you get your information. I find we live in the world of opinion which are NOT back by facts. Social Media and News are probably two areas I have found myself to have to limit because of just the pure amount of hate and negativity online.

If you notice yourself getting agitated, fearful or depleted when you're seeking news, then time for a beak. Very likely, the general guidelines of "Wash your hands" and "Maintain Social distance" will not change if you take a few hours to disconnect.

People are working to make it better

While many of us are at home remember there are those who are working diligently to find a curse and end this pandemic so we can all get back to somewhat normal. After listening to the media its easy to start to believe the negative voices like "The government isn't doing anything", "Doctors don't know what they are doing," or "People don't respect the guidelines"

There are also those stories of hope, although we have to search for those they do exist as those who give a helping hand, families coming together and sharing with those in need. Your depression and anxiety can minimize from hearing these stories.

Invest in Uplifting

As mentioned there are ways to be uplifted during this time but we need search for it by surrounding yourself with uplifting media, people , activities and thoughts can help encourage a more optimistic mindset. Find those things that bring you comfort, such as reading a good book or writing. I find comfort in Writing, Reading, teaching and remembering those positive times in my life. We can do these things and will change our mindset and get us through these dark times .

Set a personal goal

One of the best ways I have found to get through tough times is to set personal goals such as learning a new skill. Being at home does not me that is the end to self-learning or making new goals such as saving money such as creating a plan post pandemic. Continuing to take steps towards your personal and career goals can also help you maintain hope throughout all this.

Do your part

Lastly, remember that if you are reading this and looking for hope remember you are doing your part. You, along with society have all been asked to do something extraordinary and stay home, protect ourselves, loved ones and society. I can't stress this enough this will end, why add to the confusion by being angry, being a jerk in society. I get people feel powerless, but you are not focus on what is important. I know this is easier said then done as people are unemployed, low on money, can't pay the bills which are all important facts, but lets try our best to through this and live to fight another day.

Hope is on the way

Hopefully this brings you some comfort and guide to help get through this pandemic and bring back our enjoyment in life and realize what is important. Obliviously I can't tell you what is important that is up to you, but to start family, friends, living is all important. Make your plan, stick to it and before you know it we will be on the road to recovery, it can and will happen and we will prosper in the end believe that.

| 5 |

Why I Have so Much Trouble with My Self-Worth

September 5, 2021

Where it All Begin

Throughout my life from a wee lad I have always been someone who felt I had no value in this life as I grew up with a mother, father, sibling, aunts and uncles the whole nine yards. But early in my childhood after Mom and dad divorced and we moved in with my grandfather it was never the same. I admire my mom for trying to keep us safe, feed and clothed but in my opinion, she made a serious miscalculation on this arrangement.

You see my mother who was now a single mom with two kids at the time didn't have a lot of financial prospects and career for that matter, so she found a way once again for us to survive. My father was not a bad father, he didn't abuse us or anything, but I feel he just wasn't ready to be a father and it showed because it was like pulling teeth to get him to spend time with us as a family. Today its very different because we are older, more mature and he is in his senior years so life is very different for him.

The life change that changed it all for me

Once we moved in with my grandfather, a man my mother had loss contact with for many years because he was not in the picture was a man to be reckoned with was a harsh disciplinarian who acted as if he was my father with his harsh words of put downs on a daily basis. This was starting around the age of five mind you and we lived with him until my sister and I moved out, but mom stayed behind.

The damage was surely done after close to fifteen years of his insults, put downs and vulgarities took a toll on my mental health and ultimately my self-worth. Add to that that I was the overweight kid most of life, pudgy and cute but still overweight and if any of you know what that's like, teases, bullying, taunts is not a very help physical attribute when your questioning your self-worth.

The struggled continued

Late in my teens I did seek counselors to help me through that pain and until late twenties when I still struggled which was at its worse, but those feelings never went away, to this day I still feel somewhat worthless as a human being, as a father, husband, employee and the list goes on. This is not meant to be a whah whah whah poor me, but in hopes as an example of what not do to yourself.

Throughout my childhood I was always told by gramps that I was not good enough, stupid and would ever amount to anything. Although mom stepped in most of the time, she could not always be around all hours of the day. I was also house slave to labor required not to do your typical chores but hard labor around the house and then once I got my driving license, I was then his chauffer to wherever he needed to go which in most cases was his beer run and to the market. Because of my age and dependance on him and the family.

Once finally leaving home the damage had been well done, now in my twenties I self-destructed not into drugs or alcohol but deep depression which came to blows in February 2007 when I almost lost my life. Picking myself up once again trying to find some hope in my life and really picking up the pieces of how I got to that point tried to seek the positive things in my life, but in honestly, I didn't see it. From the outside one would think why I felt this way when I had more than more, a bachelors and master's in business, unemployed at the time, family who loved me but it just was not enough.

My realization of Value

I wanted to feel a sense of value, never realizing at that point that people cannot give me value I would have to seek that myself and realize that I as a human being was not more or less valuable than the next person, but and there is but. But one of the areas I have always focused on is success, such as success of myself and making constant comparisons to others, to this day I still do that.

I look at someone younger and ever my own age and see these incredibly gifted talented individuals and I can only think well they definitely are more valuable than me, I mean even look at their net worth. As you see I make constant comparisons which are self-defeating because I know deep down those feelings will NEVER help me but being a glutton for punishment continues.

Learning to Love and Appreciate yourself

Over the years I have learned to love myself more and to appreciate this point in my life and that this is where I am today, working, teaching, writing, family man, father, husband and the list goes on. I am not rich or poor although being poor is not a negative personal quality as most my childhood and adulthood I have been poor in spirit, in money and wealth but that's ok because I figured we all have a way to make ourselves better if we remember one thing, we do have value, self-worth and that we can set our mind to those things that can make us better people.

<u>Tips to get your started</u>

But here are some simple tips that can help all of remember our self-worth:

1.Rewrite your core beliefs

This is where you shall begin by slowly changing your mind set and recreate your personal mantra. Remember that new mantra, repeated it over and over again giving you the focus to retrain your thought process.

2.Reclaim what was been repressed

Take back your power and work to discover those areas in your life where you feel powerless and work towards challenging yourself to improving those areas in your life.

3.Replace people-pleasing with self-care

Being a people pleaser is not the answer to getting the affirmation of your self-worth, but to change our mindset not to put so much weight on what others think of us but make sure we are ones deciding what we want to put value in for ourselves.

4.Journal

Writing is another that I found great self-discovery into areas that I do have value and worth and physically seeing it in black and white will allow us to realize that we actually do have great value.

The reframing of your mind and Beyond

Self-worth takes time to retrain our minds from all of those in our life who may have caused the damage over the years like myself, but it is possible. The benefits of knowing your value definitely outweigh the negatives and if this is how you feel then today should be the day that you take back your power and realize your self-worth because you do have value whether you see it or not.

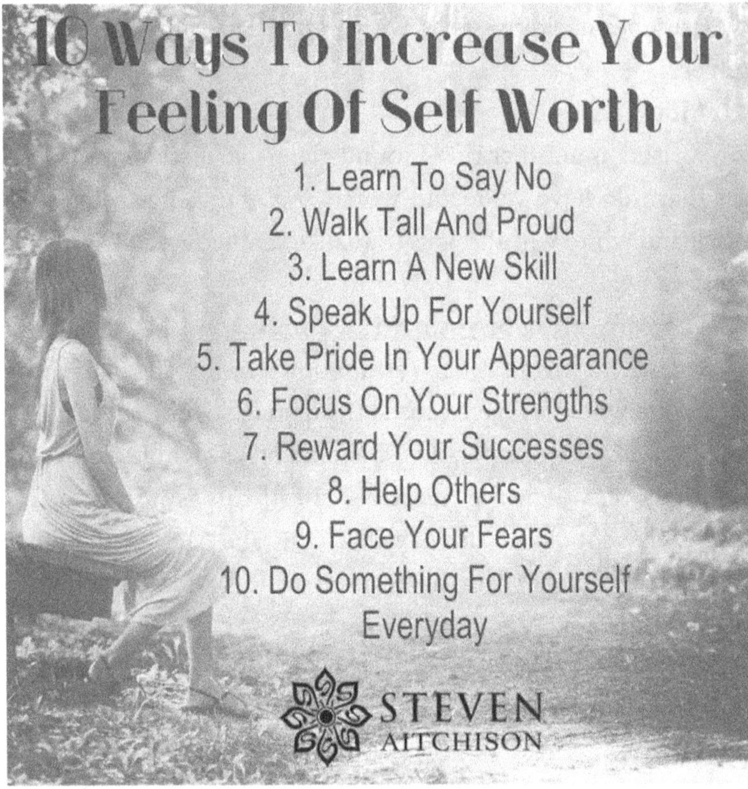

By realizing your self-worth, you will be more confident, making wiser decisions, improve the quality of your life and learn to remove those toxic things and people out of your life. It will be a work in progress, but it can be done, just look at me I work each day to push out those toxic thoughts, reframe my thinking and move forward and so can you.

| 6 |

How Self-Reflection Helps My Mental Health

August 14, 2021

I often look back on my life and think to myself how I have changed over the years, what milestones in my life help create who I am today. Some of those major life events include getting my college degrees, getting married and having my daughter.

These were some of the happiest moments in my life, but there were also hardships that defined me most recently in 2015 when my mother passed away and some of the most difficult times raising a family when financially it was very difficult.

You may be asking yourself why is this important to me? Well it should be important to all of us knowing that that five, ten, fifteen years from now you will be a different version of yourself, you may or may not life who you become.

Self Reflection Didn't Exist at First

I can say truthfully back in high school and early college years which put me at late teens early twenties I was incredibly naive and if there was one word, I could use it was just innocent.

Growing up I was always verbally abused by a grandparent who helped raise me with my mother and sister. In one way I felt I was very sheltered with not a lot of friends, mostly spending my time at home, doing chores, homework and manual labor that my grandfather had me do.

Like most teens I like music, movies and computers and I loved sport deep sea fishing but growing up felt like a slow process I was awkward in a way, certain things that most kids and young adults were doing at my age I was not like dating, going to dances, spending time with friends.

As you can see I said friends twice and that is because I feel friends have a certain affect over how we grow as individuals, I didn't really have that although I sure did try.

Going through college, I was a lone wolf so to speak, spent time at home or on my own, which again had an effect over my development in my young twenties, I honestly feel I was in a haze those years and that is probably because at those times I was also going through a deep depression which severely slowed down my ability to function at times and do things that those my age did like have fun.

Going into my late twenties and early thirties I finally found the person I would marry and have a child with and for the first time in my life I felt complete hope that I could have some growth in my life and boy did I grow.

Life Changes Forced Me to Reflect

Nothing changes you like a family and being that I was in my early thirties I seemed like a perfect time in my life to start a family, but in all honestly I was not prepared for married life, so to help me I dived in my work, working two jobs to help support us and be a good provider, it was exhausting but worth in as my daughter had her mother with her all the time.

The struggles really got to me like that do many, but depression always seemed to linger and I had difficultly coping. Through hardship's I felt myself changing in the sense of personality, how I treated my family at times and how I view my life. we

My attitude at times has been difficult, my personality went from sweet to almost non-existent just in a gloom at times always thinking about money, paying bills and keeping things together. I felt angry at times, resentful of those who were experiencing success in their lives and I always felt as I was struggling to make it.

Due to these feelings, hardships, life challenges my attitude and feeling changed and soon became very jaded, angry and although I have my family felt that speaking to them about these feeling would only concern them so I bottled them up and carried them around.

A Look Back I Finally See My Change

Looking back, I ask myself where I went wrong from early twenties to my now forties, as these years felt as though they were in the blink of an eye gone, never to return.

Each day I look in the mirror and realize I will never be the same man I was in my teens, Twenties and Thirties that I will grow and there's nothing wrong with that, but it is frightening to see how will I change, how will I change in my forties, fifties and beyond, I know I will we all will.

I just felt I needed to self-reflect as I do and reflect this with you to think, that you have a choice in your life, to think about how you want to grow, sad to say I didn't realize this until late in my life. I imagine where I would be today if I had realized my power.

Self Reflect = Wiser You!

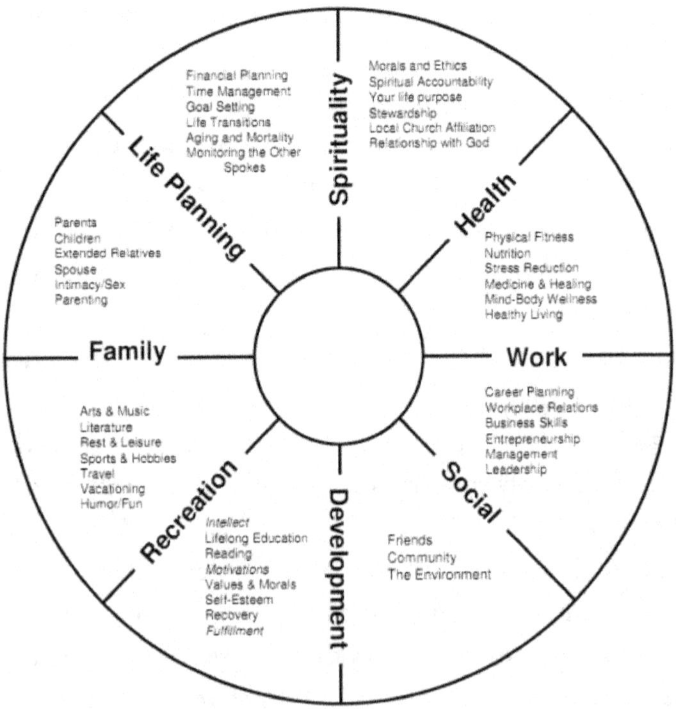

If you have gotten to the point of this blog, you will see that I find self-reflection important to mental health due to not dwelling on the past or the wrongs in our life, but the rights too. All too often time passes by as we live life and forget to reflect on how we have changed over the years, are we kinder, Angier, wiser, bitter what describes you. I feel this can be done at any age or stage in our life, but make sure it gets done. All too often we tend to do this in the new year, but really think each week, month and even day how you change and grow.

| 7 |

Why We Continue to Stigmatize Mental Illness?

July 31, 2021

Recently I had the time and urge to watch the television series Homeland on Hulu. A show that has been off the air for a few years now but one that I truly missed out until now. The main character Carrie Mathison a CIA agent who fights to keep America safe all while carrying around a secret. The secret is that is Bi-Polar.

Over the course of years I have seen both in television and movies portrayals of what its like to suffer with mental illness and the effects it can have on ones life. Some of the depictions are true because I have experienced those symptoms myself and some depictions are incredible over the top. I get that those who suffer with mental illness especially Bi-polar suffer differently and we are all not the same.

The Portrayal of Mental Illness

What really opened my eyes about this portrayal is that she pushed each day to do her Job despite the fact that she dealt with the darkest parts of humanity dealing with terrorists, death and destruction.

Carrie Mathison a fairly young women but in actuality is my age born April of 1979 or so the fandom page states as I was born in December 1979.

What makes this character so real to me is our age and many of the symptoms she experienced. Now mind you, my symptoms are not to that extreme but could be if I didn't work hard at self-care and have the love of my family like my Wife and daughter. Part of the reason I believe Carrie suffers so much is loneliness and not feeling worthy of the love of another person only experience short bouts of love in her relationships that don't seem to last all on the count of who she is.

For those who have watched this show , you will see that Carrie suffers incredibly without her medicine Lithium and without she becomes incredibly unhinged and delusional , unmanageable and down right scary to those around her. I remembered back in my late teens and twenty experience extreme depression, anxiety and my mind constantly raced with thoughts of those around me who I felt where watching me and thinking horrible thoughts about me.

I too was alone at that point in my life searching for Love and companionship but never getting that until I met my wife. I did feel unloved at that point in my life although I did have my sister, mother and father to lean on but I felt like I was battling every day until I hit a breaking point that changed my perspective because I was moments away from being on this earth anymore.

The Stigma of Mental Illness

One of the struggles I noticed immediately in Homeland and even in my own life, is how those with mental illness are still stigmatized for their illness. Many times, thought of as outcasts because their differences and their struggles that many choose not to want to be around those who suffer greatly at times. I remember times when I opened up to those, I felt cared about me friends primarily about my mental illness and before I knew it they were no longer answering my calls and they were no where in sight, something I have experienced time and time again over my life that eventually I just gave up on trying to make friends.

I wish I could understand why people reject those with mental illness and choose to stay away, maybe its too difficult to look at that person struggle and have no answers into how to support them. Those of use with mental illness need a listening ear and someone who is just there to listen to our rants at times, but even that is too difficult for some.

I get that many spirals out of control because mental illness is tough, a constant battle of our minds and our physical beings that sometimes we just give up because its too much. I gave up once and thankful I am still here to live and breath and enjoy the goodness of life and the love of those around me. Although I don't struggle like I once did, the pain is still there at times as my insecurities, my mind race at times.

I think we all need to learn to be more accepting of those who suffer regardless how uncomfortable it makes us as we are human beings on this earth trying to just make it. Carrie Mathison gives me hope to see that she lives to fight another day like many of us do.

Mental illness continues to grow each day as more and more are suffering with this ugly illness and although there is treatment and help not everyone can afford nor get the help they need. But something we can all do is just be more kind to those around us, listen more and be patient with those who suffer.

Another Mental Illness Portrayal in the Joker

One of the most recent films I have also watched the portrays a severe form of mental illness was in the film "Joker" with Joaquin Phoenix. Another incredible example of a man who has suffered and just to be clear I am in way justifying the deaths he caused due to his illness. But when I watched the Joker, I could a man who truly cried out for help was getting it and then it was cut off causing Arthur Fleck to again lose control. Again, he was stigmatized for his differences, his strangeness as people felt the need to bully him and eventually it was too much.

These two portrayals are vastly different but very similar in how we as society reacts to those who suffer and believe me there are millions who suffer with all different symptoms. I know for myself and even today I feel unworthy at times, but I do know I am love. I feel even in my daily life I am just not good enough making constant comparisons to my peers and society in general. I plan to live a long life as long as I am here not going back to those dark times in my life but looking forward no matter how tough life gets.

What Can be Done?

I would encourage anyone to look at these examples of characters who suffer and ask yourself how can help those just need help and not outcast them for their differences. Carrie Mathison and Arthur Fleck both vastly different characters but both suffering with mental illness and both living on the edge. I once lived on the edge but found it incredibly difficult and tiring as that life look my spirit away and who I wanted to be in life, I lost a part of my years due to mental illness.

Seek Help, Going alone is Not an Option

I am better now but encourage you and others to seek help if you are suffering as you don't have to suffer alone although it may feel that way. There is a brighter side to life even if we fail to see it , life is worth living.

Love yourself more, appreciate yourself more because you are unique and special just the way you are and learn to not take what others think of you personally. I know its difficult not to feel down and out at times, but you have a right to be happy in this life and you deserve.

As you can see this subject I am passionate about because I don't want to see you suffer like I did or how Carrie and Arthur suffered.

| 8 |

A Case Study for How Not to Treat The Mental Ill

July 17, 2021

Art many times imitates life and vise versa, as a film love I always tend to look for the meaning behind the action, drama and love. Over my lifetime I have tried to look at a films message as not every film as a message, some are just pointless and fun. Pointless and boring and some just make no sense as far as the plot, the logic and realism of the film. I get not every film has to make logical sense like magic or spiritualism that may not always be true and live-in reality.

A film that a recent watched was the 2019 Film Joker. First and foremost, I think Joaquin did an incredible job in his performance as the Joker much different interpretation then previous Jokers giving the character some back story to his madness. The film reflects a man who I think the world has just forgotten about which happens all too often today for many.

Arthur Fleck a man who appeared to have just had a rough life from a young child, first starting with his abandonment by his birth mother and then abuse by his adopted mother's boyfriend. Unsure what his life was like growing up, but it must have been difficult having a mother who suffered from delusions herself and being a one-time resident of Arkham asylum. Parts of Arthur's life is unknown even who may his father in the film, which is believed to be Thomas Wayne, wouldn't that be a great back story to have the great Bruce Wayne as a half-brother.

My Suffering Relates

As someone who has suffered with Mental illness and depression in my past, I somewhat sympathize with the Joker. Although the deaths were senseless especially his mother. It just goes to show you how much someone is in pain and people tend to ignore that pain. Many will attempt to justify that the pain is not real or important and to just get on with their life but its not that easy. Having been a fired clown and a failed comedian Arthur was trying just to make it and find something that brought him Joy.

In my late teens and mid-twenties, I suffered greatly from depression even though on the outside had a fairly normal upbringing living a home, food on the table and clothes on my back, but had my own torturer in my life a grandfather who belittled me from a young age something that took years to overcome. Even today I don't always have the confidence I feel I need to succeed always doubting myself.

My mind has been through hell and back so I can see a man like Arthur looking for anyone to be just kind to him. Remember fondly the seen when Arthur kills Randall in a violent outrage but allowing Gary to leave the room because he as kind to him. You see kindness can go a long way, something we in society fail at miserably. I would never justify someone like Fleck killing but it certainty is understandable especially when one feels powerless especially in the subway scene where Arthur kills the three Wayne enterprise traders. The hate for the rich still exists today as it did when the film time took place in 1981, even today the hate for the rich is stronger than ever.

Today is Only Getting Worse

Today we see all too often people are going off the deep end and going on kill rampages and murder sprees and caulk it up to people not being kind to them, but that is not it at all. The truth is we some control we are not powerless, but the sad truth is for the mentally ill to function in society we need society to just be kind. Arthur was obliviously strange in his behavior, how he spoke and his laughter which was caused by nervousness.

Growing up myself I grew up awkward myself, a loner, the fat kid with no friends sitting at the lunch table alone. I was bullied as the fat kid with physical threats, words and belittling. It hurt but I internalized that pain and held it in thinking I was just not worthy of friendship and love.

Over time I got better but I did have a breaking point in 2007 that almost changed the trajectory of my life and in 2008 and beyond my life changed forever meeting my future wife and having my daughter. Maybe that is what the Joker was looking for, in fact I know he was as he imagined life with Sophie Dumond. For myself I search for that special someone late in my teens and into my late adulthood until I found my wife, but remember rejection after rejection because of who I was, still Fat Joe, strange , quiet, reserved but not worth anyone's time.

The Joker still ends up the Same

The end result with Joker is that in fact he is insane and murderer which lines up perfectly with who the Joker becomes. The Joker does have a degree of intelligence and is not just some thug, but if you compare this Joker to other Jokers in comparison the others are thugs and murders who just wish to Kill. Arthur Fleck's mind has reached the point of no return as he is now a real criminal who would most likely spend his life at Arkham Asylum for the criminally insane.

Today we live in a world of sickness and depression that goes untreated for many only magnifying ones symptoms causing the person to get worse. Arthur Fleck appeared trying to heal his mind with therapy and medicine until those resources were cut out, a reality that happens to many today as they are unable to afford their needed meds and get the therapy, they need to maintain a healthy life.

What is intriguing about this film is that Joker forced himself to be happy each day, living a dismal life of living with his mother. Not there is anything wrong with helping mom but being that Arthur and his mother were both mentally ill it probably was not the best fit since both needed serious help and attention, like the blind leading the blind.

Having lived in a place that mimicked those dismal circumstances it was quite depressing, lonely and easy to get to a point one can go crazy being in certain surroundings. I am sure it was by design living in Gotham (New York) is a dismal place at times, although many will disagree it's a great place. I am having live-in South-Central Los Angeles for most of my life I can relate.

I would say anyone who you know who and could be the next Joker show that person kindness, compassion and understanding but putting yourself aside for once, your selfishness and think of others.

Remember to smile at these individuals because deep down they want to see that you see them as human, as a person and of value, if we had done this for the Joker its quite possible he wouldn't have turned into a psychotic lunatic.

| 9 |

Why I Never Feel Good Enough

August 29, 2021

For some feelings of inadequacy is something we tend to carry around throughout our lives, even though many will say you should not. Yes, we are all different have different talents, strengths and weaknesses. As an instructor to college-age students I have had my share of teaching students from all walks of life which has also allowed me to reflect on my shortcomings.

Growing up I can honestly say I grew up poor, I wasn't to the point of being homeless thank goodness, but growing up as a child I didn't realize we were poor until I got older and realized that there was a lot I could not have. Yes, we had food on the table, a place to sleep and clothes on our back which many would say well that should be enough.

Realizing My Worth

But when I became a husband and then a father, I realized that was not the life I wanted to give to my child. I truly feel being poor in an America is almost a crime as the cost of living is high especially living in California where the luxury of beaches and Hollywood justify the high price. My family is at a much better place now but still on the verge of going back financially when certain situations take place as our current pandemic.

Even now it's a struggle where you need two incomes just to make it or you will truly be poor with scraps to eat and the housing is not the best neighbourhoods. I know this may be true for anyone living anywhere, being poor, low income however you want to spin it is looked down upon and those who have money, strong family structure is considered more valuable in today's society.

Some of you may not agree with my opinion, because maybe you were brought up with a different family structure, a good decent living with good education with everything you could desire. Other's will feel we have all the control to get out of poverty by pulling up our own bootstraps and getting it down and there are even those that feel being poor is a person's fault.

Why am saying all of this you ask because it is my impression this has truly causing major delays in my life from getting a proper job, having the mental development one needs to be successful in this life. Growing up in Los Angeles in an area that many who watch movies will see perfectly represents the area such as Menace to Society, Boyz in the Hood and Last Watch. All these films centred in Los Angeles and if you think those films are not reality think again, they exist.

Family is Where it All Begins

I can honestly say I blame my family for this upbringing for putting myself and my sister in those kinds of conditions, but once again when you lack resources what else can you do. I know its easy to say just move but it's not always so easy.

It is my belief that others have always seen me as less than dating back to my childhood and I think it's a common problem we have today. I know it may be different for you as you may have been in a similar situation but under different circumstances.

It has been a hard road to change my frame of thought, one area I focused on was education by going to school getting my bachelors and masters but that didn't always completely help me feel more worth especially in the eyes of those we depend in this life.

Who are those people we depend on well for one of those people we need to help us in life like our bosses and supervisors who we depend on seeing us of value? I know this may sound crazy but in life, we rely on so many to help us reach our goals, it's not just myself taking myself where I want to go, someone has to believe in us, not just ourselves.

It Takes Other's to Believe in You too

I have not had many people in my career who have truly believed in me to want to help me and that I feel has truly affected my life and prosperity. It's never enough to think we don't need any help, we can do it ourselves with our own will. We need people, people who will encourage us, belief in us, bring us up to reach our full potential.

From the outside I should feel differently I have a wife, a daughter who loves me who look to be to give them confidence, encouragement, and love which I want them to have. But in the end, I am looking myself to feel adequate especially in the work I still have not received it although I have worked hard to gain it.

I tend to do the opposite in my students and family because they see their specialness and I tell them that, in my life, not many have said if I am special or what they see in me which has to lead me to believe I am not good enough. It's not enough to just believe in myself, it's nice to hear it to feel it, but I am in search of that each day.

Are you like me do you feel inadequate? Do you feel good enough? If now how have you gained that confidence? I would love to know.

| 10 |

Fear is Taking Hold, Don't Let It Take Hold of you

March 22, 2020

The world as we know it is in chaos right now due to COVID-19 as many living in fear of catching this terrible virus the orientated from China. During these times many are forced to work from home, something that can be great for many but lack of interaction we tend to lose in the process.

I will be not only working 8 hours a day but also teaching my course all at the comfort of my apartment. In addition I am also with my family, my wife, daughter and currently my mother in law is staying with us, so you can say its a full house literally.

Living in California we are definitely a hot stop for the virus due to demographics of people from all over the world as our neighbors, so we need to be especially cautious. I do live in fear in a way because you never know who may have the virus and pass it myself and I could easily pass to my family. I would be ok if this was some type of curable flu but its not it affects the lungs which can lead to death like so many have already.

During these times humanity really goes to hell as people start to horde supplies, food and even guns. You really see the worst in people come out , worse then during the holidays, as people will literally steal the TP from you, take needed supplies in greed pursuit.

Let's please practice social distancing, staying as much at home as humanly possible, wash your damn hands, use sanitizer and take extra precautions. This is about flatting the curve so it doesn't spread, don't be selfish by making this about you, how many times do we have to see people in large crowds who don't give a shit about others just for the need to go to a concert, a theme park, a party, even a wedding.

Stop the spread and we can soon go back to normal, but if people continue to spread it will only get worse. Although we can not blame ourselves for this virus we can blame the response on the U.S government for NOT protecting the American people from harm and not it has gotten worse, while other counties have a grasp on handing it, we do not.

I am tired of those who defend the incompetent administration as if they have done no harm, they have actually affected us in ways we will probably feel for the rest of the year and maybe longer.

Stay safe everyone, be kind, send time with loved ones, stay in doors, read, write and know this will pass in time if we do our part.

As someone who is mainly in doors now I can refocus my time to writing more blogs and of course finish editing my book, which I am need to finish. Wishing everyone a safe healthy week ahead.

| 11 |

The Effects of Social Media on Mental Health

August 7, 2021

Living in the 21st century Social Media has become a part of our daily lives, as we use it to keep in touch with just about everything from followers, friends and family, the news and basically anything that goes on in the world today.

For some Social Media is the best thing since sliced bread but not everyone feels that way because of some of the harm that can done. For me social media was one of those take or leave type of communications when my first introduction was Myspace, then Facebook and now Twitter. I know there is so much more to Social Media than Facebook and Twitter, as there is also Instagram, Pinterest, Snap Chat, LinkedIn and so many others to name.

Personally, I have used social media as a tool for business as a one-time Social Media Manager so I know the power of reach when it comes to getting the word out effectively and at a low cost. You can literally reach millions in a matter of seconds which makes social media so power especially from a marketing standpoint.

In my view although there are definite positives to using it, I find there are more negatives to using it, but I will say that it all depends on how you let it rule you overall. Social Media has the tendency to rule people instead of the other way around as many us are addicted to knowing what is going on constantly.

I will say I have this problem; I tend to use Twitter because as a writer I want to build a platform of for my future work of blogs and books and of course to a certain degree for personal reasons. Even using it for that purpose I tend to have information overload as it literally has tons of connections and information such as news and having real time updates on the latest.

I have grown attached to twitter because I want to know what is happening at all times, when deep down it really is affecting me mentally and my focus. It also affects how I perceive realistic expectations for my life as I look at others lives. I find it true that social media can cause depression as we look at those who post looking happier, healthier, wealthier living their best lives. Some would say yeah that's them that's not me I can separate reality from fiction. If you have the attitude where it doesn't affect you I applaud you.

Negative Effects
OF SOCIAL MEDIA
Depression
Anxiety
Lower self-esteem
Less self-control
PTSD Trigger
Overeating
Fear of Missing Out (FOMO)
Hive Mind
Irrational conformity to a group's thinking

Social media gives the impression that people are living perfect lives while looking perfect with filters and if you like me have a problem with your own life and how content you are living your own life then Social media may not be the best thing for you. In addition social media has what so many love which is freedom of expression which is great but many times people post things are simply inappropriate who push the limits of what should be viewed. I am not trying to control what people post but hope you see what I mean when others will post horrific things that unfortunately you cannot un-see.

Some of areas I found most important include:

1. Self Esteem

For those who have self-esteem issues, we look at social media and we tend to make comparisons of those we see whether it's someone who atheistically beautiful, someone who has more wealth or perceived better life then you. Does this sound like you? Maybe if you struggle with self-esteem it may be time to step away and build yourself up to not focus on the those aspects and appreciate you for how special you are.

2. Human Connection

For many of us Human connection is so important because many of us have a difficult time making friends, having conversations and Social Media may be the perfect way because you don't have the physically be there with someone, but we all need physical contact to feel connected something social media doesn't offer.

3. Memory

Social media remembers EVERYTHING which can be a good things and bad thing. The good thing is it can remember milestones, birthdays, anniversaries, pictures from the past which may also remind you of hardships I know it does for me. If you are like me I tend to dwell on the past too much think about my past failure's something social media is good at.

4. **Sleep**

Having enough sleep is so important to our mental health, but for many of us its hard to put the phone down without looking at every few minutes. Looking at social media before bed can have negative affects because its what we will think about before hitting the hay. Imagine if you will looking at someone else's life and then thinking about how you don't compare to that persons life and getting depressed before bed, I know it has happened to me maybe to you as well.

5. **Attention Span**

Although its incredible to have so much information at your fingertips, it also affects our attention span as we go from one topic, thread, subject to the next in seconds. If you find yourself checking your phone, the twitter or Facebook maybe you need to work on having more control and putting those sites aside for now or taking a break for a few days and maybe even a week to give yourself a chance to recoup and lose the attachment.

6. **Mental Health**

Being someone who struggles with mental health at times I can tell you social media does have an affect over how I perceive my life. I really do see at times it's a fight for my happiness against those I don't know on social media who have who I yearn for in my life maybe a house, a better car, money, but it's different for everyone, maybe you see beauty, maybe technology. We really have to recognize that mental health comes first and then social media.

Social Media is Here to Stay

Study after study show the negative affects of social media, but I will say it just depends on the person, but more and more people are struggling to maintain healthy relationships both physically and mentally due to social media and our addition to always being connected. Its important to unplug spend time with family and friends, give them a call and actually speak to those in your life.

All to often we lose the human connection due to social media and really give way too much of our lives online that can affect us in the future. Consider how much you use it and if you feel you are using it too much maybe put some controls or limits and ween yourself off for awhile or permanently.

I am not against social media it has a purpose but within reason we have to realise that social media is not a substitute for living life and its not a substitute for having relationships with people. I understand it's the times we live in but prior to social media we as people were mentally healthier and relationships were one on one not shared through a phone screen.

| 12 |

Accepting Yourself in Today's World

September 25, 2021

Recently I had the pleasure to watch Rocket man the bio pic of Sir Elton John and I must say I quite impressed with his life and the impact he has made with his music and just his humanity throughout the world. Now mind you I am not sure how accurate this story to the real life of Elton John and frankly it shouldn't matter, it was a great film in my opinion. What I loved was the struggles Elton had with his family and how he was able to overcome those incredible difficulties.

Family does truly make a difference in our abilities to sometimes succeed in life and be prepared for a bright future. But many in life don't experience a solid family life such as two parents in the household who are devoted to raising well balance kids. Some of you may be saying well my mom or dad were single parents and they did great and I say I am one of those who was always raised with my single mom who did an incredible feat with raising my sister and I on pennies, but It could have been better.

For those who have read my blogs you will know that I am a difficult relationship with my grandfather in which I lived with along with my mom and sister. My grandfather who I believe never genuinely loved me put me down for most of young life and most of adult life. I was never good enough and he made sure to remind me each day, but in survival my mother made a choice to keep us afloat so I don't fault her for that.

Feeling acceptance is so key to our development in this life, not only be accepted by others but accepting yourself as is.

What brings this thought to mind is that recently I had a young co-worker graduating college, starting out her life in the most wonderful way. A young women who I see as intelligent and hardworking and has the world in her hands. There is a hint of jealously in my tone because I look back in my own life and I ask myself what have I truly done in my life to be impressed about.

Yes I am a husband and father but I look back at my life and wish I could be a better provider, but One the reasons I feel I have failed is in my career. Now I am not saying my jobs that I have taken are bad or the companies I have work for are bad, actually they are decent, but it could have been better. Right now students are graduating High school and college starting major chapters in their life.

I think back when I was graduating high school as it was exciting, the future looked bright I was going to college and ready to begin my life. I was ready until early on I started to fail miserably being in college away from home, homesick and not prepared for college, so I made the choice to go back home with no resistance from family.

A choice I regret, but I know back then I was not ready and I didn't have the confidence and the self-acceptance to push myself. This was something that affected my life until today and I don't want anyone's life to be affected in that way. I encourage those who struggle with this to know you are not alone, you are special just the way you are.

One of the struggles so many deal with is comparison as in comparing yourself to others life path as I have done so much in my life. When I look at someone my age, my level of education for example and they go off to be successful while I feel stuck in neutral it hurts me. Many others may feel this way like when will I move into gear and never do at times, it may be because you have never truly accepted yourself.

Being in my forty's now, life has passed me by pretty quickly and it continues to keep going unrelenting and unstopping, so what can one do to overcome this, here are some ways.

Set an Intention

Set the intention to acknowledge that self-loathing simply doesn't lead to a satisfying life, it actually leads you nowhere. If you intention in life is to have self-acceptance which it should be we will find ways to appreciate who we are and our strengths. It starts with good thoughts and creating a chain reaction to continue those positive thoughts, its that important.

Celebrate your Strengths

We all have strengths no matter if you can't see them right away, but its important to recognize what those are. Hone in on those strengths and abilities by writing them down helps put those strengths in black and white. If you are having a tough time coming up with your list, name one strength each day. Start with something basic like "I'm a kind person" to start.

Consider the people around you

What kinds of people do you surround yourself with? Those people in your life make all the difference as mention in my personal example. Those who bring you down are not the people you need in your life even if they are family. Create those boundaries even if it means cutting those out of your life and see you blossom like never before.

Forgive yourself

We tend to be our worst critics preventing us from self-acceptance. Forgive yourself and move on, it's as simple as that. It's important to learn from mistakes, make efforts to grow and accept you can't change the past.

You make your decision best for you at the time, but I won't lie it would be nice to have a time machine to go back and correct those choices at that time maybe our lives would be different then today.

Shush your inner critic

The inner critic can be the most powerful voice for good and the bad. We all have that voice but many will push the inner voice aside, some listen constantly like I do. It's important to know that inner critic is not always helpful in your quest for self-acceptance but still valuable being self-aware.

Grieve the loss of unrealized dreams

Many of problems of self-acceptance come from our inability to reconcile who we are as compared with the idealized dreams of our youth. Maybe you dreamed of becoming a doctor or Lawyer but instead ended up in business and think about it constantly. I do that to this day, I think what if I had stayed in my first college and finished, what if I joined the military, What If, What IF's constantly if my head, but I realize that doing that does more harm then good.

Be kind to yourself

Many people are hesitant to show even a shred of self-kindness because they se it as selfish or undeserved. By the keys to self-compassion is to understand that weaknesses are part of the human experience. Coming to accept who you are involves loving yourself because of your flaws, not in spite of them.

Your Journey is Your own, Make it Count!

Realizing you have an issue of self-acceptance is half the battle, but if you look at yourself in the mirror and see that your truly can't accept yourself, then you have work to do. Going back to the film Rocketman Elton John struggled to accept who he was as he felt he always had to hide his sexuality, his fashion sense, his delicateness as people in his life told them those feeling are bad such as his mother and father. Accept yourself, your quirks, differences, strengths and weakness and embrace them right now.

Our lively hood depends on accepting ourselves and because we have a long life to live why live in agony over those feelings, its not fair yourself as you deserve the best. I encourage to look within but if that's hard at first look to those who have fought hard to get where they are today like Sir Elton John accepting himself and never looking back.

| 13 |

Being Kinder During These Stressful Times

November 27, 2021

The panic in today's world is off the charts it seems with the current events of COVID-19, high unemployment and pure instability. Now I can only speak for the United States as this is a global situation. Since our lives have been rocked in the US with over 600,000 deaths, many due to COVID-19 has left me with some very raw emotions and anger at these times.

It appears anytime we turn on the TV, go online it's pretty gloom and doom and I ask myself how am I suppose to have peace in my life during these times. I get that it's difficult to have joy in these times knowing things appear to be getting worse.

My intention is obliviously not to add to the panic and scare of that is going on, but to say that one day this will end and we will go back to life as we know it. Now I can't say if our lives will be the same, many have lost family and friends whose life will never been the same.

For those who live in the United States the news is also filled with anger, protests, riots society seems to becoming unhinged over being home, being told to wear a mask and constantly watching the ticker of deaths go up daily. But add to that we have great division among each of us at times and I also see that hate is on the rise, crime increasing and it's a scary sight.

So in today's ever changing world how can we have some peace for ourselves and family, here are some ways.

1.Turn Off the Tube

The Tube is probably one of the biggest reasons we are being robbed of our peace causing many to have higher anxiety and depression. I understand we all want to stay informed of the times, but let's remember one thing, COVID-19 and the stability of our nations is not going to happen over night especially since we have No vaccine as of yet.

Whether your watching the local news, CNN, Fox whatever it maybe we have to remember television has a purpose, one could be to deliver your local news, others are for entertainment and ultimately it is all about viewership, the more the better. I think all too often people confuse facts with opinions where many who deliver information deliver as fact when in fact its not.

2. Limit Social Media Intake

Almost with the same as television social media has a different effect on our information intake as many use it not just for information but to spread mis-information with millions of opinions it can be very overwhelming. Social media I consider it to be a tool and like any tool can be used for good or bad as there many bad characters looking to persuade us to their view causing many to inadvertently spread information true and false.

3. Focus on the Good

What is the good in your life, family, friends, your church, school? This can be a time to focus on them although we may not be able to see them every day, but what we can do is build connections with those our life and reconnect.

People are hurting right now for that reason feeling isolated and alone as if they have no one that truly cares because frankly we are all going through something. Social media can be a good tool for this or even a simple text message with words of love and appreciation. Let's all make an effort to try harder at connecting.

4. Keep your distance

I know we still have many who truly believe COVID is not a threat to themselves or their family, but lets respect the rules of keeping our distance. Now it's understandable that can be difficult at times but let's just try harder. Let's put aside situations that cause us to be in close proximity like parties, family gatherings, political rally's and anywhere else.

5. Wear a Mask

This is by far one of the biggest contentions of society the refusal to wear a mask, because frankly they don't believe it will have any effects over the prevention of getting the virus. Let's all agree COVID is new and information about it is still developing, but that doesn't mean we shouldn't respect the rules. There have been so many arguments over the use of mask and their effectiveness due to mis-information, people's belief systems and even the lack of promotion from our own leaders.

6. Be Kind to others

This may be something many may say well of course I am going to be kind, why wouldn't I until they cross someone else's ideals or beliefs they don't agree it and then kindness goes out the window. As mention this situation is difficult for ALL so couldn't we all be a little more or a lot more kind to each other.

7. Follow the Rules

The rules are meant to help us all, its not political or is there some special agenda, which is where many tend to create conspiracy theories. This is one area that I guess I can not understand especially in today's world.

Why would anything think anyone would want COVID to be around, why would anyone want high unemployment or deaths, logic appears to go out the window for many arguments and no truth to it. Yes, most of us don't like being told what to do such as wear a mask, social distance, stay home and so it goes now. But last time I check our society has never experienced anything like this recently, the last time being in 1918 Spanish flu.

8. Protect your little ones

Kids are the future and we must ALL do our part to protect their bodies and minds from harm and in my opinion, we are doing a horrible job. As adults we have a responsibility to model good morals and behavior.

Our children may not truly know what is going on and to a degree that's ok, let's have kids be kids and stop trying to force them to grow up quickly. Yes we are in unprecedented times, but many kids truly don't know that there is an invisible virus reeking damage, heck most of us adults don't fully understand, why risk it.

9. Do your research

As mentioned, it is my opinion there is the possibility of misinformation on the web and even on television, make sure you check facts. We should all remember that science has proven to be the most accurate but let's understanding nothing is 100% guarantee especially with COVID. There are many good sources of good information in your respective country, state and city so rely on that for the best information.

10. Stay Positive and Be Kind!

For those who have gotten to the end know my intention is never to tell you what to do, that is your choice, but in hopes that we all come together. For those who have lost someone to this terrible virus I am deepest condolences.

We will prevail in this fight, but in the end, we will lose if we do not be kinder to each, work together, respect each other and at the end of day come out better. I know it may be hard to see the light right now but it's there, let us stay positive and focused. A lot is happening right especially here in the United States where are future leader will be chosen, so the stakes are high.

| 14 |

Overcoming fear in tough times

December 19, 2021

I know there are probably going to be tons of advice out there not to panic with our world pandemic going on concerning the Corona Virus or COVID-19 and that may be easy to say but it seriously does disrupts our lives in ways we are not used to and hope that this situation does not last long allowing us to move on with our lives.

Living in California we are especially affected, but like mentioned this is affecting many around the world especially in the U.K. Spain, Asia and many other populous countries.

Panic has truly taken hold of many for good reason, it also doesn't help that we haven't gotten the answers we are looking for. Lack of answers has caused many to horde supplies, food and act in a horrible manner as to have the survive of the fittest example, let's not live by that example.

We All Have a Part to Play

In this time, we must be kind to others, help those less fortunate and have the mindset we are going to be ok and this will pass. Keeping you and your family safe, social distancing and keep those more vulnerable inside for the time being. For most, we hate being inside, but it actually can have benefits like spending time with loved ones, reading and writing more.

I would recommend to please limit how much news you take in not necessary to limit information but many times news and especially opinion programs will intentionally try to strike panic in people who can lead to disinformation something we don't need right now.

Living in the United States there is a great deal of disinformation that we must be careful about especially when it comes to seeking help in the health crisis.

I would recommend following proper government guidelines in staying indoors and don't expose yourself unnecessarily until we know more information and before we start flatting the curve and getting a vaccine to combat this.

Let's not live in fear but know we all have to survive for tomorrow, many in the world can not fully stay indoors or work at home, some have positions that are in the face of the public like hospitals, Food and banking to name a few.

Do What is Needed

I can't stress enough continue to live a very hygienic life washing your hands, which shouldn't even be said, but so many don't wash their hands, using sanitizer and limiting being in crowds of people especially at places like the beach, concerts, and other highly populous areas.

I know it's easy to be afraid, mad, frustrated especially when seeing others act in a manner we find unfitting to humanity, but let that go for now as those people will be called out on their poor behaviour.

Keep on keeping on

Continue to work, go to school online if possible and in time this will be a memory, hopefully, you will not be affected.

I sympathize with those who are losing loved ones due to this horrible virus and if are one of those people try to give yourself a break, knowing you did not cause this, you did not deserve for this to you happen to you, but we, unfortunately, live in a world where these situations take place.

Stay safe, be happy

Something within me wants to speak these words of comfort to those who feel like I do, a little scared even to go to the supermarket, live my life at home for now while I work and teach courses from home.

As a father, husband and provider who genuinely want to protect my family from harm in any way possible, but being a shut-in is not the answer for me as I feel I would literally go crazy as someone who used to purposely self-isolate due to mental illness in the past, it's not a great feeling.

Luckily some interaction to the outside world is important for all of us in this time, which is why I write, tweet and interact with the world community.

| 15 |

Chaos Taking Over ! What is Going on?

May 31, 2020

The world is in Chaos as we speak first starting is Covid-19 and now with recent killing here in the United States as protesters have turned this event a reason to Loot and burn anything in their way. I happen to live in San Bernardino county about 45 miles from Los Angeles the epicenter of Covid-19 and the Protest/riots taking place. This event is sucking the world in as other countries are find a reason to protest too.

I will just be sitting comfy at home as why would I risk my life and health to protest something that in my opinion it NOT change. Racism is apart of our country whether we like it or not. If we we think as citizens our government will do anything they will not because frankly those who practice racism like White supremacist are citizens and our country will NOT infringe on their rights for they killer belief system.

As someone who is has Spanish ancestry I know perfectly what it means to be discriminated against for my skin color. I have seen how I am treated at work and in my career and I absolutely hate it. But I am just trying to get through with my life. Time is ticking away as I get older and solving racism , discrimination is not something I have the power or will to change.

Why am I saying all of this because I know I have no power to changes these situations, Only GOD can change the course of our lives. The times of today are Nothing new, but I believe many are becoming woke to what is going on, but its not enough, we need to open our eyes even more to other injustices like income inequality, ageism, Sexism and many other ism's.

From my standpoint we have a racist in the top office as president who chooses not to condone racism. Further more we have racist in our congress as they may choose not to call themselves that but reality they are. As you can see this subject boils my blood because I see NO point in burning down buildings, Shooting and Murdering Cops, Rioting, what does that have to do with Racism. In my opinions just shows how ignorant people are to do those things and think it will change things.

How would you feel if you had a business and some random person decided to just burn your business down all in the name of racism, how does that help the cause, IT DOES NOT. We have a deadly pandemic happening as we speak and the streets are filled with protestors catching the deadly virus as we speak that that same virus into their home, into communities leading to what could be worst case scenarios death or serious sickness.

As you can see I am really worked up about this as this situation truly does anger me. For those saying well what about the man that died due to police brutality's and yes that angers me too, but the peoples response I think is complete overboard making matters only worse. I believe in the sanctity of human life, but what about society as a whole this is healthily especially with everything going on in the world, I think NOT.

Wishing everyone a safe and prosperous weekend ! See what's in store for the coming weeks and months as our country continues to unravel. Stay Safe.

| 16 |

Why Its Important to Listen to Your Own Voice!

August 21, 2021

Today we live in a world of social media, media and influencer's who do everything in their power to influence how we view ourselves, how we should live our life and what we should consider as important. At times this angers me as someone who writes blogs for Need to Live, I work to give you a realistic perspective on what everyday Joes and Janes go through instead of living through the alternate reality of social media where not everything is what it seems where people will go out of their way to deceive you into thinking.

This also goes for media in general too like reality shows, the news and other media sources. Although we are a media source too I like to think we write from the heart not necessary to get more likes on our social media sites (I have no social media sites).

The Pandemic and The Damage

Over the course of this horrific year of Covid-19 and the pandemic many which were forced to stay home out of safety gravitated towards the one thing most of us have access to the internet, social media and other forms of at home entertainment. Social media such as Facebook and twitter usage have increased exponentially filled with some truth, but in reality its my opinion there are voices that that go out of their way to shape the way you and I think or should think especially with politics.

It is my opinion that instead of listening to our own voice, many have chosen to listen to lies and misinformation labeling It as truth. I often think as society especially in the west where I live we are supposed to be smarter than that, but maybe I am wrong because if you watch our News programs to will see that many choose to believe in conspiracy's.

Many of you may say well that's their choice to believe in what they want even if its not true. Yes, all can create our own belief systems and values hopefully they are based in reality but it seems its only getting worse.

Where Did We Go Wrong or Did We?

I often wonder where we as society went wrong where we stopped believing in truth and our own voice and replacing it with those that have no direct contact with our life like family and friends. For example, many listen to influencers and celebrities for their daily living advise such as you should eat this, dress like this or act this way to get somewhere in life and why cant we all follow the beat of our drum, why must we follow someone's else's.

Each day we all have a choice how to live our lives but why do many feel they need be validated by what others say and how others live their lives as if they are a source guaranteeing success. I know to a certain degree we should listen to experts because they have truly studied subjects to make us better people like health and fitness, there is a science behind it.

But what has really triggered this thinking for me is politics. Living in the United States Politics has become a divisive tool that once was to help the people but have turned into Us Versus them, believe this ideology , follow this political group, being a liberal versus conservative and if you are one party you are bad and horrible human being. Add into the fact that religion that has in some part made people turn from the true principles of helping us be better people.

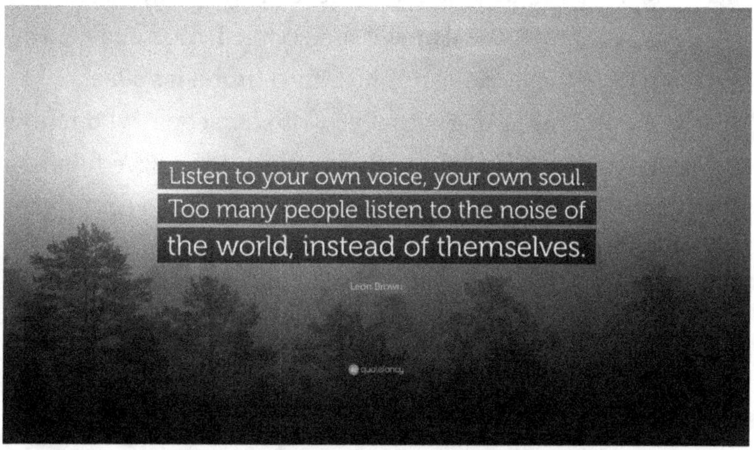

I know, I know I am going on a tangent here and some of you may not agree, but hopefully you get my drift that we must work to refocus on how to live our individual lives once again and stop relaying on those outside forums and really focus on those sources that are known not to spreads lies and misinformation to you.

For example the Need To Live works to provide you information and voices of those who live life , who struggle with everything things that you and I want answers too.

One may ask well what is the difference between Need to Live and other sources on the internet and many I say try to persuade you to take up their ideology and spread it to others which can be dangerous at times especially if you see what conspiracies can do to society.

Let's Put the Phone Down once and Again

I am in no way trying to tell you how to think, I am merely saying that we should really put away social media and those means of media that actually to do damage to our thinking. Studies have shown the damage society media has and continues to do to society, that is not just my opinion it's a fact.

It is my intention that we all grow to be people who follow our hearts and minds to those things we need to have fulfilling lives. Each day there is a new piece of technology, a new app or device that makes life easier which is not a bad thing until we start relaying on those things to replace our own voice.

I believe that social media is no longer a place to voice our own voice, but to take up others voices, spread lies and misinformation and ultimately spread hate in the form of free speech.

Better Devoted Time

That is why I devote so much of my time to reading and writing so that my voice stays my voice and doesn't get lost. I understand I still use resources found online in my research for my blogs and my writing because the truth is still important when I write to you and myself.

Thank you for always listening and your support in my quest for truth and knowledge and my hope is that you all see my intention to make you and I better people in the long run, where we are not conformed to the ideas of others but our own beliefs and value systems, something I think many don't take too much stock of today.

Maybe for once we could go back to the future and redo history in the sense of learning of our wrongs of today and correcting them as its not too late for any of us to turn back and do a 180, or our we outta time!

| 17 |

Don't Let Imposter Syndrome Bring You Down

October 24, 2021

Starting a new job and career can be on the most nerve-racking experiences one can have in their life no matter how many jobs or career changes you have. For some and even many, you may experience what is called Imposter Syndrome. Don't worry it's perfectly curable and it's more common than you.

In my view, I have often experienced this in much of my career but I will say this it will subside in time when you soon begin to see in your abilities in your new profession. As someone who has a Masters degree in business, I shouldn't experience but like all of us I still have to learn skills, a profession to get me to where I am today.

IMPOSTOR SYNDROME

Also known as impostor phenomenon or fraud syndrome.

Impostor Syndrome:

High-achieving individuals are marked by an inability to internalize their accomplishments and a persistent fear of being exposed as a "fraud"...sound familiar?

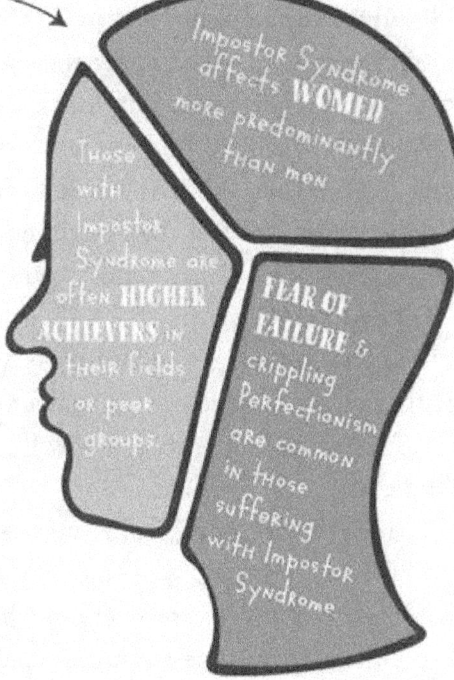

Remember this:
Your **LITTLE MESSAGE** is an important piece of the **BIG PUZZLE**!

I have always been one to take on roles that were outside of what I learned in school and felt it was important to challenge myself in roles that many would not normally take, which in part has to lead me to feel like an imposter.

The definition of Imposter Syndrome would be:

Rewrite your mental Script

Retrain your mind to enjoy the opportunity you've been given. For example, instead of thinking,

"There are going to find out you have no idea what you're doing and fire you," think to yourself, "Everyone feels this way, it's natural and I got this. You might not know everything, but you can learn, the company chose you for a reason.

Take out the Trash

When self-sabotage bubbles up in your brain, drag it out. Get those fears out and talk to someone, a friend, family anyone you trust and those thoughts will soon begin to disappear in time.

Failure is a stepping stone to greatness

Why not change the way you view failure, where failure is what it takes to succeed and everyone that is anyone had to fail? Throw the idea of success out the window for a moment and discover the meaning of failure: A steppingstone to greatness.

Show yourself

Visualize your victories big and small and you shall see yourself succeed in whatever you set your mind to. Focus on the positive and don't look back, it can be hard but take those nerves and think about the bright path in front of you and go for it.

Trick the brain

When all else fails, fake it until you make it! Don't wait for confidence to drive over. Our confidence will build when we take risks but changing our behaviour and your mind will follow.

Give Yourself a New Perspective

To give you some perspective to a time I have felt like this to an extreme level was when I took a role that was very technical in nature learning code, minor programming and it was something I had never had formal training in. I was that position for 18 months and each day I felt like an imposter even though I learn how to do the job. I felt like I didn't belong and many times others made me feel like I didn't belong either so the imposter syndrome never went away.

It soon took over my work because I felt I just wasn't good enough, I made mistakes along the way but I kept pushing forward eventually it no longer was a good fit for but I will always remember that I took a risk to learn.

That fear I have subsided in my new role, another role I have taken where I had no normal training but that's ok because in my eyes I must overtake this fear of me not being good enough because I can learn to adapt and move forward.

Have you experienced these feelings, did they affect you in the long term or short term? How did you overcome those feelings?

At the end of the day, remember this: You are here for a reason. In this job, your business, your life, you are worthy. You are better than you think you are. You are smarter thank you think you are. You are more than you give yourself credit for. Remember that. And remind yourself as often as you need to.

| 18 |

Is Body Positivity Social Movement Toxic?

October 16, 2021

Growing up I was often the overweight kid as I think back over my life, taking a looking into my history and the photo album. Pictures of my youth as a young boy who had a normal weight, thin and healthy but as I got older my weight ballooned as I looked no longer healthy. Some who may look that those photos may say to themselves well you're a growing boy.

I get we are all different with all different genetics, some who grow up mimicking their parents in many ways. My family whom I love has always been on the heavier side from both my mother and fathers' side so naturally one can understand that could it runs in my DNA.

Being Bullied on the account of being me

I was bullied at school for much of my childhood called all too often "Fat Boy" , "Fatty" ,"Pig" and you can only imagine what else I was called. I was often put down by a verbally abusive grandfather on a daily basis. One could imagine my self esteem suffered and I my weight went up as I turned to food for comfort. My mother who I loved did her best but struggled herself with her weight and had so from her own childhood.

I often think where the positive body movement was back then, would it have made a difference or today is this a toxic ideology. I course have no problem with loving yourself because we are all different, and many times growing up many of us are told to love ourselves, accept ourselves for who we are inside and out, but I ask this is helpful.

Diets, Fasting and Starvation

Over the course of my adult life I have dieted, fasted, and even went so far to try to starve myself to meet the image of society wants to see. I see we live in a world where It has gotten dangerous that many accept obesity and being overweight as normal and to just accept it.

For this year I have dedicated myself to getting healthy, losing weight, getting myself to a point of looking, feeling and be healthier. Some may argue that having a normal weight does not guarantee healthiness and have ready that even someone who is obese or majorly overweight can be healthy which goes against all logic to be healthy, because how does one's heart remain healthy by carrying more weight than naturally a person should.

Family history dictates what I know to be true

My mother whom I love passed in 2015 struggled with her weight for most of her weight, also having my aunt who suffered dying young in her forties on the account of Obesity and other health issues, a cause I think about every day.

Today it appears we live in a body positive movement where influencers and even the media make it acceptable to be overweight, obese and just to have self-acceptance. I guess my question is why should we accept ourselves like that?

Why can't we look ourselves in the mirror and want better for ourselves. I have been told that those who struggle with their weight can not always help their weight due to thyroid problems or other health issues that causes a person the inability to lose weight which I can understand but what I can not understand is how we are telling future men and women generations that its ok to live this way.

This may come across as judgmental and why can't people just live their lives they choose fit, thin, fat, obese, overweight, small, big you name it we all have a right to live as we see fit and you would be right, but again I pose the question shouldn't we all choose to live better, healthier lives that will give us all the best chances to live longer lives.

<u>The Dangers of the body positivity movement</u>

Some of you may say well you're missing the point of the body positivity movement, we are supposed to love ourselves and accept ourselves as is, skinny, overweight, obese since we are all different, why should one size of person rule. I can certainty understand that argument, but frankly I think promoting unhealthy lifestyles and acceptability in being obese is wrong because of what this teaches future generations.

I have seen time and time again influencers who promote overeating, social media and even the media that says its ok to live unhealthy. I guess one can say to each their own, it's their life let them be, why do I care so much, and the question is I care because I have a young daughter who is growing up in this world and will be affected by those choices she makes and frankly I wish not for our family to repeat our history. Would I see love my daughter of course, but do I wish to see her have a shorter life to the amount of strain it can have on her life and health, no I do not wish to see that.

Here are five reasons what body positivity has done and not in a good way:

- **People who are heavier-set refuse to accept the detrimental reality.**
- **It's taking a toll on people's physical health.**
- **Social media makes the situation worse, especially for young women.**
- **It takes a toll on one's mental health, and not always in the best way.**
- **The health of our younger generations is at stake, and we need to step up.**

My opinion is my own, many will not agree

Many of you may not agree with my opinion, deep down I can be honest and say I hate the fact that I was the overweight fat kid in school and how horribly I was treated. Struggling each day with seeing the ugliness of my body, the fat rolls and for a young boy and man the man boobs. I have struggled, fought to be at a healthy weight and feel finally I am although I feel my weight loss journey is not done yet.

Looking back at my own family whom I love, only wish for them to be healthier giving them a longer life expectancy. There are even those in movies and television who were simply taken too soon as I often reflect on those like actor John Candy and James Gandolfini in addition to others who died from heart disease on the account of their weight.

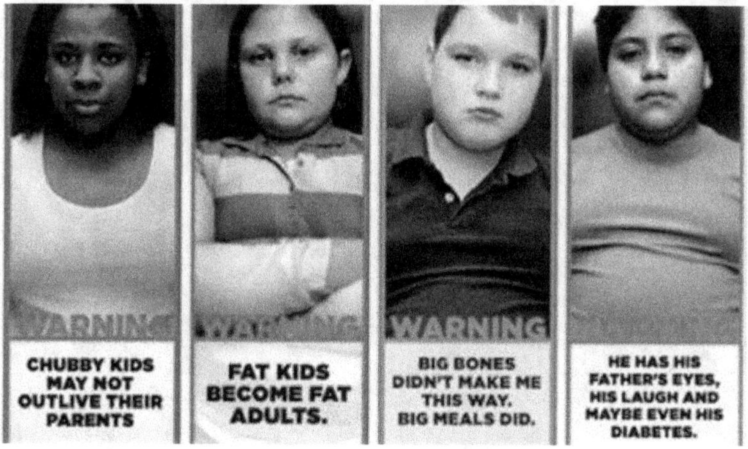

What is the point?

Each of us has the choice on how to live our lives whether to consciously think about our health, our weight and the food we eat. Many choose not to think about it filling our bodies with junk, but I can't fully blame ourselves as we live in a world of convenience of fast food disguised as quick and healthy, but its anything but as the healthy meal is made at home with fruits, veggies, meats and grains, one could call it clean eating. I admit for many its not possible to cook at home every day and fast food is quick, cheap and easy so why not.

Let's really begin to think about what we eat and no there is nothing wrong with your favorite fast food once and while, the point is not to deny but to make better choices, giving us a healthier chance to live longer for ourselves and our loved ones. Ultimately if you love your pudgy, overweight and or obese self well good for you, because you should love yourself, but love yourself enough to see you can be a better, healthier you.

The question I give all of you is the body postivity movement helpful to society and to yourself? and if not what are you going to do about it.

| 19 |

Gluttony is Eating Us Alive, How do We Overcome it

May 30th, 2021

As of late I have been really thinking about the word "Gluttony" and how much it brings true to the United States and world. I would go far as saying as many of us are gluttons one way or another, but there is extremism. Why am I suddenly thinking of this, well its because right now I am in my weight loss journey to lose 60 pounds, that's right 60 pounds!. I have already lost close to 40 pounds and thinking about how much weight I have gained have made me realize how much of glutton I have become, but not by choice. Over the years like anyone else who doesn't exercise every day or most days, the pounds slowly pack on and add to that I was not consciously watching what I was eating. If I wanted a burger and fries, why not. If I wanted ice cream and cake, sure bring it on and add on all the sugary drinks the more caffeinated I was the better.

My Beginning to Gluttony and Food

I have always struggled with my weight from a young age being the fat kid in school, being called names like fat boy, chubby, oinker and you name it I was called it. Growing up chubs was difficult always having to buy large clothes, having a belly and boy/man boobs. Always embarrassed of my body , never ever taking my shirt off in public, even in gym hiding and dressing in private or a stall. I was also bullied as a child and even by family who went out of their way to embarrass me. Those feelings took a long time to change, and I guess deep down I have always tried to accept myself.

I understand we should all accept ones self for who we are , but it seems in America especially gluttony seems to be celebrated especially obesity. This may sound hypocritical, but I love my family who has also struggled with weight most of our lives and it all started from mom and dad and other family members who didn't appear to have a problem with their shape. I have seen firsthand what more weight does to a person, to their appearance and health especially with my mother, who I love but I saw the struggle with her and the plain discrimination she faced for her weight. My mother endured and I think what helped her was the fact that she was fair skinned, but society is and never kind to the large folk.

My Attitude Change

Over the years my attitude towards bigger folks has changed over the years where I have had to correct my perceptions of people who I feel are gluttons and cant control themselves, but I know its very easy not to control ourselves in todays world. As an example a very special family member works at McDonalds part time and I must say the line NEVER Stops and this McDonald's is 24 hours and the line still never stops. Many eating Big Macs, Double quarter pounders, McFlurry's, and fries galore. Now one may say well why do I care its their body, its their life they should be able to eat and do what they like.

I understand for many who work late and getting their dinner or breakfast may be starved for a meal after a long day and night, but what about those who are sitting home and have a craving for Big Mac and a Large Fry and lets not forget the Large sugary drink to finish off their meal. Destroying our colons as we speak. Now I am not against fast food even though that is the worst food one can eat full of fat , sodium and whos know what else. I can enjoy a Big Mac once and again but now I have chosen healthier choices and I will say that eating Micky D's once in a while doesn't hurt but some eat it every single day as their daily meal.

Here are some stats to bring perspective:

- **The fast-food industry revenue in the US alone makes about $110 billion annually. (Statistic Brain)**
- **50 million Americans eat fast food every day. (Statistic Brain)**
- **A complete fast food meal is 37% of your daily calories. (Statistic Brain)**
- **McDonald's is more recognized than the Christian Cross. 88% of individuals in a survey correctly identified the fast-food giant's logo compared to 54% who recognized the Christian symbol. (Marketing Week)**
- **Fast food restaurants are expected to keep growing at 2% annually through 2020. (Brandon Gaille)**
- **There are nearly 200,000 fast-food franchises in the US as of 2020. (Statista, 2020)**

Now again myself and my family can never fully just give up Fast Food especially with my daughter of eight who loves her Happy meal which I have been enjoying since a young lad and my hope is one day my daughter eats normal food like her mom and dad but that has been a challenge because is my belief fast food as addictive chemicals that keep allowing you to come back for more. Now not all fast food is created equal some are not very addictive but McDonalds, Burger King, and other fast-food restaurants truly know what's in their food regardless of what they put on the label.

The Studies have shown

Here is some more information:

Studies of food addiction have focused on highly palatable foods. While fast food falls squarely into that category, it has several other attributes that may increase its salience. This review examines whether the nutrients present in fast food, the characteristics of fast-food consumers or the presentation and packaging of fast food may encourage substance dependence, as defined by the American Psychiatric Association. The majority of fast-food meals are accompanied by a soda, which increases the sugar content 10-fold.

Sugar addiction, including tolerance and withdrawal, has been demonstrated in rodents but not humans. Caffeine is a "model" substance of dependence; coffee drinks are driving the recent increase in fast food sales. Limited evidence suggests that the high fat and salt content of fast food may increase addictive potential. Fast food restaurants cluster in poorer neighborhoods and obese adults eat more fast food than those who are normal weight. Obesity is characterized by resistance to insulin, leptin and other hormonal signals that would normally control appetite and limit reward.

Neuroimaging studies in obese subjects provide evidence of altered reward and tolerance. Once obese, many individuals meet criteria for psychological dependence. Stress and dieting may sensitize an individual to reward. Finally, fast food advertisements, restaurants and menus all provide environmental cues that may trigger addictive overeating. While the concept of fast-food addiction remains to be proven, these findings support the role of fast food as a potentially addictive substance that is most likely to create dependence in vulnerable populations.

So how do we change from being stop being gluttons in todays day in age, is it as easy as flipping a switch, I think not. I perceive that gluttony will only get worse over time as you can see today wealth is even greater problem today. Now I am not saying that being wealthy is wrong, but which people have much they want more and more even those who could buy whatever they want while the country and world continue to get poorer.

I encourage each of us to observe the world from the standpoint of gluttony, are we getting better or worse. Some of you may not even care and why should you since it's difficult enough to focus on our own lives then those perfect strangers gorging themselves on food, drink and wealth. But we are also the problem, do we take part in gluttony, pig out, want more, more and more. I get that many of us do want more in life because simply we are not content with what we have and look at the Joneses and what they have, I know I do. Now the concept and idea of gluttony is nothing new like I mentioned before it has only gotten worse so what can do to change this.

What Can We Do?

According to **John Piper**, there are a lot of reasons for obesity in our culture. It's not just that we eat a lot of bad food. We're also pretty inactive and don't do a lot of walking, running, biking, etc. Oftentimes obesity issues are connected as much to activity issues as they are to what goes into our mouths. Muscles are designed to burn food, but if they aren't being used then any amount of food is going to result in obesity.

But "gluttony" is a better word to use in this context rather than "obesity," because overeating is where the problem is, not how much you weigh. There are all kinds of reasons why a person might weight too much or too little that is not a result of gluttony.

So how do you fight the battle? I think it must be fought mainly not with the word "No" but with an alternative "Yes."

We need to cultivate a range of appetites for great and good things, things like good literature, people's fellowship, reading the Bible, nature, work, etc. Discover these other appetites so that things other than food can satisfy you.

Lastly, this blog is not meant to say I am better than thou, its more of lets all try to open our eyes and be better , get healthier , lose those extra pounds and see the difference in how you feel. It will take time, effort and patience. I know the road to healthy eating and lifestyle takes time, discipline and dedication but we can all do it but we must start somewhere and no way am I saying go do the extreme and starve yourself to death. I have personally seen each pound melt away one by one, week by week, month by month, it will get discouraging at times because we want to lose weight quickly that in my opinion is not realistic.

Again you can apply these principles to any form of gluttony you experience.

Enjoy your Memorial Day weekend and remember don't be gluttons with lots of drink and food although I know that is the fun part of holidays but remember the meaning of Memorial Day to honor those who served our country. God Bless.

PART II-SOCIAL CAUSES

| 20 |

Homelessness, The Sad Reality, Don't Look Away!

July 15, 2019

Homelessness is a tragic and terrible thing that has wreaked society not just in the United States, but through out the world. But on a closer note to how it affects where I live, having lived in Los Angeles, now I live about forty five miles away from what is called Skid-Row. Having grew up in Los Angeles, homelessness was nothing new, I guess it wasn't until I got older that I started to notice the affects it can have on society and the damage it continues to do to people's lives.

The Reality Of The Numbers Homeless

Especially in Los Angeles, there are approximately 58,000 who are homeless and about 5,000 are children and 4,000 are elderly. In Los Angeles it continues to get worse each year as the cost of living continues to rise, and more people are beginning to live out of their cars but still continue to work to survive.

https://www.youtube.com/watch?v=8WkvjD1ZK5o

Last year there were approximately 16,000 , that's right 16,000 people sleeping in their cars called Safe Parks, accounting for 1/3 of the homeless population. But that kind of accommodation is only scratching the surface to what can be done due to space limitations, which in this case there were only 85 spaces. These parking lots have to meet certain safely standards , such as having security guard and many cases restrooms. Imagine living like that and for those who read this and have experience this I am so sorry and hope that in time you are able to recover and live a life of peace and safely. https://laist.com/2019/01/09/la_county_opens_another_parking_lot_for_homeless_to_sleep_safely_in_their_cars.php

Surviving Today comes at High Price

Many times it's easy to take living in a house or an apartment for granted, for many who still live at home with mom and dad, there is definitely a high cost of living that is making it very hard today. It's not just in California but all over the United States. Not every state is on the same level and height of Homelessness but California continues to get worse, as the price of a standard studio apartment is about $1400, one bedroom $1600 and two bedroom $1800 and up. Now I will say not all counties are this high, this is particular in Los Angeles, but housing prices continue to go up as Landlords continue to remove housing off the market, sell those properties and those new landlords raise the rent again making it affordable.

Some of reading this may be thinking how do people in California survive there, and you made my point, it's not easy and it's not easy just to pick up and leave to another state, such as some of the more modestly price states like in the Mid-west, where housing is considerably lower. But again back to homelessness, this is an issue that goes hand in hand with stagnant wages that have not gone up for many years for certain industries which have left people stuck and many who can't survive on those salary, even with government assistance.

The Struggle is Real for Everyone!

Although I have never been homeless the struggle is real, I am an educated person with a masters degree in business, but unfortunately wages for myself have been stagnant, but the price of goods, housing has gone up, leaving me at times with a negative balance in my pockets and that's working two jobs. I know the struggle exist for me imagine what its like those who may not have the education or skills or survive.

Homelessness is not always caused by Drug addiction or mental illness, it's caused by hardworking folks who lost their job, had no savings, just trying to make it and were forced on the street. There are approximately 1200 veterans in Los Angeles that are homeless people who have fought for our country and are left to fend for themselves.

The Vulnerability of Women and Children on the Streets

One of the most vulnerable groups like I mentioned is Women and Children who are homeless, approximately around 18,000 women. 18,000 who have to deal with the following while homeless

- 40% are survivors of sexual assault
- 55% are survivors of domestic abuse 40% are survivors of sexual assault
- 68% are survivors of child abuse
- 91% have experienced physical or sexual violence in their lifetime

In addition to those things listed above, there is also abuse in shelters , as high as 35% of women reporting feeling unsafe in a shelter and experiencing sexual abuse. Imagine being on the street and having to deal with abuse and trying to leave abuse in the home and just trying to make it and this happens, it's a horrible scenario.

Per the L.A. Times :

All the great social issues of American society play out in homelessness — inequality, racial injustice, poverty, violence, sexism. Naturally, life expectancy for the homeless is short:

about 47 years, according to skid row doctor Susan Partovi, compared with 78 in the population as a whole.

Helping Those in Needs Comes at a Cost

The challenges are enormous not only for those who are homeless but those who are trying to help, because unfortunately there is no magic formula to help those in need, it takes time, money and those in the private sector to make a difference in helping the homeless like Missions and churches, soup kitchens, all who have a heart for the homeless to help them off the street and survive. One of the best examples I have seen who is doing this is the Union Recuse Mission https://urm.org/.

The sad fact is society is so used to seeing Homeless on the streets many just don't care and feel like it's not their problem, but unfortunately the truth is anyone can end up homeless, as many are one paycheck away from being homeless. The homeless deserve respect and our attention to their needs as we go home and live in comfort with a roof over our heads and with our families.

Some of the questions that get raised about homeless is, Where are these homeless people's families, and the sad truth is many of those homeless are abandon and cast out by their own families, some are runaways, some were trafficked on the street and escaped only to be left homeless to fend for themselves. In Los Angeles homelessness is a sad part of our backdrop everywhere we go there is a homeless person, many counties today are actually trying Not to help the homeless but cast them out because residents complain about their property values going down because of Homeless, like in Orange County a very affluent part of California. It's quite sad to see counties try to physically move Homeless out of sight in certain cities because they don't want their businesses and home to suffer, essentially pushing the problem aside.

The Stats are Frightening

Some stats to bring it all in perspective since 2013 Homeless has gone up 49% in Los Angeles and within the United States, 3.5 million are considered homeless according to National Law Center on Homelessness and Poverty. The figure does seem high and it's possible, but by https://endhomelessness.org/homelessness-in-america/homelessness-statistics/state-of-homelessness-report/ , Homelessness is estimated around 552,000, which represents 17 out of 10,000 people. Lastly on a worldly estimate, its estimated that 2% of the worlds population is homeless, however about 20% lack adequate housing.

So you may ask yourself, so how does this affect me, why should I care, we should all care about those in Need especially Living in the United States, considered one of the richest countries in the world. It appears especially in the United States we have criminalized homeless by putting them in jail, throwing away their belongings and leaving no access to restrooms, shutting windows to beggers on the freeway. Yes we feel bad, but unfortunately many don't consider the homeless people, as many homeless experience attacks, being spit on the chastised, told to get a job without a loving touch for those in need.

We need many factors to solve this problem, but lets start with being kinder to those in need, doesn't necessarily mean giving money, but a kind word. From there we can work with local cities to help the homeless get out homelessness, but its going to take time, money resources and those in the business and private community to do more. I won't leave out our government because they too have a large role to play here too, but unfortunately fall short on caring about those who need the help.

Take a look at some of the sources of my information and get informed about your own communities and states and countries so we can at least have knowledge. https://www.latimes.com/opinion/editorials/la-ed-homeless-crisis-overview-20180225-htmlstory.html

This blog will hopefully bring more awareness and hopefully open our heart to more understanding to those in need 365 days a year, 24 hours a day.

| 21 |

Fear, Hate and Dignity: Opening our Heart

August 29, 2019

The pain of how we as people feel at times. Many of us struggle, rarely does anyone live a perfect life, perfect for me is not perfect for others. My perfect life would be to live a day where I don't have to worry about those things that many worry about like Money, taking care of a family and have a successful career.

Don't get me wrong I am not complaining, Life is what it is for everyone, there are those who struggle a lot worse than I do, like someone who is Homeless or has a deadly illness ticking away their life each day, Also fortunate to live in the United States, even though there are country's who have strong society and take better care of their citizens.

Again I am grateful and thankful to be here, but it can be a stress living here and see our country turned upside down by politics, people who are crazed fanatics and don't seem to have anything else to do with their time but to focus on our political Leaders, I wish I could tell those people go get a hobby, read more, spend more time with your family, Love More, Stop the Hate, be unified and stop being US VS Them mentality.

Get a Hobby

You may be asking where am I going with this? Well I will tell you where it starts, throughout my life I have NEVER been about politics, to be frank I could have cared less, I lived in a bubble for many years where I had no idea what was happening in our country, To this day I find politics very stressful and damaging to our culture and mind, where now it seems people are focused in putting their faith in those who run the country and not in what is important like focusing on the good, live your life, go to work, read, write, start a company do something more valuable in your life.

Reading that you may say well Joseph, I do take care of my family, I do provide for them, I do spend time with them, I do Love them. OK, that's great! So maybe there is one thing you do more often that is not healthy like watching to much TV, watching Political commentators tear each other a new one, create Hate for Profits and at the end of the day it's perfect ok because it is entertainment after all, no one takes that really seriously.

Oh but people do, we have seen it, and it's unfortunate we have to live through these times to see, because it appears other countries don't have to deal with certain issues like Gun violence, Mass murders like we do. I will Not say other countries don't experience it just not to the level we do.

The Fear is Real

I fear for my family, especially my Wife who immigrated from El Salvador in 2002 and is Now a U.S. Citizen. It is my belief that she has a target on her back for racism and hate because of where she came from. Even I worry for in her jobs where People I see have an image of my Wife being different, unworthy to work with them because they were born and raised in the Good Ole U.S.A.

Growing up I believe we are a nation of immigrants Legal and Undocumented, but ultimately we are a nation who gives chances to those who want a better life because other countries are either too poor to offer resources or don't have the structure to help those in need.

I have no problem with people wanting a better life, those people who come here searching for that, only wish to work hard and do jobs no one wants to do, unfortunately its what we call modern day slavery for low wages that NO American wants, the biggest argument I see well these people are taking jobs, they are taking American Jobs, that could go to us first. Ok yeah well that may be true to a certain extent, but many self intitled American would work 16 hour days for $12 bucks an hour, Not many I guarantee you that.

Marrying someone who came from the Norther Triangle El Salvador, Honduras and Guatemala those countries are poor, corrupt and could care less about their citizens at time, but ultimately there are good hard-working people who cannot feed themselves let alone their families.

Many Don't want Facts

What many don't realize is that people from El Salvador have a major Gang problem that strikes fear in people every day, stopping people from living a normal life, something we take for granted at times. The good people of El Salvador have to fear death itself each day, be exhorted, robbed and even not allowed stay in their own neighborhood without fear of being Shot and mutilated as those gangs could care less for the people its own citizens about their lives.

Don't get me wrong, I care about the issues affecting our country especially gun violence, homeless and our own gang problems, but what gets me is the heartlessness for others who are human beings and the hate that has taken over.

https://abcnews.go.com/International/el-salvador-murder-capital-world-gang-violence-life/story?id=39177963

It is my belief that the Hate and racism has bubbled up in our country has always been there but has been enhanced because those in power who have made it acceptable to act. People feel emboldened to act this way, but it doesn't make it acceptable or Right.

The History Speaks for Itself

History of how we treat people in the United States can be kind of appalling to how we have treated African Americans to Latinos to Native Americans to Immigrants, to Color of people, to Races of People, the list could go out, but for Immigrant that is nothing new, but you would think over time we would learn, one interesting piece of history called Operation

Wet-Back https://en.wikipedia.org/wiki/Operation_Wetback - Yeah you read that right!

Operation Wetback was an immigration law enforcement initiative created by Joseph Swing, the Director of the United States Immigration and Naturalization Service (INS), in cooperation with the Mexican government. The program was implemented in May 1954 by U.S. Attorney General Herbert Brownell.[1] The short-lived operation used military-style tactics to remove Mexican immigrants—some of them American citizens—from the United States. Though millions of Mexicans had legally entered the country through joint immigration programs in the first half of the 20th century, Operation Wetback was designed to send them back to Mexico.[2] The program became a contentious issue in Mexico–United States relations, even though it originated from a request by the Mexican government to stop the illegal entry of Mexican laborers into the United States. Legal entry of Mexican workers for employment was at the time controlled by the Bracero program, established during World War II by an agreement between the U.S. and Mexican governments. Operation Wetback was primarily a response to pressure from a broad coalition of farmers and business interests concerned with the effects of Mexican immigrants living in the United States without legal permission.[3] Upon implementation, Operation Wetback gave rise to arrests and deportations by the U.S. Border Patrol.[4][5]

Yes we are a country of laws and order, but the question I ask myself is many of us who are born in U.S. say that we follow the law and we are all Law abiding citizens, until we become a country that people stop following the law. The United states is NOT immune to becoming lawless even though that may never happen, because of our structure and the checks and balances that exist and our incredible law enforcement, but what could happen is people feel more emboldened to harass, spread hate and I Believe it has already begun with Social Media.

Open Your Hearts and Minds

As someone who is married to someone from Central America, these people are called horrible horrendous names, yet you never really hear anything from those being harassed. You never hear people from Those countries spreading Hate but Only wish to come here to survive. Yes Survive, not coming here to get rich, but just live, provide for their families.

Having been with my Wife I have come across many here who were undocumented , many barely scrapping by to eat as the jobs they have or had were changing from week to weekly, not a lot of stability, taking odd jobs no ones wanted, you know the type the guy cutting your grass, the painter who does a pretty good job painting and not charge you fortune. The women cleaning your crappy toilet's or picking up after you as if you're a five year old.

Film depicts struggles of Immigrants

I am reminded of a film I love call "Pretty Dirty Things", https://en.wikipedia.org/wiki/Dirty_Pretty_Things_(film)

A story about a man named Okwe, an undocumented West African Immigrant living in the UK, who drives a cab in London during the day and Works in a Hotel at Night. The Hotel is staffed with immigrants, both legal and illegal. A doctor in his home country, he was forced to flee after being falsely accused of murdering his wife.

In London, he is pressed into giving medical treatment to Poor immigrants, including fellow Cab drivers. Throughout the film you has very close friends Juliet a prostitute, Senay a Turkish Muslim seeking asylum, who works in the hotel as a cleaner. Throughout the film provide examples of illegal immigrants fear trying to survive and really being used for cheap labor. There is so much more to film without giving it a way, but a recommended watch.

The point is immigrants legal and illegal In woven into each society because other countries don't fulfill their objections to care for their citizens forcing people to leave.

Many people across the globe share the thought well they should just stay in their country, stay in their country to Die, to starve, to be exhorted, to be raped, abused and who knows what else.

These countries may have laws but those in power are corrupt, except in a recent change in El Salvador where the new president is working to curtail those coming to the United States, trying to stop gang violence and clean up the country. There is NO magic ticket for this to happen it takes time, but it's being done.

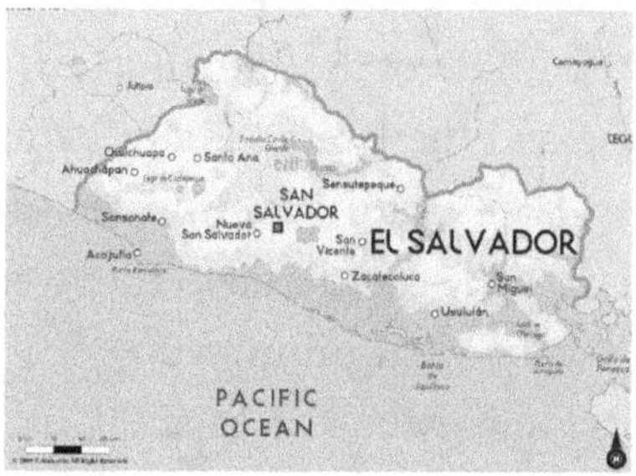

So Getting to this point, you may be asking what is the point of what I am saying, I am saying that as an American, a Father of an American and My Wife as a Naturalized Citizen, we are American's, but we are human of course, I hope the time will come that we treat those who are different looking, different culture, different education with respect and dignity. But I question if

our society is too far gone, I choose not to believe that but may be proven wrong.

We all deserve Dignity

The argument that someone doesn't deserve to be treated with dignity and Kindness, many of those coming here are not here to cause harm to you or me, but to work, to survive without fear of death each day. If we were in an alternate universe and the United States became unlivable due to lawlessness, Hate, extortion, Murder and making it unlivable surely we would leave to a place that we had peace in our lives.

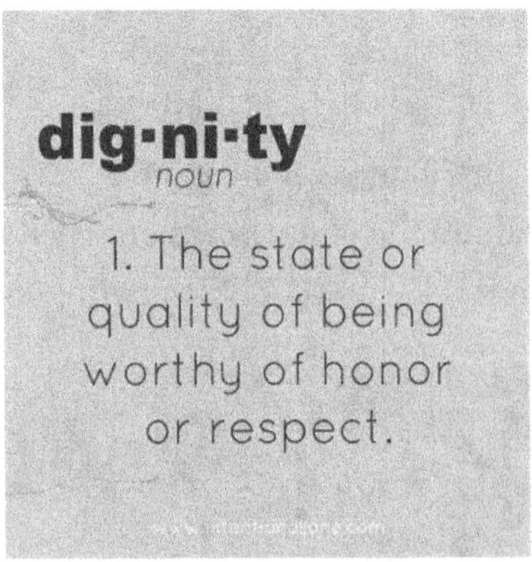

Lastly, what prompted this impassioned Blog well It's about equality, not being seen less valuable because people of different cultures are not from here, because your are wrong. We as Americans may have to abide by the rule of law in the United States, but I nor you own this country, it doesn't believe to us it belongs to God.

As someone who was raised here, I see myself how I am treated as If I don't belong here and even more so by my wife by how others treat her with infuriates me as if they are more worthy then her, they are not. Each day I guide my wife how to deal with those who feel empowered to look down at her, and to those people I say Scream them, they are the ones who have no value because this is not how we treat people.

In the end we all get put in our place, no matter where we go, there will always be someone richer, more educated, higher in power who looks at us and looks down at us, why must people continue to do that when we are all just trying to get through life with as little hassle as possible to survive. I think to myself do people have nothing better to do then hate, and then I think to myself maybe they don't maybe Hate is ingrained into their being that it's easier to hate, it's easier to blame others for our misfortunes.

I don't blame anyone for my hardships, I blame myself, I made choices, Living in the United States I had opportunities that I either blew or succeeded at but at the end of the day those were my decisions. Those who choose to come here for a better life to escape hate, violence and death, came here to live, survive away from Hate.

Those who practice this towards others hate when it's done to them, are we just filled with a hate filled world, I choose to think we are better than that, but let's try a little harder to respect those around us, to like and even love those around us who are different.

| 22 |

How Evangelicals Accept Hate in Politics

uly 11, 2020

For those who have read my blogs you may have noticed that I write about a variety of topics from Creative writing, Short Stories, Bigfoot and almost anything on my mind. Based on the title of this piece you will see that I am a Christian and take my faith very seriously.

I am far from perfect, so I will start there and I know that. As a person we are not meant to be perfect, only GOD is perfect, despite what people may say that he is flawed because situations in their favor are not happening. GOD and Jesus one in the same are perfect, omniscient , Loving, Patient, knows the Past, Future and Present and in my view everything is in his control, nothing is in our control .

What triggered this post and yes I will use the word triggered because I truly see the church going in a horrible direction and although its GODs church not Mine nor man, God has surely placed men and women in charge of his church to preach the word of God and save souls. I am not a pastor I am just a Jesus follower who knows right and wrong something that many christians today don't seem to know the difference.

How I was Triggered

I am absolutely disgusted with the fact that we have "Christians" who follow our current president Trump. I have had the opportunity to speak with many through social media primarily Facebook and they are unlike any christians I have seen before. Many appear convinced that Trump can do no wrong, his lying , cheating ways are no big deal simply because he is doing their bidding such as filling the courts with conservatives , abolishing abortion in society, which in my opinion that will never be abolished, protecting religious freedoms, having a relationship with Israel. All Many agenda points which most christians fight for. Now don't get me wrong they are important to me, but at what cost should those things happen, a loss of morality, a loss of ignoring what Jesus says and what GOD hates, which we have all but ignored in this president.

I truly see them as Sheep and although many who read this will see religion in general flawed and that is because Christians are meant to represent goodness but failed and are failing to do that. I am NOT saying there are no good Christians out there, are obliviously are and those who fight for the voiceless. But as a Christians how can you explains how people are treated today. I have faith in my GOD Jesus because he has NEVER let me down, but I refuse to treat people like they don't matter of any race, color , sex and creed, every man and women matters so how is that many today treat others like 2nd class citizens and this goes for minorities too.

I am appalled at how evangelicals have treated those in need like at the border, even the homeless where are they today? where are those fighting for the voiceless and yes I mean the unborn but what the kids at the border who are being abused as we speak in detention centers, who got stripped from the parents and pawned off to foster care which in my opinion is like kidnapping. If you are not aware what happens when an undocumented person crosses the border and caught, the child is separated from the parent and basically given to foster care were others adapt them while we deport the parents back to their country, OH its happen as we speak. I am angry as you can see as we have come to a point that Christians have been consumed in politics Right VS left, Hate.

What GOD Hates

As a Christian I am too have strong convictions about hating evil and GOD is very specific that we are to HATE what he hates which include the following from Proverbs 6:16:19

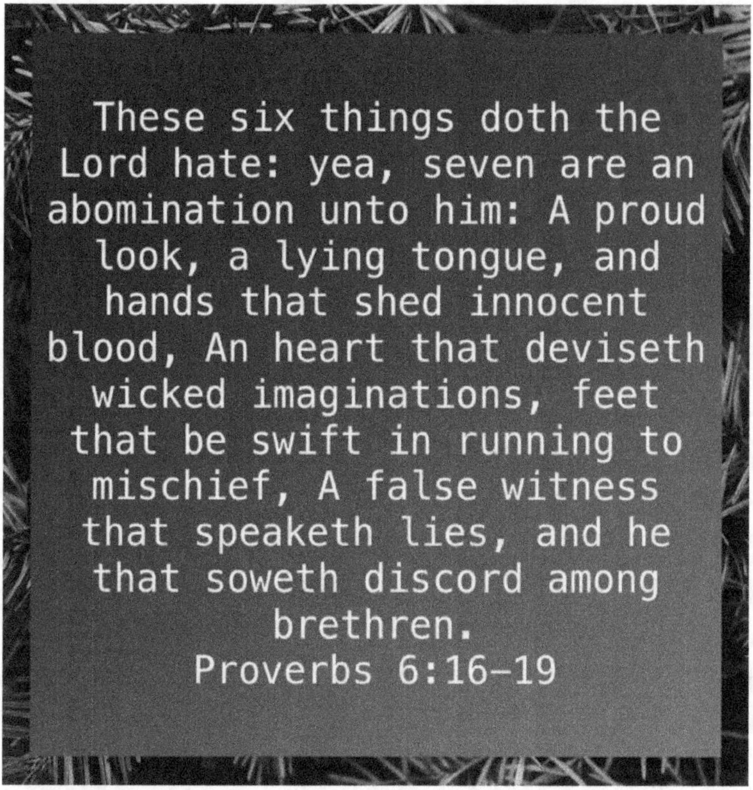

These 6 things the Lord Hates and I do everything in my power to say clear of what GOD hates, again I am not perfect and we all fall short in the glory of GOD, but he gives us specific standards to follow.

You may be asking where is all leading to, its leading to how many Christians today do not even resemble what god hates and those who even follow hate. I see every day especially in the United States who professes the name of Jesus yet does all of these things.

I see it in the church when they proclaim they love Jesus yet they are completely silent on some of the biggest travesty's happening in our country especially those who follow President Trump, a man I personally didn't vote for and would have never voted for due to a man I have seen as evil and who could care less about anyone than himself and time and time again has proven that.

It angers me when I see Churches, evangelical leaders support and continue to support a man who has caged Men, Women and Children without an ounce of humanity or dignity. Despite the difficulties of the situation has made things worse.

I will not pretend to understand what happens on the Border, I am sure it's horrific, but these are human beings are not pawns in his political game of hate for the brown man and women. He has also Lied over 10,000 times purposely mind you, continues to cause conflict in the United States and the world. Continues to run to evil and do evil things that are coming to light every day, yet, people still support him spreading hate, increase in violence and unfortunately many of those are so called Christians.

I am Not Bashing Christians, but those who proclaim to be ones and don't follow God's word, these are NOT Christians, they are followers of Man. I will say that I hope many will see the light, but just like in the bible where Sheep were referenced, that is represented by us, because Sheep are considered the stupidest creatures. But JESUS loves us and if we follow him, he will never leave up for forsake us, that is why I continue to follow him, Not Trump, Congress or anyone else.

I truly believe times will get worse and they are expected to per the Bible, eventually Jesus will come back for his church and his Bride Groom which is us, but no ones know the day or hour, only he knows.

As a Christian I understand God has a purpose for everything, even placing a man like Trump or any other King or Queen in power, because he has a purpose.

<u>What Jesus Stands for!</u>

Being a Christian can be difficult but worth it, because I know deep down what Jesus stands for is Love, building a relationship with him, following him and loving him. He gives us a choice that will always stand, it is my belief that you can not love two masters, you either are for Jesus or against him, you not have any feelings towards Jesus, so that means to you are against him.

As a Christian I am not here to preach to you, but to love you, be an example of Christian living even though I will fail, because I am man and will fail, but I will always try.

In today's day and age Politics has infused Christianity into that platform, many times spinning God's word to fit the agenda and to make money, two things God surely hates. I see it now and really has always been around, where there will be those trying to make a buck on God's name and people surely fall for it.

I have also seen churches incorporate politics in their messages, not always outright telling us to vote for someone but leaning towards that direction, not giving direct access to other party like Republicans and Democratic candidates. In addition, there is what's called the Christian Elite which are mega churches who have a lot of influence push an agenda and again telling us who we should really root for and I absolutely despise that.

I understand as a Christian we have a mission field to go out and preach the gospel, but what does voting for Donald Trump or another candidate have to do with God's word, in my opinion Nothing.

God Is in control again he will place whoever he wants in power and we will just have to deal with it. It's my educated guess that God will put people in our life for reasons to teach us even if it affects us negatively like Donald Trump who continues to lie, spread falsehoods, self-dealing and really only cares about his base, constantly putting down minorities, Immigrants. Democrats, journalist and anyone who doesn't agree with him.

Again God is in control, so only he knows what the future holds, because we live in republic we have choice which is of course wonderful, but choices have consequences when we make mistakes just like in life.

As a Christian, I live my life devote to Christ, My wife , Daughter, Family who are the core of my life, God Comes first and what he wants for my life.

Getting to the end you may be asking what is the point of this blog, the point was to simply release this burden on my heart over what I see is a sad state of affairs in Christianity in the United States. I say the United States because in certain country's being a Christian is deadly like countries such as Iran, China, even Russia, because the Bible is considered controversial for its principles, where these governments are so afraid of an uprising and people opening their eyes to the truth. It is written Jesus will account for those places that have little or no access to the word of God before the end of days.

I pray the country does turn around fast, our churches as well, but most importantly you and me who will open our eyes to what is happening around us. Of course we are to Live our lives, be busy unto the Lord until his return, not to Fret or do not be afraid which is mentioned 365 times, meaning we are not to be afraid each day of week, because again he is in control.

Again this is not to bash Christianity, its to shine a light on those who profess they Love God, but don't reflect anything godly but worldly, that goes to the Government, those in the church and of course the world. It's time to wake up Christian, open your eyes to what's happening and stop falling for lies of the enemy, pray more, open your bible more, put the phone down and focus on building godly god fearing lives.

In today's society I was against social media for so many years like Facebook and Twitter for the same reasons I am today its divisive, it sucks you to be negative and that goes for be a Christian. Christians are hated online and sometimes it becomes overwhelming to be online but I love the interaction for my writing.

There is some truth online but we have to be very careful and there is lots of misinformation but there is also truth to how people especially Christians act and are silent on important human rights issues.

For those who follow me online you will see that over the past few months I have gotten very political in my posts against our current administration but many evangelicals follow him like sheep in my opinion. He goes against everything Christ stood for. Yes Christians want to abolish abortion , put the bible back in schools and so many other things. Many take choose to have a platform to hate in the name of Jesus because they feel they can justify it but they can not.

Jesus was called for us to LOVE not hate, he was called to die for our sins yet Christians seem to be the best offenders at times especially from what I call the Christina Elite, those mega churches who feel they own Christianity and their voice is what matters. GODS word is what matters, man will always be weak and have self interest even if you are a pastor of a major church, ONLY Jesus is selfless.

Over the last few months I have grown increasingly angry over what I see happening in the church today and even by those who call themselves believers. Now I am by no means a perfect person and I am NOT self righteous in my pointing out flaws because I know what the bible says when it comes to pointing out the log in my brothers eyes:

So I know I should focus on my own flaws before I start pointing out others flaws, but it pains me to see Lost people especially believer who practice hate, who follow a man who lies to them as president and those choose to ignore the pain of others in need instead to practice what god hates.

I know we all fall short in this world and in the eyes of GOD, but we can all ask for forgiveness and we are forgiven on the shot, what a great GOD. If would only practice what we preach we would all be better people. I can't expect those who don't believe to practice not doing what god hates, but I see many non Christians do which put many to shame.

What is the point of the message is NOT to point out what we shouldn't do, but really a message for myself to remember that I am not perfect, I too do things GOD hates and I need to stop. I am NOT holier than thou, but I am a man who strives to be better each day and some days I do take a step back but I move forward again. This Blog may be more geared for believers but for who don't believe this may go to show you what GOD hates and how we can strive to be better.

Lastly I know that many may not like this Blog because NO likes to be told what GOD hates, because many will equate that with GOD being unloving but that is quite the opposite because GOD loves all of us regardless of what we think. GOD only wants the best for us and to rely on him for our needs when it can be difficult its easy to rely on ourselves, but I see seek him, Pray and see what happens God is faithful to us.

I know from reading this many will say hey your just a Trump hate, first and foremost I DONT hate anyone I Hate that we have a man as president who practices ALL the things GOD hates and yet Evangelicals are accepting of him. I have truly interacting with many online and although its a small percentage I speak to and I can not speak on behalf of all Christians and I choose NOT to, this is what I observe. Now If this is the direction our church is going into then we are in serious trouble. What will happen when Trump is NOT in office will the church recover from the years they practice to hate fellow man, to accept a man who they followed for years and destroyed the rule of law and republic. I am being over dramatic some of you will say I am, but I see what is happening around me and its scary. Here is a scripture I truly see today taking place and although this scripture is true to any generation, day, year and time, it is even more true today. There are literally hundreds of scriptures if not thousands that talk about evil in the world and those practice it. I am not self righteous in understanding my faults I know I am flawed seriously, but each day I work on my relationship with Jesus to be a better man, husband, father, brother and son.

What has been so shocking to me that those I do speak with say I am lost, I am letting the devil working through me because I am making an attempt for others to open their eyes to deception like this this wolf in sheep's clothing.

Yes I am triggered each day and maybe I need to lay off the social media, I am NOT a news watcher but I see Twitter and Facebook have the same negative affect. I know social media is NOT reality but those are still people voices many negative who appear UN-rational. Many will say I am being UN-rational people have a right to believe what they want, what right do I have to tell people what to believe, but at the end of the day there is still right and wrong, truth and lies, what will you choose to believe, many will believe the lie without thinking, without investigation that is NOT me.

Thank you for taking the time to read this and know that is has been in my heart and mind for quite some time and it will continue to be on my mind and heart for years to come. I do believe that one day Christ will come back and take us to heaven it could today, tomorrow or a hundred years from now only GOD knows but in the mean time I am here and continue to search for the truth and not believe the lies of the Devil or what the world tells me to believe.

For those out there who are Christians I hope you see my heart and where I am coming from . Those who are Non-believers know my concerns come from what I see in our country taking place and refuse to bow down to a man who I see only cares for himself and only has an agenda to help himself be enriched for his own financial gain, something many followers of Trump have said I am wrong, and with everything I say there has been research, studies even to his mental fitness which I believe he is unfit to be president, but I respect the republic because people voted for him, hopefully a learned lesson to what can happen when we choose the wrong people.

I am open minded, I am intelligent in my assessment of what I believe, but wrong is wrong, never will wrong be just ok or right as long as Christian agenda is made. GOD is once again in control of what happens in our life although we all have a choice and thank GOD because many countries take away a persons right of choice and we are republic with freedoms that I see are at stake each day due to the corruption taking place in the office of presidency, congress , senate and our country, lets wake up!

Lastly be kind to each other , love one another and in the words of the great Fred Rogers:

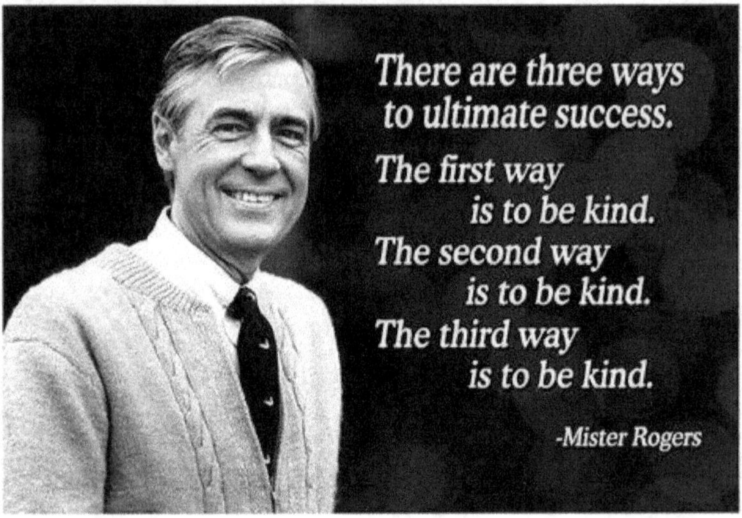

Thank you once again for taking the time to letting me unload my heart as this blog has been sitting in draft since May of 2019 and finally could no longer hold on to my feelings. Until we meet again!

| 23 |

Being a Christian Doesn't Give You a Right to Hate

June 13, 2020

Since 2009 a most memorable year in my life as this was a time I would meet my future wife, but this was also the time I became a christian and gave my life to Christ. I don't talk about my faith much on my blog for one because I find it very personal. For those out there who may not have any faith in religion or God for that matter this piece may not be for you.

As a christian I have grown in my faith and have relied on GOD for my needs even though it has not been easy. Since getting married that has only strengthen my faith in Jesus to be my crutch in my life. Like anyone else I have had my good times and bad times.

Over the years I have developed what I interrupt to what GOD wants for my life and what direction he wants my life to go into. Again I have made mistakes along the way for not listening to GOD on my life direction and took my own path at times and frankly have failed even when the warning signs were there and when I went against my wife's advise which I don't recommend.

Over the years I truly opened my eyes to the Christians around me, the hypocrisy that takes place in the body of Christ. I get we are all human, we all make mistakes and we are imperfect, only GOD is perfect. But I really seen lately the huge disappointment in fellow believers especially since Trump became president.

I never thought so many would become Sheep of Trump and follow him to the ends putting aside GOD's love to meet an agenda. What agenda do I speak of well the abolishment of abortion for one, which as a Christian we are taught that abortion is against God and in some way It is because GOD values our life and life and it is sacred.

Now I am not here to get into the abortion debate, because one thing GOD gave us was free will. Free will to choose how to live our lives in the hope that we would turn to him and give our lives. Abortion as much as I may not like it is Not my choice and we live in a world where abortion is allowed while other country's do not allow it. I am not here to judge or condemn those who do, but I have a point so stick with me.

My point is back to the disappointed in fellow Christians as they have thrown love, patience and kindness out the window to Make American Great Again. I have watched one of my churches which I used to attend turn into a full MAGA church which pains me to see as many who go to that church I have had some interaction online and they spoke some of the most vile things to me to defend their Trump Loving pastor.

Now I admit we ALL have a right to listen to, follow whoever we want as so I am, I choose to follow GOD and my pastors keep politics out of the pulpit. But if you have seen how what I call the Christian Elite act is disgusting, those like Franklin Graham, Jack Hibbs, Greg Laurie all Trump followers and advisors.

Some of reading this may say well its a free country, to each their own why let it bother you. It bothers me because as the body of Christ we are to be united and I frankly don't see that. I don't remember anywhere in the Bible where it said it perfectly ok to follow a man who Lies, Cheats and Steals from the American people, Puts kids in cages and who has ignored the rule of law.

In my opinion any good they try to do with wiped away with lies as our President constantly does. In addition we not only have a corrupt president who a cabinet who only take advantage of the American people. As you can tell I am NOT a Republican and prior to Trump becoming president I had NOT interest in politics, I actually have Never VOTED. But I will vote this November as if my life depended on it and so should You!

I don't hate my brothers and sister in Christ I just feel bad for them they followed blindly hook, line and sinker for a man who who doesn't give a damn about them only as a Vote nothing more , nothing Less, its all about him, his selfish greedy self. I actually find joy when fellow pastors and believes call out the Bull shit they see and bring a voice to Trump.

As a christian body the main argument many say is well Trump is fighting for our rights, he is fighting to make our world better. People are in a better place now more than ever and I say again bull shit. We are in a far worse place then we were 4 years ago. No president is perfect, they all make bad decisions because they are human trying to do their best, but Trump only has Trump to worry about.

As of late I have grown angry with politics and I will say its on both sides Dems and the GOP, both living in their ivory towers looking down on us while they collect their fat paychecks. I get our country is at a huge disadvantage with the GOP in senate and a Dem House nothing will get down because frankly both Parties don't care. At Least Dems try while in my opinion GOP lies , cheats and steals from the American people.

I see hate on the rise, violence, Racism increasing all while COVID-19 is taking place, a recession is here , 40 million out of work yet Many Christians are happy to see that the end times are coming. Yes I know we should all be happy as Christian the end times are coming, but what a world to leave behind especially with my wife and seven year old daughter.

Add in the recent riots, protests and murder of innocents and when I look at the Christians I see finger pointing, blame of Dems rarely GOP. Even the 15000 kids in cages are ignored by the Christian Right not a word or care as many of their positions are well their illegal, they shouldn't have come here, they get what they deserve instead WHO CARES.

Some of you out there may say well how do you know what those Christians feel? What right do you have to say that. Let me ask you this if they cared so much where are they? where are they on Fox News, OAN and other networks talking about the injustice, you just wont find it. Again this goes to both sides, but as Christians, which literally means CHRIST LIKE , where are those Christ like people, NO WHERE to be found.

Our world has both beautiful images of how Christians have helped those around the world and many do I am not discounting those who go into the mission field and preach the world. But what about here at home? It appears many Non believers have the right message for fighting for those who are voiceless, those fighting to have food on the table to feed their families where in Amerika we have an abundance of food and resources to help those in need but choose not to because what are we some charity to the world, well we used to be.

Sorry getting off topic again as a Christian we are to follow the word of GOD, be Kind, Be loving, be peace makers, where is that in our country and our world, I know its out there but where we need more of that today. We need for pastors to stick to preaching the word of GOD, the mission is to save souls not bring souls down with why Trump is the best president since Abraham Lincoln.

A lot of world hates because of politics, dictators presidents, people who are put in power. Ill admit GOD almighty put Trump in power to teach us a lesson. When you choose a lying, selfish leader who get someone who will not care when things go bad like with COVID-19 due to his inaction we have failed. This whole sick experiment over the last four years has been on sick experiment to teach Christians to wake up or else.

I know this may seem like one big rant, but this goes to show you I love my faith, my God and although I fail as a christian, I know who leads my life ultimately as he is the only one who can save so one day my soul has a place to go in Heaven. I know many may not believe but I hope you do to know Jesus died for you and me so we could have eternal life in heaven one day.

Christians need to wake up even though they think they are Woke they are not , they are lost, but many will say I am lost because I choose not to follow a lier in the White House. Sad days are truly ahead for all, but pray they get better.

| 24 |

Is Christian Nationalism The Ruin of Christianity?

July 19, 2020

As a Christian for 10 plus years now I have a strong understanding of what it means to be a Christ follower. I am by no means perfect and I will never claim to be, I sin like every man, women and child in this world even if you think you don't you do. Christianity is extremely sensitive topic to talk about and for some it turns off people lumping Christianity into a bigoted religion whose only intention is to limit people, spreading hate and fear. First and foremost that is NOT Christianity but those who profess to say they are why they hate, be bigoted and only wish to hurt others and churches are filled with those people.

We Are a Christian Nation

I will say this I do believe as a nation we were built of Judaeo-Christian Principles and to this day those ideals are still part of our culture and our government, but what I am going to discuss here is something so much more than that. I respect others ideals, beliefs alike and although I am believer in Christ, I believe in treating everyone with dignity and respect. For those who read the bible we are follow what Jesus says and Jesus was about LOVE and his message.

We are all taught as Christians we are all apart of the body of Christ and whose who profess to love Jesus need to live a certain way. The way in NOT perfection but in Love, respect and honor to Jesus and to treat those around us with Love. The bible is filled with beautiful scripture which I consider to be GOD's love letter to us as he truly does love us all even when we as people don't always love him.

One would think that we should all have unity in the church and be one big happy family but unfortunately that is not true. Yes we are a family and like any family we are all different, even having the weird uncle and for the most part whose who truly profess to love Jesus do and I spend my time with those.

But where I have truly seen a shift is the moment the Trump became president as he pushed hard to get evangelicals on his side make promises to gain their vote. Now I am not saying its necessary wrong to vote for a president who appeals to our needs as a person and country in most cases that is why we vote for a specific candidate whose ideals align with ours.

A Shift To Christian Nationalism Under Trump

In Trumps case he has NO ideals, he in my opinion is a cheating, lying , womanizing rapist who has a long history of abusing those around him. For many who hear this I would be called an anti-Trumper and I am ok with that, because deep down I see his game who completely baffles me in how he game evangelicals but I believe I see how and its NOT just him appealing to that base. As a believer we are taught abortion is wrong, be prolife, love Israel, fight for religious freedom which seem to be the biggest issues and I will add the sanctity of marriage between a man and women.

All of these beliefs are not just tied to Christianity, other religions believe similarity but Christianity is by far one of the largest groups with this belief. I am not saying I don't believe that Life is important, of course it is or marriage or having religious freedom and of course we must support Isreal because as a Christian you Can not Say oh I love Jesus and Hate Jews and the Country we Must want and pray for those things.

The problem lies in our culture, our world that unfortunately we are not going to change, although we can try. We can try to set laws to limit abortion or even eliminate it, we could make marriage between a man and women ONLY, we could even create laws to limit the rights of the LGBT community and bring the Bible back to schools. But lets remember we live in a nation of Not just Christians, so we CAN not force other to believe in what we believe and that is why many times whose who fight for Christians and their right lose battles because our courts and laws are geared for all of society not just one sect.

Trump since in office has tried to change that but attempting to put conservatives in the supreme court and federal courts in a way to tip the scales in his favor so when certain cases go to court there is a most likely chance he can win, but

NOT always. He is NOT a Christian and it is my belief he could care less about Christians and their beliefs they are just ponds for his re-election.

What is Christian Nationalism ?

He plays on the platform of Christian nationalism. Some of you may or may not be familiar with that term but you are probably more familiar with Nationalism. Nationalism is simply identification with ones own nation and support for its interests, especially the exclusion or detriment of interest of other nations. If you would like more information on nationalism please visit Wikipedia here : https://en.wikipedia.org/wiki/Nationalism

So nationalism is in line with Christian Nationalism which is similar in the sense of the following:

Christian nationalism is Christianity-affiliated religious nationalism. Christian nationalists primarily focus on internal politics, such as passing laws that reflect their view of Christianity and its role in political and social **life. In countries with a state Church, Christian nationalists, in seeking to preserve the status of a Christian state, uphold an antidisestablishmentarian position.[1][2][3] Christian nationalists have emphasized a recovery of territory in which Christianity formerly flourished, historically to establish a Pan-Christian state out of the countries within Christendom.[4][5]**

https://en.wikipedia.org/wiki/Christian_nationalism

Some of you reading this are probably asking so what does this mean and for every country its different, but for the US it primarily focuses on the following:

Christian nationalism in the United States manifests itself through the promotion of religious art and symbolism in the public square, such as the displaying of the Ten Commandments and the national motto "In God We Trust",[28] which came into force in order to distinguish the United States from the state atheism of the former Soviet Union.[16] The Foundation for Moral Law, for example, was founded for this purpose.[29] The ideology also advocates for public policy to be supported by religious beliefs, such as enshrining the sanctity of life in law through the buttressing of the pro-life movement.[28] Christian nationalists support Sunday blue laws in keeping with traditional first-day Sabbatarian principles; the Lord's Day Alliance (LDA) was organized by representatives of various Christian denominations to this end.[30] In 2018, the Congressional Prayer Caucus Foundation began Project Blitz to achieve these goals.[28]

Basically what Christian nationalism is the promotion of Policy which as mentioned deals directly with changing laws, adding conservative judges to the federal courts and in the supreme court. Trump has been systemically picking apart our courts for this reason to make evangelicals happy so they will once again vote for him despite his racism, his narcissism and hate for people of color and women I might add. For many who follow him they will deny he is racist, that he loves this country, that he even loves GOD, but he only loves himself and has only wish to enrich his life through the US government.

I implore others to learn who Trump is but many times Christians are blind to who he is and frankly they do not care as long as their agenda is done.

Why should you care you ask? Well because we are republic of people that's why, we are a nation of immigrants, people in all walks of life, rich, poor, you name it and what I see is he could care less about those who truly need help. I understand that as a nation and a state we have leaders who are supposed to fight for the small guy or gal when people vote them in office and they usually don't and haven't. Trump is the president which makes him the leader of our nation and he has failed us ALL. He has failed especially in this pandemic placing blame on China, on Obama and willing to blame anyone unwilling to be accountable yet Christian Nationalist vote for him.

The Issues Are Important

Do I believe Christians should care about the issues, of course I do. Do I believe we should all VOTE and be apart of the political process, of course. Do I believe in choosing leaders that align with our values of course, but this where I don't agree.

I believe for anyone in office, the person requires a moral compass for a nation to lead, a person who doesn't necessarily need to be in politics but someone who LOVES people and wants to make a difference in the lives of all man, women and children for the betterment of humanity.

We don't have that unfortunately; we have a fear mongering president with fascist tendencies who loves the attention of dictators like Putin and Kim Jung Ung among others. WE have someone who allows other countries to hack our systems and I believe allow bounties on our US soldiers abroad, in addition to the final nail in the coffin he was Impeached.

Many Christians choose to look the other way all in the name of progress for Christians, when ultimately GOD has the power the shift the powers of man for good or bad. This has all been a lesson for true Christians in who you choose to lead a country. Someone who does NOT lead with love and compassion can NEVER been a true leader. I am not saying Biden, Kanye, Warren or anyone else would be better they are all different but one common factor I saw in all of those Except Kayne is they LOVE people and want to better society. We may not always agree with everything they say or do but at the end of the day they are moral people with a conscience and a moral compass something we need in our lives and the lives of our leader.

Where Should We Stand

Sorry I get off topic but my point is Christian nationalism is NOT the answer, because I will say this policies and laws do NOT lead with compassion and Love in many cases they are used to help only certain parts of society. Now I love people, I love Christ and only wish to follow him and lead with a love heart for others whether your straight , gay , transgender,

Black, white, brown, white whatever you are deserve respect and compassion not to be put down further.

With Christian nationalism is really about our values being placed at the top of the pile and putting everyone's else's ideals and beliefs at the bottom. Our beliefs are NOT more important than yours. Yes I want others to come to Christ, go the heaven, live in eternity. But at what cost. Am I will be vote for some who is willing to toss others aside like a piece of garbage, NO! The only prime example is what has happened in our borders, Detention centers, abuse of children and adults all in the name of building a damn useless wall and living in fear and using hate and racism against who are less fortunate and poor. Yes I get we have laws and yes to a certain degree those who came here illegally broke laws, but does that deserve someone to be abused, have their kids taken away, NO!

Lets lastly go back to WHO Christ is, would he condone or accept what is going on today, I say he would surely hate it and does. We have failed even as Christians to do what is right and unfortunately this is what happens when Christians choose to stop following the bible and choose to follow a man, instead of allow GOD to have control.

I am sick over this, I am tired of turning on the news, seeing in social media and see the destruction that has taken place waiting for Christians to stand up and say ENOUGH! But none, I hear only silence especially in the border issue. What so infuriating is kids at the border who are innocent being locked up and abused by those in government.

Christian nationalism Does NOT work, believer in Christ, following your bible does, praying works and leading with love and compassion as Jesus commanded. This was placed on my heart in what I see today, I am filled with both anger and sadness over what I see each day in the body of Christ. Only GOD knows what the plan is, will our country recover, get worse, only GOD knows.

Praying for everyone affected in this world, COVID-19 and who struggle with what I do each day. Thank you for reading.

| 25 |

Are We In The Era of Orwell's 1984?

September 7th, 2020

As a writer and a reader, I often find that fictional imitates real life as something one could think is unimaginable to imaginable to our world. In addition to loving books, I also love film which is where many films created are taken from books. One book I surprising have never read until now is 1984 or Nineteen Eight four by George Orwell.

I have only just begun reading the book and have already watched the film with the late great actor John Hurt and Richard Burton. The film gets incredible close to the book so far, I know many of you will probably tell me about the inconsistencies if any. But like I said I have only just begun the book.

What is so incredible about this book so far is the incredible frightening resemblance to the times we live in today. Now mind you I live in the United States and the year is 2020. Our country on the verge of snapping in two as right and left are at hateful odds, its Democrats VS. Republicans, The Haves and Have Not's. Many will say that my comparison is preposterous and there is no comparison as we live in democracy not a authoritative state, but we are not far off if you look at things and where they are headed.

The Age of Trump

We are in the age of Trump and for many of you that's perfectly fine, as Biden will bring destruction to the world and U.S. which I find laughable. I am an intelligent man with an MBA in business, years in business from education to finance to Software I am no dope. I am smart enough to know that history can repeat itself with those in power who will allow it.

We the people the citizens are really at the mercy of those who run the country as we have to go along with whatever changes are made which includes are freedoms or lack of freedoms. Right not it may seem like everything is normal in a sense but everyone is on edge , but hate has amplified in our nation to new levels.

I truly believe that hate always existed in our country, but now people are free to hate and display that hate even so more than, gone is the civility of our world and country. Many are happy to have to be civil and the pleasantry's of being kind to others, caring for others and loving our fellow man.

One of the most stand alone parts of 1984 is something I came across last night which is:

"In the old days (it ran), before the glorious Revolution, London was not the beautiful city that we know today. It was a dark, dirty, miserable place where hardly anybody had enough to eat and where hundreds and thousands of poor people had no boots on their feet and not even a roof to sleep under. Children no older than you had to work twelve hours a day for cruel masters who flogged them with whips if they worked too slowly and fed them on nothing but stale breadcrusts and water.

But in among all this terrible poverty there were just a few great big beautiful houses that were lived in by rich men who had as many as thirty servants to look after them. These rich men were called capitalists. They were fat, ugly men with wicked faces, like the one in the picture on the opposite page. You can see that he is dressed in a long black coat which was called a frock coat, and a queer, shiny hat shaped like a stovepipe, which was called a top hat. This was the uniform of the capitalists, and no one else was allowed to wear it. ***The capitalists owned everything in the world, and everyone else was their slave. They owned all the land, all the houses, all the factories, and all the money. If anyone disobeyed them they could throw them into prison, or they could take his job away and starve him to death. When any ordinary person spoke to a capitalist he had to cringe and bow to him, and take off his cap and address him as 'Sir'. The chief of all the capitalists was called the King,*** *and –"*

If you focus on the passage in bold, we live in a capitalist country and like today the capitalist own everything and everyone else was their slave. Now you and I work for the man may think well I am no slave, but in reality, we are slaves. We rely heavily on organizations to pay us for our labor but ultimately, they have the control. Many capitalists own the land, the factories and all the money. We live in a time of greed, wall street, lobbyist and nothing happens in the world without money.

Who Really Control's Society?

As you know we have no shortage of billionaires and millionaires and many more are born each day in the land of opportunity. Now some of reading this may say well they deserve their wealth who am I to tell them they can't be rich and wealthy. How does another billionaire affect us you say well just someone else owning the world and doing everything in their power to swift the balance of power from the small guy like you and me to know, rigging the rules for their benefit.

If you think that the rich don't rig the system for them you are sadly mistaken as many of them pay little or no taxes, but the argument is well they provide thousands of jobs with companies like Amazon and Walmart, making slaves of their worker to depend on them knowing they will Never have the power of someone like Jeff Bezos.

Now mind you Jeff Bezos is an intelligent man and used his talents to get where he is today but he had lots of financial help such as his parents and venture capitals making him the riches man in the world and getting richer each day.

So once again what does that have to do with Orwell and where we are headed. There are those who will continue to create a class system as in the book which includes the upper class inner party, the middle class outer party and lower class Proles who make up 85 percent of the population and represent the working class. As the government , the party control the population with four ministries: The ministry of Peace, Ministry of Plenty, Ministry of Love, Ministry of Truth.

Like government each ministry has a purpose to keep control over the people, ultimately Big brother Is the one who watches all except the proles but everyone else they are pretty much under control. We do have a form of big brother watching us, listening to us each day and if you think what you write online and in social media posts is not watched or recorded you are dead wrong as companies like Facebook, Google and Twitter willfully sell our information to the government.

Yes we live in free country for now but for how long, this has really been on my mind for a while now and after watching and reading 1984 we are closer than ever to one day falling under one rule which in my opinion we are not out of reach of someone like Trump.

How the Media Rules Our Age

If we truly lived in the age of 1984 I would never be able to write this, Gestapo type men would be kicking down my door and taking me a way to reprogram me or worse yet kill me and incinerate my body. What is incredibly interesting is the amount of Hate for Media in our day in age and I understand why. I know the media is far from perfect, they lie, distort information to benefit their viewers on TV and on print, they are money driven and must do anything to stay in the game.

I will not call the media the enemy of the people because there are bad actors in all professions, we live in a world of profits, capitalism and greed. To stay in the game of life one must do what it takes to keep the customers coming and although most organizations are in a sense honest they are not out of reach to ripping off the public if they had to. When it comes to the media they rely heavily of viewership, ratings and endorsements and if they don't have that they go out of business.

I make every attempt to not watch CNN , Faux News, MSN, or any major media because deep down they all lie, its not right VS left news many times its lets spin our opinions as truth and fact and its NOT. There are factual news media who tell it straight but in all honestly I choose to try to do my own research when finding out facts on the issues. Social Media is another form of media of verges on the edge of propaganda spinning lies to get more likes and RT's.

Our Attempt at Rewriting History

What is interesting to what is going on today and in 1984 is how the Ministry of Truth rewrites history all the time so that no one ever knows what the real history is. This is what Winston Smith does as an editor of revising historical records to concord the past to the contemporary party line.

We as society have a real problem will history because many times our history is not pleasant , but whose history is as we make attempts to erase the horrible things our country has done such as allowing slavery, eliminating native Americans and removing them from their land, add in racism, wars and so much more that many wish to erase like it didn't exist so a new narrative can be written in its place.

I often think of how history books are written today, what has been removed and kept as I have truly been out of grade school for decades now I can only imagine what is taught today in schools. I find no problem is learning about the horrors of what our country has done, but I also know we have done good too but lets stop try to erase history, but if you think about it any way we are similar to 1984.

Reflections

As I continue to read the book I will surely reflect more on our differences of the book and today in our society and where we are headed. Again if I lived in 1984 I surely couldn't even have a blog, have social media or anything that lets me think and express my thoughts. In 1984 there is only one thought the loyalty to the party nothing else and if I am not loyal I am once again reprogrammed or killed.

Imagine all those who try to speak today in our country and world who are eliminated because their voice doesn't want to be heard by heads of states and governments, its not out of place that we one day become a country that will eliminate peoples voices of thought because there is truth to it.

As you can see I have thought seriously about this, I hope you think about it too as we begin to go into new eras of those who will try to quiet us who have thoughts.

Many who read this post may not find this far reaching, thinking that we can never mimic such a fictional world as 1984 , but in reality countries do exist such as this, who make it a point to control the narrative, control information, try to quiet whose who think differently. Although we may not try to assassinate those we disagree with like others countries have shown to do like Saudi Arabia , Russia and even China.

The Attack on The Free Press

In addition many of those countries prevent free press , something that if things continue to go we could one day lose free press. But you say no Joseph its in the constitution we will never lose that, well I will say that we can lose it because when governments stop following their founders original intent and start making up the rules as they go along or discarding laws and rules than it's very plausible to get rid of those freedoms.

Yes if that was to happen there would be literal turmoil in our country even more so of what is happening now such as more protests, which is our constitutional right, but where there is NO constitutional right is looting and rioting, I condone those actions and only take attention away from those who truly are trying to get a message out about injustice.

Just in today's climate with protestors which again I agree are allowed to protest peacefully, but when looters and rioters come out and destroy property, fight with authorities, kill people in the name of justice, complete anarchy. When situations like this happen states and the federal government then feel the need to take action which can be extreme at times, no one should ever have to die to protest yet we see it happening.

I will not say the police involved is perfect, they obliviously have a job to do to perfect the citizens of our towns and states, but some police can take it too far because deep down they feel empowered that nothing will touch them, that is what happens when law and order go out the window and giving so much power to police. Now I understand we need police to protect us from the bad people, but we don't need police to mimic criminals in the name of justice taking a vigilante approach, that is what is making society made.

So again sorry got off topic, going back to 1984 there can be scary differences to how society was once civil, ruled by law and order and slowly became ruled of one man or a group of men or women. In our case corporations rule the working class which would make most of us proles who are the worker bees making up 85% of society.

U.S Government Vs. Orwellian Government

Within our society we have structure of a government in our case of the United States we have three branches the Legislative, judicial and executive. Most of us know this is out we separate powers building a system of checks and balances, something that has appeared to have gone away with this current presidency. Although many will say well the president of the United States has authority to make choices on how he or she chooses use that power and in my opinion that is a flat out NO.

The presidency doesn't not give that person unlimited powers to misuse those branches regardless if they don't like the rules. That is one of the big issues when leaders break those rules and no one stops them, when in reality most of us who break the rules are penalized , put in jail or go to prison why is the presidency any different, it isn't.

The sad fact is that congress is very powerful as well it should be, but they there to protect the citizens of the countries from harm including an authoritative president or leaders but when they choose to not do anything because of loyalty to a person we all fail as a country and more harm is done to our republic.

In comparison to 1984, there are what are called Ministries similar to our branches. In the book there are four ministries which include:

The Ministry of Love

The Ministry of love serves as the interior ministry. It enforces loyalty to Big Brother through fear, through security and repression, as well as brainwashing. In the book this ministry has no windows and is surrounded by barb wire entanglements, steel doors, hidden machine gun nests and guards armed with "jointed Truncheons".

The interior lights are never turned off, it is considered the most powerful ministry, controlling the will of the population. The thought police are part of this ministry. This ministry is misnamed since it is largely responsible for the practice of misery, fear, suffering and torture. In a sense, however the name is apt, since its ultimate purpose is to instill love of Big Brother, the only form of love allowed.

Each of these Ministries or Branches serve a purpose I found quite interesting and if you have never read 1984 I would high recommend to see the incredible prophetic vision Orwell had in 1949 when he wrote this book.

The Ministry of Peace

The Ministry of Peace serves as the war ministry and is in charge of the armed forces, mostly navy and army. The primary principle in this ministry is the principle of perpetual war, using all surplus resources, keeping most citizens in lives in constant hardship, preventing society from learning enough to comprehend the true nature of society.

Perpetual warfare also helps preserve the special mental atmosphere that a hierarchical society needs. What this means is the balance of the country rests in the war, which is in charge of fighting the war, making sure to never tip the scales.

Again the ministry of peace if opposite of its name, since its main objective is in charge of maintaining a state of war. Perpetual war is what keeps the peace and the balance of power in the world, and since the other major powers also use warfare as a means to maintain the status quo.

The Ministry of Plenty

The Ministry of Plenty is in control of Command Economy which is considered an economic system which the government controls and regulates production, distribution, prices and etc. This ministry oversees the rationing of food, supplies and goods. The central theme of Oceania's idea that the poor, ignorant populace is easier to rule over than a wealthy, well informed one. Telescreens often make reports on how Big Brother has been able to increase economic production, even when production has actually gone down.

Once again this ministry is misnamed, doing the opposite and is responsible for perpetual poverty, scarcity and financial shortages. However, the name is also apt because, along with the ministry of Truth, The Ministry of Plenty's other purpose is to convince the populace that they are living in state of perpetual prosperity. In addition this department is in charge of the state lotteries, very popular among proles who buy tickets in hope to win big prizes, which is a vast hope as the big prizes in fact are not awarded at all.

Ministry of Truth

The Ministry of Truth is the ministry of Propaganda. Responsible for any necessary falsification of historical events. This ministry spreads a new language amongst the populace called Newspeak, which, for example "Truth" is understood to mean statements like 2 + 2 = 5 when the situation warrants.

The Ministry of Truth is involved with the news media, entertainment, the fine arts and educational books. Its purpose is to rewrite history to change the facts to fit Party doctrine for propaganda effect. For example, if Big Brother makes a prediction that is wrong, the employees in the Ministry of Truth correct the record to make it accurate.

Looking at these ministries one would think well yeah these are perfectly plausible to a country who wishes to control its people, taking away ones way to learn the truth instead providing the truth they want society to know and if society chooses not to embrace their truth they can brainwash them.

Are we not in a state of brainwash ourselves in our country believing that one party for example Democrats Vs. Republicans and how Republicans preach that they are the only party that can bring peace to the country, smearing the Democrats as being socialist and against Law and Order, and against this and that, but ultimately have shown they are ones who wish to keep control and try to bend the will of the people by controlling what society can and can not do like voting.

One can say well everyone in the US if eligible has a right to vote and yes that is true, but suppression does exist as states run mainly by republicans try to make it more difficult for some to vote especially in minority populated parts of the country doing everything in their power to stay in power.

I know of you may feel I just making up conspiracy theories about our rights but in truth the reason why its not a bigger issue is because we have really our own Ministry of Truth which is the Media who attempts to control the narrative of what they want the people to know about, this is where it gets to Orwellian with our reliance on Media to get what we need and why its so dangerous to take all the media as truth, in truth everyone has an angle right.

Although I live in the United States, the land of Free, nothing is free , there is a cost to it and in our know right we have our own Big Brother watching us use those resources to say in the future well group X used this amount of resources versus Group XY and so we should take way Group X resources and control them.

Such as control which groups can be in power keeping poverty a perpetual part of world and country when we have the resources to solve homelessness for example, but again every state and local government has that power to decide who we can help and not help.

But once again the control is in corporate America as they really choose what society will be provided , what wages they decide to be appropriate to keep certain groups just having enough to barely make it relying on the government for other resources like welfare keeping those classes in place.

Ultimately I think in 1984 its about the classes of people and keeping it organized so that certain classes will rule everyone else, because once you let the proles rule society will truly only start be fair in sense for everyone, we don't live in fair society of world, as it repeated in 1984 "War is Peace" Freedom is Slavery" and Ignorance is Strength" these government slogans.

War is peace is best examined as the government believing the people must believe that war is peace meaning one must tolerate the horrors of war. The idea is that one must make terrible sacrifices in order to have a peaceful nation.

Freedom is Slavery on the other hand is meant to represent the message that the party imparts to the community that anyone who becomes independent of society's control is bound to be unsuccessful. A society that is based on free will result in chaos and the development of society.

Lastly Ignorance if Strength is meant for the citizens to subvert their will and their awareness to accept the contradictions the government puts forth. They are expected to bury the truth and accept irrationality such as in demonstrated in these three statements.

Ignorance is therefore strength as it is the willing ignorance of the people who ignore obvious contradictions. It is this ignorance that maintains the power of the government and the seeming coherence of the society. Its through this ignorance that people can find the strength and live in a totalitarian society where the government oppresses them even while communicating to them how fortunate they are.

How many times do we in society hear our government how great we all have compared to other countries; how much we are provided and what they are doing for us. In some sense government has an obligation to help its citizens, not necessary to be rich and wealthy but to survive.

Governments know the power they have to help their citizens like provide healthcare, food and shelter but in the U.S. will they ever truly do that probably not because that would resemble socialism which our country is clearly again in principle but in a sense we still bail out corporations and agriculture in forms of financial help, so socialism is still part of our fabric whether we see it or not.

The point I am try to making is the many similarities and possibilities of where society is headed and how ultimately we have our form of Big Brother , government watching us, listening to us and even corporation who have taken it upon themselves to watch us like Google, Amazon and Apple, but that's ok because they are multi billion dollar companies that we know we need here.

I am not against capitalist or capitalism its what makes our country great with the ability to have wealthy and a life of freedom, but eventually our freedoms will come at a cost because of control, control is something someone always wants such as government. The question is when control will more be allowed in our lives and what are we going to do about it before turning into the era of Orwellian government control, its not far off.

I appreciate you listening to my deep thoughts on the matter and I know as I read further into the book more enlightenment's will take place and I am looking forward to it, but I recommend you read the book, watch the film and see those comparisons.

| 26 |

Amerika, Democracy in Name Only!

September 26, 2020

We are one of the most difficult times, as a forty year old male I have seen anything unlike I have like today's days. But to be honest I guess prior to 2016 I didn't pay much attention because I was so focused on trying to live my life. We are coming to a point where are livelihoods may be in jeopardy, some of you may think I am being over dramatic as if nothing will happen. We are of course in an election year which adds much more stress to the future of the next four years but also what the next ten, twenty years will be like. We are on the cusp of our country falling into further decline then I have ever seen before where hate, racism continue to rise and it appears civility have all but disappeared from society.

Taking the Good with the Bad

Living in the United States built on good and bad principles that will forever be in the fabric of our society, certain freedoms that are key to our happiness will one day disappear I suspect. Many of you say well that's why we have the constitution but even our constitution can be rewritten and outright ignored if we allow it. What is so unfortunate that we make everyone to be evil and by that logic you and I evil.

We live in a world of fear mongering, that I see comes from the right and the left, Democrats and Republicans constantly fighting ideology finger pointing each other as being evil. As a Christian I am very conflicted over how our society has grown over the last few years. I truly believe the arrival of our current president only magnified our society to be more bold to hate more , be uncivil and I see it only getting worse.

I must stand on my principles which are becoming shaky at times relying on the word of god for my goodness in knowing I am not alone and he will forever be faithful to our lives. Many of you who read this I know may not believe in GOD and many have the attitude that church, GOD, Christianity are useless something I would disagree with and remind those who think that we live in a fallen world ruled by sin and evil the Devil.

Christian's Vilification of those in Society

Stay with me for a moment, we are all human beings who deserve respect despite what Christian right make those who are different such as the LGBT community as they continue to vilify them each day. Even If I don't agree with their lifestyle who am I to tell them how they should live their lives just we expect the same respect with our lives.

Just is the case of those who choose to have an abortion , yes as Christians we are taught that that babies life matter and surely it does, but what is often gotten in those who preach pro-life is the life after birth, such as those kids who grow up hungry or live in situations that harm their lives like drugs and alcohol, what about those lives of refugees who come here for a better life and are told to go back to you country, no room is that respecting life it doesn't appear to be but the Christians remain silent on those issues.

I have seen horrible things how we treat humanity without an afterthought the consequences to those lives especially with immigrants who are treated subhuman. I get that for much in this world we require others to also care and continue to push for those issues that help human kind such healthcare, housing and having food on the table all of which seem to be systemically taken away from society, yet we have no problem giving billions to the military when people at home are suffering real loss like homelessness but if you watch the media apparently homelessness only happens in Democratic states and the federal government has no responsibility to help those citizens.

Democracy in Name Only Begins

When I say that we are a democracy in name is because we truly are, where is the democracy when trying to help the citizens who needs real help right now from job loss, from be evicted from their home and for many will say well the government did prevent evicted during the pandemic, but what happens afterwards when those same individuals with no income owe up , who is going to save them then especially when our federal government makes the judgment that additional aide is a hinderances to those individuals wanting to go out an get a new job, these are clearly the thoughts comes from the GOP, so little faith in the American worker yet we have no problem giving 1.5 trillion tax break to the top 1% and what effect does that show that helped Americans, there is none because that tax break helped no one but the rich.

I will say that congress is another issue as on the both sides of aisles you have Dems and Republicans who rely heavily on corporate donors to help keep them in office, money truly talks and when you have donors contributing millions to a candidates causes compared to a new comer with not nearly enough in comparison what chance do they have.

Money Makes Dreams Happen

Not to get off track my point being money makes the world go around, you can truly buy the presidency or seat at the table in congress with money regardless if you good ideas or not on how to truly help society we see it everyday many congress sit together contributing nothing but collecting a nice paycheck. In the need those seats are still vulnerable when the people choose to vote them out. That's our power right there to vote and keep voting never being happy with those in office until they truly start fighting for the people of their state and country.

At the moment you have seen horrors that are happening under our watch with the Trump administration who has sway the republicans and people to believe they are truly making a difference, but I don't see it. Yes from a Christian standpoint, Trump has been their mouth piece to fight on their behalf in eliminating the rights of the average Americans and propping up Christians like we've never seen before.

Honestly I have GOD to provide for me I need no man to speak on my behalf and Trump doesn't speak for my beliefs and values, what he believes goes against everything good about what Man and Women try to do each day, I truly believe he has I allowed more evil in this country giving the citizens a brazenness to treat others like garage , to spit on society and say well who's going to stop me.

Evangelicals Continue to Condemn Society and Don't look at their own shortfalls

What is so hard to swallow is the message I constantly get from Christians which is You are going to hell if you are a democrat, Trump is the only answer to saving society, Trump is going to fight for your rights, Trump is the moral compass we need in our country as he is fighting for us to end abortion, project your religious freedoms. I don't believe that one and that's my right, I choose to believe in what history tells me about man, which is give a man or women an inch they will take a mile.

Allow man or women to get a free pass on being held accountable, he or she will continue to go further and further next time. Look at the behavior of a criminal with no accountability they will go out again and again to commit more crime leading to worse behavior because whose going to stop me.

This is exactly what is happening in our White House with the justification of breaking laws, ignoring the rule of law, bypassing barriers that protect our constitution and protect we the citizens from going from a republic to a fascist state, think it cant happen, you would be dead wrong.

What people don't fail to see with it comes to fascism rising that its really not that hard, it all lies in those who are in power and who give power to one man or women giving them free rein to act in the way they see fit. If you look at Adolf Hitler, he was an incredible speaker and many knew it being drawn to him more and more people soon followed making it almost impossible to fight against him as his party became the majority.

Violence Continues to Wreak Society on All Sides

Not I am not about to say Trump is Hitler but can he have the same tendencies to using violence to get his message across and its being allowed, especially with those on the border whose human rights have been taken away. Our rights are slowly being stripped away as we are being told in subtle ways that free speech shouldn't really be free if you speak against the government like Trump who wishes to silence social media companies from allowing who speak against him.

Now many will say he would never do that, he is not trying to do that, stop stop stop that is the attitude of many Trumper's who think he is not capable of doing that, but we all know he is if he is allowed which doesn't make it right. Look at what is happening to our free press as we speak which is being daily bombarded with threats from society over their disagreement with how Trump is portrayed in the media being called the "Enemy of the People". Again if you think that Trump administration wouldn't try to slap sanctions or create laws to limit or silence the free press think again, it just takes those in congress to work to make that happen, but thank goodness we have a Democrat Majority and a GOP senate Majority, but that has meant nothing gets done hence of where we are at today.

Will we Ever Learn?

One of the most striking things I have seen in the last four years is the amount of lies that continue to fill the minds of Americans and that includes conspiracies. Truly never believe Americans could be that stupid but I guess we will as a country will never learn from our past and our mistakes following like sheep. What is interesting is a large majority of those following the lies are evangelicals who repeat those lies in their pulpits, sad but truth.

I currently attend two services online at the moment Calvary Chapel Rancho Cucamonga and Calvary Chapel Downey, but who I consider teaches the word of God. What is so different about those two pastors is their messaging where one stuck to the word of God with the infusion of thought on the coming elections while the other spouted conspiracy theories concerning COVID-19, Voting in subtle words for Trump and leading with your conscience and what the bible says. Both respectably stated we should vote based on the bible says concerning the issues. What I don't understand is that bible states should love our neighbors, love the poor, treat the foreigner with Love all principles that goes against what Trump has done and acted in his life time.

Kleptocracy is Our New Norm

I am smart enough to know that Trump knows he has the Evangelicals by the cajones as they follow him without question, although they say they follow GOD their words and actions say otherwise. Many would say well Joseph your not really a follower if you don't vote for Trump as he is the best person to fight for your religious rights, Biden believes in abortion , but I truly believe although he has made NO attempt to outlaw it doesn't mean he accepts it. We must all remember we live in a republic with the Citizens of the United States, laws meant for every citizen not just a sect of people like Christians. The United States not Christian, we are not a Theocracy , we are now a Kleptocracy which is defined as is a government whose corrupt leaders (**kleptocrats**) use political power to appropriate the wealth of their nation, typically by embezzling or misappropriating government funds. Sound familiar, it should because that is exactly what is happening to our country as we speak.

I like to think its not to late, but greed does have a powerful effect over society to keep the gravy train going and it doesn't appear anyone is going to stop it for the Trump administration with no condemnation from Evangelicals and the GOP. It is my thought that the GOP is no longer the political party of GOP but the Trump party with no ideals of their own as long is it pleases their dear leader.

I continue to think deeply about our country, pray for it to turn course and open the eyes of evangelicals who follow Trump without question, no longer Christ followers but Trump followers wholeheartedly.

I continue to reference my bible for the end times, which to non-Christians that may sound crazy but our earth, our time will eventually come to end on this earth whether its 2020 or 2045 or the year 3000 only God knows until then I keep focus on my faith, my family and keeping my eyes open to what future horrors hold for our country, I personally don't have a lot of faith in humanity at this point but hope to be surprised.

I know there so much more we could discuss over how society, our country and our world continues to go downhill as those from the right, the left, the center, the evangelicals look to place blame on anyone but themselves who I am sorry to have made add a new degree to hate to the conversation by working to attempt to take the rights of those who don't share their beliefs.

But as whole most of us are aware of the wholesomeness of society is gone due to the affect over the media especially social media who continues to have their grip on society in what we see and believe. I am tried folks, tired of the division, tired of hate and racism, tired of someone always try to make attempts to control us to follow their agenda.

Only time will tell if we can ever return to a true democracy or if our country will continue to spiral out of control which will ultimately lead us to a fascism.

Many of you who will read this will read is disbelief even if you get this far thinking that everything is just ok, Trump, the republicans and even the Evangelicals are not a threat, that I am the one fearmongering over what may never happen. I will say that anything is possible, we relay on those in power meaning congress and government to protect the rights of the people and not allow the spread of violence to our cities and states. I will not go as far to call BLM terrorist's, but in my opinion the real domestic terrorist's are white supremist.

I get that BLM and those who represent the cause have not been the best representation of what their message is about because many will equate BLM with mobs and destruction when you look at what as happened in our cities, but a majority of society I believe want to live in a nation of fairness and equality, we can no longer ignore the issues that are causing our nation pain. Its not about shutting them up but really listening, As a nation over 200 years old we were built from Judeo-Christian principles but we were also built with racism from the indigenous people to the African Americans to Latino's and it will continue no doubt.

We as a nation try to ignore that part of history because lets face its not the best part of who we are as a nation and what we have allowed and continued to allowed. Many will have the argument well Blacks, Asians, Latinos have the same rights as everyone else and although that is true they are not always treated with fairness and equality they are treated guilty until proven innocence when other races are innocent until proven guilty we have two separate systems here , one for the rich and poor, but embedded in that system we have a different system to treat each race differently placing a value on each race as being more valuable to society.

Even today we continue to have a main indicator which is the wage gap which continues to affect women and people of color who are generally paid less than Caucasian. Until we start putting aside this type of value system people will never be treated fairly and equitable. One can think we all have the same opportunities in America if we just work hard and that is not true because we relay on a system of people working together, helping one another to reach their goals and dreams, but when society has the idea that because your Latino or black that you don't deserve the same help as others who have a higher value in society those individuals have a higher probability of failing.

The problems we go through today are not new, society continues to ignore it and they will only get worse over time, causing more unrest, more violence and hate. I get that those who suffer should not be adding flame to fire by spreading hate and conducting violence that will not help, but what else are these individuals to do when they are ignored and those who are supposed to care about these issues do nothing.

Our Freedoms Slowly Disappearing

We no longer will in a democracy although many will say yes we do we still have freedoms, we have the constitution, we have rule of law and I say for how long? How long until those in power ignore the rule of law and break the rules because no one will stop them. If I wasn't a moral man I think I would be breaking the law now because again whose going to stop me since the rule of law isn't even respected by those in government such as people in congress and especially our president. Luckily my moral compass is lead by a relationship with GOD,

Jesus Christ is the one who I take direction from. You may think that is an out of place statement but if we have no way to tell us right from wrong then its easy to choose the wrong path, GOD is the right path, because he is righteous, the ultimate ruler of law and order and one day Jesus will come back and rule the world where every knee will bow.

I know our country and world is failing each day because its ruled by men and women who have no moral compass who look at their people as means to get more money out of them, to suppress their voices and take away their will. Our will , our privilege's, our rights will slowly or rapidly decline depending on if others will protect our rights if no ones does than we will have anarchy in this country.

Yes we currently have it with riots taking place and it appears state and local governments just let it happen but one of the main reasons for those people going unchecked is because government has to make tough choices do we pepper stray rioters and protestors and devote our police and fire to those causes or do we devote those resources to those in need like the sick. I could never understand what it means to rule a city, state or country but I do know it takes empathy, compassion but much more than that it takes someone willing to listen.

I highly encourage everyone to read 1984 by George Orwell, a perfect example of what our country and world will be become and has become. You may say well that's just fiction but art imitates art in many ways. I also would say add in the film Metropolis (1927), a another prophetic film that details what rich only wish to do to those in the lower classes and to a certain degree that has already happened as the powerful, the rich rule over the Proles. For those who don't know what a prole is, its detailed in 1984 and as those individuals are considered the working class as society is divided into three separate classes the inner party, the outer party and the proles.

Those in power only want more power which is no secret and they are willing to take powers such as rights and privilege's from the lower class because ultimately they feel we as people only squander our rights who they must be taken away. I am not trying to make this sound like some big conspiracy but many in power already think they can do as they wish and no one will stop them because again we have two types of laws for rich and poor.

We are no longer a democracy remember that!

PART III -BIGFOOT, MONSTERS AND FILMS

| 27 |

Metropolis and The Reflections of Today From 1927

July 24, 2019

I am a lover of classic films, black and White, silent with just the sounds of instruments and subtitles. The love of silent films is not for everyone, some have a hard time adjusting to not hearing talking. I find these films most intriguing imagining those actors and actress act out those roles, knowing that that they just have to look like they are speaking and subtitles will do the rest. I am sure it's more involved than that, if you have ever seen the film Chaplin with Robert Downey Jr. as the great Charlie Chaplin (English accent).

The Film of The Future

Metropolis is a film from 1927 directed by fritz Lang, a story that considered a pioneer in science fiction films. Ladies and Gents this is where many of our films and stories came from. Although Science fiction the genre has been around for centuries beginning in ancient times fusing myth and fiction together, which is what it is today. From the books and films out there it is my belief Science fiction has not fundamentally changed, but has grown more graphic in how we wish to display and tell stories. We have some of the best films and books in science fiction, and I find this genre creative in the sense that you literally create something that doesn't and can't possibly exist such as in "Aliens" the film. But Science fiction has had some of the greatst pioneers to write it including H.G. Wells, one of my personal favorites.

Metropolis is an incredible film that I never grow tired of watching, there is actually two versions, one which has the original score and one that create with a pop soundtrack in

2010, both are great, but being a generation X-er I love the pop version the most.

The History is Just as Important

The film details Made in Germany during the Weimar period, *Metropolis* is set in a futuristic urban dystopia, In a city called, what else "Metropolis" wealthy industrialist and business magnates and their top employees rein from high-rise towers, while workers work underground to operate the great machines that power the city.

- Alfred Abel as Joh Fredersen, the master of Metropolis
- Gustav Fröhlich as Freder, Joh Fredersen's son
- Rudolf Klein-Rogge as Rotwang, the inventor
- Fritz Rasp as The Thin Man, Fredersen's spy

- Theodor Loos as Josaphat, Fredersen's assistant and Freder's friend
- Erwin Biswanger as 11811, a worker, also known as Gyorgy
- Heinrich George as Grot, guardian of the Heart Machine
- The Creative Man
- The Machine Man
- Death
- The Seven Deadly Sins
- Brigitte Helm as Maria[Notes 1]
- Heinrich Gotho as Master of Ceremonies in Pleasure Gardens *(uncredited)*[13]

There are a few main characters that you will get to know in this film, all I should are spectacular and although we have terrific actors and actresses today, these actors really had no sound or a voice to convey the message of what the characters where going through. The following characters/cast include:

The Story of Freder and Maria

Joh Fredersen is the city's master. His son Freder idles away his time at sports and in a pleasure garden, but is interrupted by the arrival of a young woman named Maria, who has brought a group of workers' children to witness the lifestyle of their rich "brothers". Maria and the children are ushered away, but Freder, fascinated, goes to the lower levels to find her. On the machine levels he witnesses the explosion of a huge machine that kills and injures numerous workers. Freder has a hallucination that the machine is Moloch and the workers are being fed to it. When the hallucination ends and he sees the dead workers being carried away on stretchers, he hurries to tell his father about the accident; Fredersen asks his assistant, Josaphat, why he learned of the explosion from his son, and not from him.

Grot, foreman of the Heart Machine, brings Fredersen secret maps found on the dead workers. Fredersen again asks Josaphat why he did not learn of the maps from him, and fires him. After seeing his father's cold indifference towards the harsh conditions they face, Freder secretly rebels against him by deciding to help the workers. He enlists Josaphat's assistance and returns to the machine halls, where he trades places with a worker.

The film follows the attempts of Freder, the wealthy son of the city master, and Maria, a saintly figure to the workers, to overcome the vast gulf separating the classes in their city and bring the workers together with Joh Fredersen, the city master.

In the film it's a powerful story of the wealthy who only wish to use the workers to keep the city going, as they work themselves to death. As the workers work, the rich play. The story centers around a ***Maschinenmensch***, which is a gynoid, a female android, who is made from a image of a real women, which she uses her power of percussion and sexuality to entice the men , attempting to control them in which one scene she dances in a very risque bra and shirt, but for 1927 this would be considered scandalist. Maria had a great deal of influence to the workers. In the film, she was basically copied to give the illusion it was her, but wasn't because she was robot could be controlled

Today's Representation of Yesterday

I look at today as a example, that really not a lot has changed for centuries, there seems to be always one group attempting to control those around them and those who are vulnerable such as the poor. In the film workers

believe are slaving away attempting to keep the city going why the people above enjoy life. So you may ask well whats your point, that's just the way things are , people have to work, to eat , to survive and many times we are at the mercy of those we work for. I see all too often, Although I live in the United States, land of free, that freedom comes at a huge cost, I am not talking about politics, just what it takes to survive in the big city.

History is a great indicator of what is to come, but it seems year after year the rich get richer and the poorer get poorer, while costs continue to sky rocket out of control for those just trying to survive. It seems each day we hear about a new millionaire or billionaire. Which many of you who read this may say, well I don't care about that, who cares, those people started companies, invested their money, they are fiscally responsible and that was their reward for their hardwork.

To the extent you would be correct, we can all start a company, think of a great idea , market it, sell your idea and products to the highest bidder and become fifthly rich. I always wondered where that term fifth rich came from, those people are not necessarily dirty people, but probably just means that they so much money they know what to do with.

The Prediction's Continues

I ask myself, if this film was made in 1927 and clearly depicts the wealthy still reminiscence of today, it's amazing this film was almost like telling the future. I am sure back in 1927, it was probably implausible that a society would be that way. I can only imagine if we went back in time, if we could tell those in previous centuries what our society is like too. Again not all bad, we have modern medicine, technology, industrialization and we continue to grow and change in to a new society.

I encourage you to watch this film, breath it in, enjoy and look the similarities of that film to today. Now we may or may not have people work under ground to keep the city going, but we do have people, little people who make the world turn and without them we would no where. I am grateful for those who do jobs no ones wants to do and keeps society maintained in a way to prevent sickness or death, such as those pick up our garbage, those who keep our electrical grid going, those who make sure our water is somewhat drinkable.

For those who have seen this film, watch it again, study it if not just for the culture significance but for majestic way this film infuse science fiction into a great story and dynamic actors and actresses. I think we should think critically too about if we were to make a movie today to show those in the future what kind of film would you make. This film by Fritz Lang had vision of the future, what is your vision? As a writer we are called to visionary's of the unknown, of the unseen for those who will one day see or read our work. It definitely encourages me to write and think about what has society not read or seen.

| 28 |

Cryptozoology: My Love of The Weird and Unexplaine

August 15, 2019

Love for the strange is something I am fascinated with from a young child, growing up watching movies, reading and just really be curious to what is out there. Some who read this may not have an interest, but if you do, then come along to learn with me.

The best way I can sum up those things are the unexplained in my eyes would be the word **Cryptozoology** which is defined as ***"the search for and study of animals whose existence or survival is disputed or unsubstantiated, such as the Loch Ness monster and the yeti."***

Now just reading the sentence you may be like WOW! I have no interest in things that may not exist, and some of you may be like I have an open mind to learn about what is out there.

So let's be clear, someone who believes in Cryptozoology are not Crazy or Nuts, so don't lump me in like that, I just happen to believe in the possibility of something that exist where I don't necessary have to see it to believe it. I will start with my belief in Bigfoot; some of you may have read my other Blog on this subject, so I encourage you read it here: https://adventuresinwriting675191505.wordpress.com/2019/07/04/bigfoot-fact-or-fiction-the-existence-we-should-all-want-to-know-about/

It all Begins with Bigfoot for Me

Bigfoot is a Bi-pedal animal that has been around for most likely centuries or longer due to the numerous reports especially coming from Native Americans. I would question Bigfoot if it was wasn't for the Native American cave art that has depicted Bigfoot and have actually made it part of their culture. Although I have yet to learn about all the Native American tribes and culture which I find absolutely beautiful and tragic at the same time for how they have been treated, I find their testimonies valuable.

I attempt to get information from different sources, some from books, film and Television, which one of my favorite shows happens to be Animal Planet's Finding Bigfoot with a group of investigators which include my favorite investigators Cliff Barackman, James "bobo" Fay, Renae Holland and Matt Moneymaker. This shows which ran for six seasons explored around the world, much of which was in the United States https://www.animalplanet.comhttps://www.animalplanet.com/tv-shows/finding-bigfoot//tv-shows/finding-bigfoot/ .

Although they didn't find an actual Sasquatch, they came close to discovering the elusive beast. If you happen to watch the show they will go to communities and get witness statements from the locals which in many cases are credible, doing reenactments trying to separate the truth from fiction from those witnesses who may not be telling the full truth or who embellish what they saw.

Let's Dive in The Loch for Nessie

There are other types of Crypto's out there are not heard of as much, many of those people tend to laugh at, but there have been many witnesses, one of those examples is Lochness Monster. Nessy as the animal is called is a **Loch Ness** (/�l�x �n�s/; Scottish Gaelic: *Loch Nis* [l���x �ni�]) is a large, deep, freshwater loch in the Scottish Highlands. A Loch is the Irish, Scottish Gaelic and Scots word for a lake or for a sea inlet.

Hence where they get the name Loch-Ness Monster, which has also been in popular culture with many sightings and just until recently learned that researchers in Scottland and United Kind are more inclined to believe in Lochness than Bigfoot and that is just because they have been more widely seen. One a recent episode on the podcast Bigfoot and Beyond with Cliff and Bobo, they had a quest and Author of the book "Beasts of Britain" by the name of Andy MacGrath discussing the various cryptos in the UK.

https://youtu.be/nQ4O0YqI_hY

Mr. MacGrath talked extensively about Lochness and sightings. Just a little history on Lochness. : Loch Ness is known as the home of the Loch Ness Monster (also known as "Nessie"), a cryptid, reputedly a large unknown animal. It is similar to other supposed lake monsters in Scotland and elsewhere, though its description varies from one account to the next. Popular interest and belief in the animal's existence have varied since it was first brought to the world's attention in 1933.[6]

Aside from it being a part of Scottish culture it too has been of popular culture such as Books, films and television, which has many times created this monster to be loveable sea creature, but I doubt that, as the monsters seem to be ancient from another time, probably being able to live extended lives longer than most animals.

The Unknown Gets Stranger

There are a few others in the media that you may have heard of such as Mothman, Chupacabra, British Big Cats, Monkey Man, Dog Man and many other different mans for Bigfoot/Sasquatch type criptid's . Another I like to add would be Tommy Knockers and Skin-walkers.

Skin-walkers I find particularly interesting because they are part of the Navajo Culture and their belief that Skin-Walkers are people who have the ability to transform into animals, but in a way are controlled by evil, as they really don't like speaking about Skin-walkers out of fear one will come after them.

Do you Know a Skin-Walker?

Skin-walkers are the following: (courtesy of https://thoughtcatalog.com/jacob-geers/2016/10/14-facts-about-skinwalkers-that-will-100-scare-the-shit-out-of-you/

1. A person with the ability to transform into different animals at will.
2. They are most frequently seen as coyotes , wolves, foxes , eagles, owls or crows.

3. Some can
   also steal faces of different people, and could appear as someone you know.
4. If you accidentally
   lock eyes with a skinwalker, they can absorb themselves into your body and take
   control of your actions.
5. Rare
   Skinwalkers can also have the ability to enchant the powder of corpses and use
   the substances as a poison dust on victims.
6. The
   legend Originates from Navajo, a southwestern Native American Tribe.
7. In the
   Navajo language the word "Skinwalker" is Yee naagloshii and translates to "He
   who walks on all fours"
8. Skinwalkers
   have only enter the public discourse relatively.
9. Skin
   Walkers can run at great distances, some say 200 miles in one evening.

I would encourage you to get more information; I found this website that seemed pretty credible and fellow word-presser Jacob Geers: https://thoughtcatalog.com/jacob-geers/2016/10/14-facts-about-skinwalkers-that-will-100-scare-the-shit-out-of-you/

Skin walkers are real in the eyes of the Navajo people, they do not joke about them, another course was with Finding Bigfoot and Beyond episode.

https://youtu.be/-8bQM_jDmXw

Some Creatures That need to Found

There are of course other creatures out there which I will briefly list and give some information:

Moth-man - In West Virginia folklore, the **Moth-man** is a creature reportedly seen in the Point Pleasant area from November 12, 1966, to December 15, 1967. The first newspaper report was published in the *Point Pleasant Register* dated November 16, 1966, titled "Couples See Man-Sized Bird ... Creature ... Something".[1] The national press soon picked up the reports and helped spread the story across the United States.

British Big Cats- also referred to as **ABCs** (Alien, or Anomalous, Big Cats), **phantom cats** and **mystery cats**, are reports and incidents of Felidae not native to Britain but supposed to inhabit the British countryside. These sightings are often reported as "panthers", "pumas", or "black cats".

The existence of a population of true big cats in Britain, especially a breeding population, is believed to be highly implausible by experts owing to lack of convincing evidence.

There have been some incidents of recovered individual animals, often medium-sized species such as the Eurasian lynx but in one 1980 case a puma, which was captured alive in Scotland. These are generally believed to have been escaped or released pets that had been held illegally, possibly released after the animals became too difficult to manage.[1]

The Kraken - is a legendary cephalopod-like sea monster of giant size in Scandinavian folklore. According to the Norse sagas, the kraken dwells off the coasts of Norway and Greenland and terrorizes nearby sailors. Authors over the years have postulated that the legend may have originated from sightings of giant squids that may grow to 13–15 meters (40–50 feet) in length. The sheer size and fearsome appearance attributed to the kraken have made it a common ocean-dwelling monster in various fictional works.

The kraken has been the focus of many superstitious sailors passing the North Atlantic and especially sailors from the Nordic countries due to their proximity and its Scandinavian origin. Throughout the centuries the kraken has been a staple part of sailors' superstitions and mythos being heavily linked to sailors ability of telling a tall tale.

Jersey Devil - In Southern New Jersey and Philadelphia folklore, the **Jersey Devil** (also known as the **Leeds Devil**) is a legendary creature said to inhabit the Pine Barrens of South Jersey. The creature is often described as a flying biped with hooves, but there are many variations.

Jersey Devil - In Southern New Jersey and Philadelphia folklore, the **Jersey Devil** (also known as the **Leeds Devil**) is a legendary creature said to inhabit the Pine Barrens of South Jersey. The creature is often described as a flying biped with hooves, but there are many variations.

The common description is that of a kangaroo-like or wyvern-like creature with a goat- or horse-like head, leathery bat-like wings, horns, small arms with clawed hands, legs with cloven hooves, and a forked tail. It has been reported to move quickly and is often described as emitting a high-pitched "blood-curdling scream"

Get Your Research and Find Them!

There is just so many Cryptids to choose from many of which have a distinct story to why people believe them, I would recommend researching some more, most of them are interesting, https://en.wikipedia.org/wiki/List_of_cryptids

But there are so other great resources such as Loren Coleman of the http://cryptozoologymuseum.com/ and of course Cliff Barakman who is currently working his Bigfoot museum https://northamericanbigfootcenter.com/. These two incredible sources I trust, but know there is so much more out there too see.

I hope this peaked your interest to know more, my thought is if people can believe Alien Lifeforms, why can't people believe in this different Cryptid's. I know some seem really unusual and probably implausible. But others like Big foot are completely plausible because research backs it up.

| 29 |

Saying Goodbye To The Evil House

July 6, 2019

Today marks a chapter in my life with the selling of my fathers house in South Los Angeles, a house that my father has lived in most of his life over forty years and he is now 63 years old. This house was my grandparents house who raised my Father Moses, Sister Elizabeth, Rachel and my Grandparents Moses Senior and Isabelle. This house I have grown up and actually lived in here is its story.

For many will say a house is not evil, a house has no feelings and is not a person, but a house can house evil depending on who lived, this house was created in 1913, so there is a lot of history there some of which I never was able to find out. My grandparents bought the house in 1961 , so who knows who lived there before. My Grandfather was a WWII vet and meat butcher and my grandmother a cafeteria worker and Sunday school teacher. My father is a man who never like change very much, from knowing him all my life, he has been the same man all his life, I will leave it at that, because this is not about my father.

It Didn't Start Out Evil

Growing up in that house, I was grew up there from birth, walking, crawling, running until recently up until a year ago I lived there with with my wife, daughter and my father, who we cared for but is fully able to care for himself. We moved in because we have a financial setback in 2014 raising our daughter and I was the one working to support us. I have no qualms about supporting my family but I needed help , but the house was a mess before we moved in.

Evil Making It's Presence Known

Throughout the years,weird occurrences would happen, as we slept we would hear sounds, such as three knocks, footsteps in the kitchen and multiple times violent bangs on our bedroom door as we slept as if something was telling us to leaving. For a short time my sister moved in as in transition and she too heard knocking in three.

One point taking a shower in the early morning I heard Knocking on the door and faint voice sounding like my wife, but she was sound asleep still. We would hear whispers in the night and early morning, and Dark Figures my wife States stood over her and she felt a pressure holding her down unable to scream. There was even a time on Christmas morning we were taking Live Pictures and we could hear a baby crying in the background of the picture, but there was no TV on and no sounds from outside.

For many of you, this may sound quite bizarre and unbelievable, for those who do believe and have experience similar experiences, you know what you felt. I believe my senses are heightened to those unseen things around us, I don't see dead people, but I know there is a spiritual world that exist, this house was Evil, since being sold I have had dreams as if it was calling me back to visit one last time, pulling me in to go back, but I refuse too, The house is Evil and hope whoever lives there doesn't experience those evil, only time will tell. One last observation is that our house was at the end of a long Street, as house on both ends of street, my brother in Law once mentioned that because of that, there could be all these negative energy coming from all of those house, which I fully believe, imagine the anger, hate, hardship, frustration all being push down our direction as the evil house feed on that, giving it to my wife and family.

It is my belief that there also exist residual energy, energy that builds up over time in a object and place, and without a cleansing will always stay, but even that may not help. We never conducted a cleansing, as Christians, we are believers in God's cleansing and protection, even though we prayed for change in that house, I feel the presence of whatever was there was too strong, not to say God is Weak, just that Evil is strong and it was unwilling to leaving knowing it was affecting us in a negative way is probably why it stayed until the end.

I can't say if I will miss the house, part of me does for the shear fact of my childhood growing up in that house with the love of my grandparents and the memories, I will NOT miss the city, congested city that continues to get more congested. I say goodbye House of Evil and riddance, may you not inflict your pain on us no longer and give peace to those now live there starting fresh!

This blog is a very imitate portrait of my life for really my life, some don't get the opportunity to live in the best neighborhoods or the nicest houses growing up, but its what I had. For those who read this blog I know judgement will set in because maybe you never had live like I did and some may say I have lived through much worse, for which I am truly sorry.

| 30 |

Bigfoot, Fact or Fiction

July 4, 2019

Just by reading the title many of you may say I pass on this blog, there is no way Bigfoot is real, he is just a myth, perpetuated by storytelling just to scare people. Many who believe including myself are afraid to be lumped into those who believe in the Lochness Monster or the Chupacabra and Skin-walkers, Tommy knockers. Many of you are probably saying wasn't Tommy Knockers a movie. But I have found there are legitimate reasons that Bigfoot has been around for so long, going back to the Native Americans. For those who wish not to read a whole Wikipedia on Bigfoot and Native American culture, I will give you a small lesson.

Bigfoot is a common to folklore of most Northwest Native American Tribes. Legends describing the creatures 6-9 feet tall, very strong, uncivilized and often foul-smelling, usually living in the woods. Native American creatures are almost always said to be unable to speak human languages, using whistles, grunts and gestures to communicate.

There is where the intertribal Bigfoot similarities end, however. In the Bigfoot myths of some tribes, Sasquatch and his relatives are generally shy and benign figures. Over the years Bigfoot has come by many names depending on the region you will find Bigfoot or Sasquatch, most of Western American will be known as Bigfoot or Sasquatch, but there is also Yeti of the Himalayas, but in Native American Culture they have many names such as Boqs, Chiye-Tanka, Hairy Man. http://www.native-languages.org/legends-bigfoot.htm

Native American Culture and Bigfoot

I have always been a believer from a young age, although I live in Southern California, I guess my first real impression of Bigfoot was from Film, "Harry and Henderson's". Although this is a heartfelt comedy and although we would all like to believe that Bigfoot is a gentle giant and many ways they are, I is my impression that you can never bring Bigfoot home, which is what Dr. Wright wood thought, until meeting him, finding him to be lovable but known the less people that he was some nut, but he knew what he saw and didn't care if anyone believed him.

From the point of view of that film I needed to know more, because Art Imitates Life in many way of what is real at times, not always. But because of the number of sightings that have taken place over the centuries, he is not just folklore, but a real phenomenon. The question many would ask is well if he's real by hasn't anyone caught him or why is no bones. Well, whose say there isn't, in the words of Dr. Wright wood, "Have you ever seen a baby pigeon?" asking George Henderson and his reply was "No", but they exist right, simple logic, Unless you have seen a baby pigeon and I stand corrected and Bigfoot would exist. But many times Bigfoot lives very deep in the forest, distances most would not go, but there have been many cases that live nearby.

I would like to believe I live in Rancho Cucamonga and behind me is the Foothills of the San Gabriel Mountains, I imagine is looking down on me from the mountains, away from the public. The other reason Bigfoot may stay unnoticed is his/her ability to blend in. Recently I was listening to Finding Bigfoot stars Cliff Barackman and James "Bobo" Fay and there were mentioning on a recent Podcast of Bigfoot & Beyond with Cliff and Bobo they explained how Bigfoot hair has a certain reddish or orange tone that when the light reflects the sun off bringing out the natural elements in Bigfoot allowing him/her to stay hidden. It is my belief Bigfoot is very aware when people are near, probably have great senses to people when it comes to sight and sounds. I have been a watcher of Finding Bigfoot on the Animal Planet for many years.

Back to the research provided by BFRO (Bigfoot Field Research Organization) http://www.animalplanet.com/tv-shows/finding-bigfoot/about-bigfoot/
bigfoot-field-researchers-organiza-

tion/?_ga=2.245324613.1936752951.1562193787-863149309.1562193787

Most Native American Tribes across North America have stories in their oral traditions describing giant hairy figures. To Quote BFRO "The tribes are spread across all the linguistic groups of native languages. Every native linguistic group has its own name for these figures, suggesting the stories of these figures did not all arise in the same place.

"Sightings continue to happen on certain native reservations in the United States and Canada — those reservations with an abundance of natural food sources."

So you may say to yourself, I still don't believe and that is fine, but I would encourage you to research more on the subject and see there are thousands and thousands of accounts of sights every year to see how of these people are not crazy. I admit some are crazy with B.S. stories even on finding Bigfoot the team had to weed out the crazies just to get a shot on T.V. and some of these people who would believe they did see one because they live in areas where Bigfoot would live.

The Evidence of Patterson and Gimlin

There have hundreds if not thousands of studies on Bigfoot, but the biggest exam of the search came from the Patterson-Gimlin (also known as the Patterson film) is an American short motion picture of an unidentified subject which is walking across the forest which is Bigfoot. The footage was from 1967 in Northern California and has had been subjected to much scrutiny and many attempts to debunk it, which have mostly failed.

Researcher have studied that film, zoologist, cryptozoologist and many others have review the film and by most accounts is authentic. The film makers were Roger Patterson (deceased) and Robert Gimlin. The story goes in the early afternoon for Friday October 20, 1967, Patterson and Gimlin were riding generally northeast on horseback along the east bank of Bluff Creek. At some time between 1:15 and 1:40 PM, they spotted Bigfoot crouching beside the creek estimated Bigfoot to be six feet to seven feet, but later raised the estimate. The film shows what Patterson and Gimlin claimed was a large, hairy, bipedal, apelike figure with short silvery brown or dark reddish brown hair.

I have seen this evidence and it is widely available so you be the judge yourself, but it is my opinion that this is No person in a costume, because of when the figures walks you can see muscle definition, something you would never see in a costume.

Bigfoot in Pop Culture

Over the years there have been other kinds of video proof of existence and pictures, but nothing to the magnitude of this film. Many in today's society refuse to believe he exists and not keeping an open mind. Bigfoot will be around for years , decades and probably centuries to come, as those out there continue to search for him and will continue to be in pop culture such as movies like Harry and the Henderson's, Yeti , The untold, Exist, and most recently Small foot, so there stopping pop culture.

I have found in today's culture is much more enjoyable than some of the films today that promote death and killing, which is not always bad, but have an oversaturation of those films as it is.

So after reading this, if this peeked your interest I encourage you research, take a short hiking trip and go searching, learn the calls of Bigfoot such as whistle, knocks and yelps and Howls, you will find much of would I speak of on Finding Bigfoot, serious researchers looking for answers with a skeptic on the cast who has come across evidence she can't explain.

As you can I am a firm believer, but I what I have not done is actually go out an search, which I would love to do, brave enough to take on the elements, sleep in the wilderness and wait for Bigfoot to walk in my path or at least let me know he is watching.

It is my belief Bigfoot is not meant to harm you and that he is more interested in us and that is why so many sightings have been around people, the interest of who we are and what we want in his neighborhood, so if you ever camping, stay calm and Keep Squatchin!

| 31 |

Krampus and St. Nick: How both Figures can Teach

December 11, 2021

Happy Krampusnacht or if you celebrate the feast of St. Nicholas.

Christmas time is here! Oh Christmas time, Oh Christmas time. For many and much of the world I know it can be hard to celebrate and why should we with Covid-19, Lock downs, high unemployment, people on the verge of losing everything. One could say Joseph where are your priorities, Christmas should be canceled this year.

I say hold on now, let's not get crazy and remember the reason for season which is Not only the celebration of Jesus our savior but of kindness, generosity towards one another. We are certainty in difficult times, and this will NOT be the last time society and the world suffers at the hands of a health crisis, but we must try to remain positive. I know this year will not be the same, but in hopes that next year will be better.

I particularly like Christmas and I do not at the same time. I like Christmas in the sense of the traditions that we celebrate with the people we love. I don't particularly like how Christmas is one big, commercialized time of the year to stick to the man or women to spend spend spend. Now some of you may say well you don't have to spend money if you don't want to and although that may be true, its usually a requirement in the United States. I mean how many of us like to receive but when it comes to giving back we decide to close our purse, it doesn't feel great.

The other reason is for many years growing up, frankly I can not remember one good Christmas, it seems like one big fog. I do remember those times being very sad and happy as my mother would cook delicious food, there would be presents, but there was always the presents of the Devil (my grandfather) who made the holiday's unbearable at times.

The Reason for the Season

As a Christian I do know the meaning of the season and I must remember that, but I also like to kind of the sillier things in Christmas like Santa, Elves, Magic, the north pole and all my love for Christmas movies and music.

But one of the figures in Christmas I am quite interested in is Krampus. Having grew up with Santa from a young age, obliviously I would like to believe he is real and in a way he is. Santa or Saint Nicolas was a real figure a 4th century Greek Christian bishop of Myra. Famous for his generous gifts to the poor, in particular presenting three impoverished daughters of pious Christian with dowries so that they would not have to become prostitutes.

He was very religious from an early age and devoted his life entirely to Christianity. Saint Nicolas legend carried on into many different forms throughout the ages from Father Christmas, Sinterklaas and many other well-known names depending on global origin. Being in the United States, British and Dutch versions of the gift giver merged further, eventually becoming Americanized into "Santa Claus".

I believe most of us know the history of Santa Claus, but how many know the history of Krampus, other than seeing the movie which added to my interest in this mythical figures or figures. Like anything else Santa is a gift giver while Krampus is a gift taker among other things.

Who is Krampus?

Krampus a central European folklore is a horned, anthropomorphic figure described as "Half-goat, half-demon" who during the Christmas season, punishes children who have misbehaved. This contrasts with Saint Nicholas for oblivious reasons.

The history of the Krampus figure has been theorized as stretching back to Pre-Christian Alpine traditions. It is said that the myth of Krampus was the son of Hel, Norse goddess of the underworld.

Although Krampus appears in various variations, most share some common physical characteristics. He is hairy, usually black or brown, has cloven hooves and horns of a goat. His long, pointed tongue lolls out and he has fangs.

Krampus carries chains, thought to symbolize the binding of the Devil by the Christian Church. He thrashes the chains for dramatic effect. The chains are sometimes accompanied with bells of various sizes. Of more pagan origins are the Ruten, bundles of birch branches that Krampus carries and with he occasionally swats children. Sometimes Krampus appears with a sack of a basket strapped to his back; this is to cart off evil children for drowning, eating or to transport to hell.

Krampusnacht, European and American Traditions

The feast of St. Nicholas is celebrated in parts of Europe on December 6th. On the preceding evening December 5th, Krampus night is when the wicked hairy devil appears on the streets. While Krampus is responsible for the bad. Nicholas dispenses gifts, while Krampus supplies coal and Ruten bundles.

Milk and Cookies for Santa but what do you give Krampus, well Schnapps of course, a strong distilled fruit brandy.

Europeans have been exchanging greeting cards feature Krampus since the 1800's. Sometimes introduced with Greetings from Krampus, the cards usually humorous rhymes and poems. Krampus is often featured menacingly over children. He is also shown as having one human foot and one cloven hoof. In some Krampus sexual overtones; he is pictured pursuing buxom women. Over time, the representation of Krampus in the cards have changed; older versions have a more frightening Krampus, while modern versions are cuter, more Cupid-like creatures.

In American it's quite the opposite with a picture of Fat jolly Santa eat cookies, with his reindeer, elves living in the north pole, so many different variations. In addition to Santa, cards typically have imagines of Jesus birth, three wise man, Star of Bethlehem in addition to a winter theme. Suffice to say you will never see Santa leering at Kids or buxom women as we have to remember that Santa originated with Christian principles.

As you can see the two difference between the two figures, obliviously there is so much more on Santa and his origins. Krampus is a folklore which wouldn't physically exist, but in sense if you believe in the devil like I do then its perfectly possible that Krampus could exist but I think I probably would have met him by now since all little boys and girls are good.

Krampus in Popular Culture

Reflecting on the 2015 Krampus film which ignited this blog and because it's the Christmas season of course, this film perfectly personifies rotten kids and family who are ungrateful with Max who wrote his letter to Santa but his cousins, aunt and uncle ruin the Christmas season, thinking to myself, Thank God I don't have a family like this. The film itself perfectly creates Krampus, the elves and creature alike in such a perfect way. I think personally we need to have more visits by Krampus in our world to teach people to be more grateful for what they have in this life especially today, where ungratefulness is at an all time high.

Watching the film and learning about Krampus I can't help but to think what kind of bad kids would lead Krampus to eat the children , drown them or transport them to hell and in reality if you think about it the Devil truly does wish to take anyone down man , women and child by whatever means to take us to Hell. Interesting how St. Nick and Krampus both appear to have some form of Christian roots especially dealing with Hell and a demon who wants to punish and take.

As a society we are supposed to learn our lesson how to be for giving and selflessness but truly do we ever get to that point, appearing that much of society is rotten to the core at times, I will not say everyone and really I have no idea what the true difference between the U.S. and lets the UK or China, but I would say that wealthy nations do have the propensity for much more greed than lets say other countries whose society may have less, but that is just a theory of course. The reality is anyone rich or poor can truly be ungrateful even for the breath we have each day.

Krampus is still celebrated today in traditional parades known as the Krampuslauf, where young men dressed as Krampus parade through the streets, scaring spectators and sometimes chasing them, although the tradition has been arguably appropriated for celebration.

What I find so beautiful is our beliefs in the United States versus those who live in Europe and have a different belief system involving both St. Nick and Krampus and wonder why do we find Krampus no so menacing here, almost like a joke, but I truly feel if Krampus entered the good ole U.S. there surely would be much better behaved kids and families appreciating what and who is in their life.

Have a fantastic Weekend and thank you for always going on these strange journeys with me and my fascination with strange which typically involves some type of horror movie that I get my influence. More to come as we kick off December and on to Christmas and the New Year!

PART IV – ON WRITING

| 32 |

Embracing My Writer Life, The Real Me

August 22, 2019

For those who follow my Blog you will see that currently I have a Weekly feature Stories from a child's past, My writings from my childhood. From a young child I remember back I believe was around ten years old, I have had a love of story telling and writing. I also love and Loved to draw, trying to be creative in my own way. I didn't think I was very good but it brought great solace and peace to my life.

> **A writer never has a vacation. For a writer life consists of either writing or thinking about writing.**
>
> - Eugene Ionesco

Life was hectic, stressful even for a young boy living in a house dominated by a verbally abusive home, but always had the comfort of my Mother, my defender. Growing up due to how I was treated grew up to be very sensitive, But I always attempted to keep a straight face to my emotions as many times those around me asked what was wrong. It was very frustrating growing up when people who ask what is wrong, why do you look sad or mad, well there was a reason, but I had terrible shyness and I think many times because I was so shy people equated that with me being unintelligent.

Writing was Always There for Me

Writing always seemed to be there for me, I could literally write a world into existence, create characters from scratch and live in that world. That is why I try to do with my writing, and what many writers do. I have push being a writer away for years, dabbling here and there, writing things that fit those things which I was apart of like Work. I am sure if my writing wasn't about a fictional world, it would be about business, economics, leadership, but I wrote.

Writing is almost in a way like an addiction to me, because I am starting to see my gifts in writing, well at least I think I am building those gifts. Such Gifts as being able to write on the fly, as a Pantser, I can write pages and pages of free thought flowing. I can structure what I write in readable and understandable form so its enjoyable to read. Many times I do go overboard with writing but that is me, its part of my makeup and how I write.

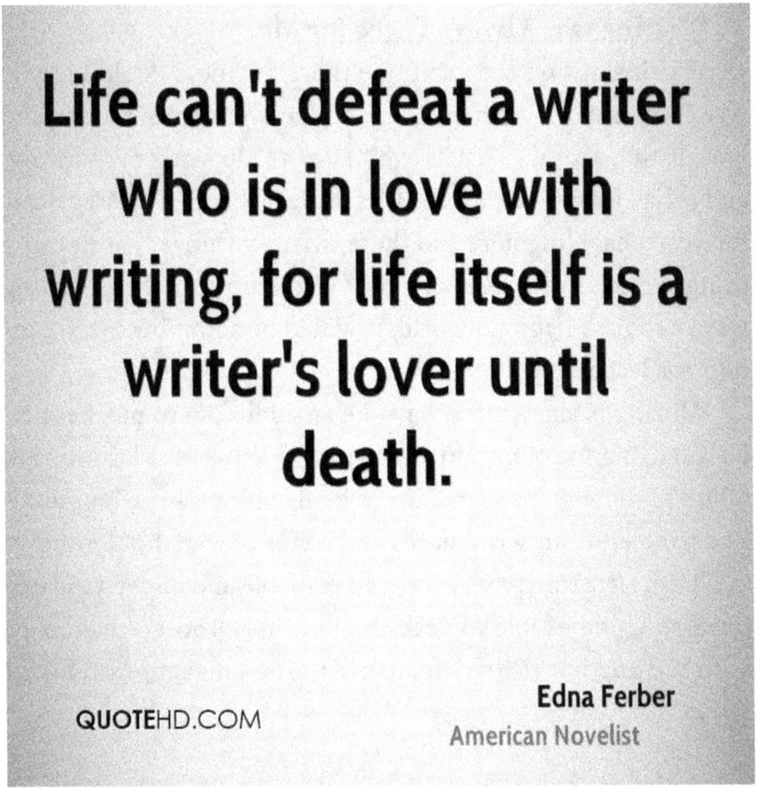

I know we are all different in our writing styles and techniques such as being a plotter or Pantster, so who are incredibly organized in their stories where every detail is laid out perfectly giving those writers focus on the task as hand. I on the other hand try to think of my characters as living beings, who feel who hurt, who are speaking to me to create their destinies.

My Journey Will be Great!

Since really taking a serious look at my writing about 9 months ago, I feel I have growth in my thought process, I have opened my eyes to create something that didn't exist.

I have really made an effort to being a better writer, working with the process of writing, learning better punctuation, Dialogue, Sentence formations and structures and what it takes be good at writing.

I will have my failures, there will be plenty of that when my book is done being told, I am writing sucks. But I look around to those who don't write yet criticize those who do and I just think what do you know about writing.

I look not only to the world of writing but being a reader too, how many people write and put out content, which may seem like a lot but it's probably fairly small because writing is difficult, Writing takes patience, perseverance , it takes failure, lots of failure to be good.

I now have a greater respect for what it takes to write a book. As a writer I love reading because it continues my love but allows me to have an appreciation for what that write went through.

My Words will have Meaning

I believe it was long days, nights, mornings, writing that book or piece no matter what, knowing those words matter and had to get those words out to the world. I hope my words have meaning, they do to me, but to those who one day read my work.

I continue to embrace my love for writing each day, each moment so I show myself I am not Worthless, I have a gift that others will love, to empower those who read my work. I always want to lift others up, especially because I know what it means to be put down. I was put down for so long, thank you for sharing this journey with me, to me this is our adventure in Writing.

| 33 |

How Writing Helps Ease My Mind in Times of Trouble

July 18,2019

Am I doing to much? is a question I tend to ask myself a lot, but most of the time I feel like I am not doing enough. Although we are all different with different struggles, personalities and traits, we all are human and have certain limitations. Some of us have a ingrained spirit to not stop, slow down, relax. Some on the other hand can easily sit back relax and noting seems to bother them. Some of you may say, Well Joseph you don't know me, I can sit back and relax because I don't let certain things bother me.

The Pressure is Real

For myself having a family, a wife and daughter to support the pressure is always on, go, go , go. I have for years tried to look to see why I push myself to the brink of exhaustion. I guess it goes back to a time in my childhood where I was always on and doing things, not by choice, but at times by brute force.

For those who have read a little bit about me, I grew up living with Mother, grandfather and sister. I put grandfather in a lower "g" even though not grammatically correct, because the value I placed in him in my life, which is pretty low.

For those reading, say with me, there is a point and this is not a blog just to complain, at least part of is not. Growing up from a young age, I was taught responsibility, put away childish things and "Grow Up". You will respect me, and if you choose you not, I will bully you until you do. Imagine doing that to a young child growing up until adulthood, the child is bound to walk away with issues of self worth. Of course my Mother was there to defend and protect my sister and I, but it has a high price to her, because she usually go the worse end of the abuse, being called worthless until she died in 2015 at the young age of 56.

The Childhood Years Make or Break You

During the years I lived in the Hell House, I was tormented with not Chores, but work, physical work, sometimes hard physical labor. I had a pretty regular routine, go to school, do my chores, do homework and if I was lucky after a long day watch some T.V or Go online. Sounds pretty normal right, to certain degree it was, except during those days I was home which was most of time he would constantly berate me, call me names, continue to have me do things until I was exhausted. I believe living in that house my mother had to pick her battles which I understood and realize now, no use getting in a verbal fight every time I was told to do something.

Weekends were no better, wake up at 6:30, as he acted as my personal alarm knocking on my wall, (I didn't have a door to my room) "Time to Get up". From there I would work outside from Morning until night at times, doing whatever he wanted, no complaints or I would possibly get hit or verbally assaulted. This went on until I finally left the home, getting married, but until that point I was also his chauffeur, driving him here and there, take me here, I need to get this and buy this. Over time I grew to resent, I grew to hate the man, who people, society says you need to love, because he is your Grandfather, but he was not a grandfather, he was a torturer, a manipulator, a bully, a lier, a verbal assaulter, a user. Over time I have grown to see those people for what they are, people you can never trust to tell the truth, even over my life until he passed, never gave me a kind word, an ounce of love.

Due to living this way, I grew to live a life on the edge so to speak, depression set in, anxiety, constant worries, never voices in my head, but slight paranoia what people thought of me. I continue to have this slight paranoia today especially in my job, where I look for some form of validation to see that I am doing something right, but I hardly get anything like that. Due to this slight paranoia that is probably what drives me to continue to push myself, so that I can validate myself in some why, but truthfully it has Not worked.

Growing Up Takes Time

After getting married, that's where I feel I changed, I grew up, which happens to most I will say, I was now responsible for a person, let alone myself, a big responsibility. Growing up I did not have the best examples of marriage, so I said I was going to be different. I was going to work hard, provide, be a good husband and eventually father. At first life was grand like many who get married, a new beautiful experience, having that person in your life who you will spend the rest of your life with, which I believe most who get married want. I am still married of course and I love my wife and my daughter, but over time it has gotten harder, because frankly marriage is hard work, throw in a child or two or three or four, I have only one and the pressure is on.

From 2011 until the recent closure of my college Mt. Sierra College, I worked two jobs, one full time and taught at night from 6pm to 10pm, pretty typical for adjunct faculties sometimes four days a week, which didn't leave a lot of time for family time. Being the sole provider, Rent, Car, Bills, student loans, you name it, put a big pressure on me and I think it continues to this day. My wife and I made a choice together that she would take care of our daughter full time and I would go to work, a decision I Don't regret, because my daughter had the love and attention she needed for her most precious years, until she actually went to school.

Many of those who read this may not agree with my choices, because in today's day and age both parents work full time and drop the kid(s) day care and that is part of life. Due to high cost of childcare it would not be financially beneficial to do that and I have stuck to that, but now that my daughter is in school, my wife can and wants to work, great!

Hardships are Not for Faint of Heart

From 2014 to until 2018 life was hard, a moved out of my beautiful apartment and moved into the house of hell in Los Angeles, where you can read about in one of my other blogs. During those times money was tight, I decided I wanted to get trained in a new field which is where my life took a dangerous turn to fight to better myself and hopefully get better opportunities for myself and family.

Working day and night, I grew tired, my mind grew even more tired as I pushed, pushed and pushed myself for betterment of my families life and to gain what I felt I needed self worth and value. Although my wife and daughter bring me happiness and are a support to me, I feel something is missing, a sense that I am going in the right direction in my life.

From 2010 until Now, life has been a bit of roller coasters, first in 2014 when I attempted to go back to school at Northwest Lineman School, leaving my family temporarily to move to northern California to be an electrical Lineman, I failed by dropping out due to the strong advice from a faulty member, after leaving my full time job to take this risk, going back home to rebuild again. I was able to find part time work, two part time jobs, then eventually a full time job, things were looking up. But I took a hard hit financially after this risk and it affected myself and family for a years and will probably affect me years to come. I had choices I felt would help us but in the end hurt us.

But these events I have pushed myself , forced myself to grow, first with a new position in a field I have never done before, a huge learning curve, but finally getting it. On top of that taking Nightly online courses for web development and programming, on top of that begin to write again, taking a serious shot a something I have always want to do is write a book, an ambitious endeavor, this is something I do 7 days a week, on top of that have not taken a real vacation, my brain is fried. I have noticed differences in my performance at work, constantly tired, stressed and starting to feel like I once did when it came to my anxiety.

I feel I am on a hamster wheel never stopping , because I can't stop, if I stop I fail, I fall. My Mind feels as though its constantly going, not even able to stop in rest. I feel over the years, I have pushed myself , putting myself last and although my family is there, there is not much they can do to control who I am or how I feel. I refuse to go back to antidepressants or meds, those were apart of my life at one point when I was at my lowest, a time I truly want to forget and taking pills will be a daily reminder.

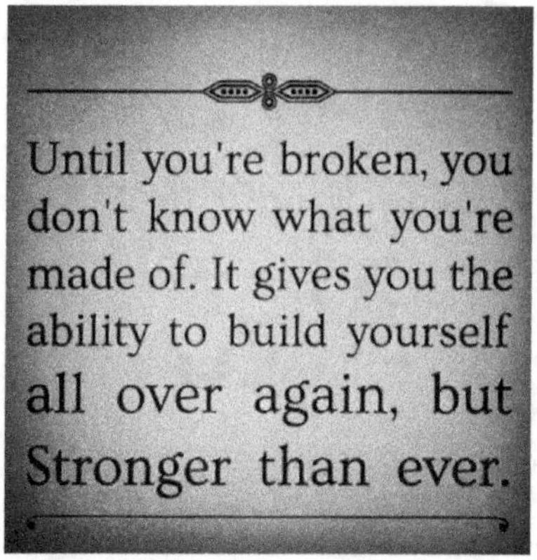

Moving Forward

I write this to say the struggle is real, if you are going through what I am going through, I pray for the light at the end of tunnel, I pray for peace, I pray for a day where I can enjoy life without the constant worry. I believe I am stronger than I think and probably would have given up a long time ago but refuse to take that path, a path I can say lead me no where but possible death in the end. My life I lived before, lead me to where i am today, a wife , a daughter who is my copy, so how can I not push myself to the brink of utter exhaustion at times.

I hope eat day I live this life, I can find the joys and the peace to know it will get better, it may not get easy, but I have my writing , I have my passions, I have the drive to hopefully get me where I need to go, thank you for listening.

Other ways I have been able to cope is exercise, eating right, putting aside the little things that don't matter, live in the now, spend time with those you love, try to enjoy life and know tomorrow will be better and know in the long run you are stronger then you think, I know I am. I think the Joseph from 2007 would have cracked by know will all the pressure I have now taking care of a family, jobs, money stresses, but at the end of day my life is better here on earth with them and those around you feel the same way.

Invest in yourself, as for myself, that is why writing is one of passions, that allows me to express myself each day, something no one can take a way.

Be strong, Your are strong!

If you do feel like you can't cope please speak with someone like a as Pastor, due to my faith, has strengthen me in having peace in my life, although life will never be perfect, there are those who care and who will listen.

| 34 |

Reading: The Tools You Need In Better Writing

July 11, 2019

Reading! something that many simply do not like to do, but most of us our taught at a young age the importance of reading, something I impart on my daughter who is six years old. It appears my daughter loves to ready and be read too, something I admit I started late doing to her, because although I love to read, having worked in education, I was always studying up on my course material, creating my courses, relearning subjects that I hadn't taught in years, I was a challenge to learn.

Having worked in Higher Education for almost 10 years, I always valued education, especially when I went for my masters degree which I have fond memories of, meeting new people, learning from those who were veterans of industry, hoping one day I could be just like them. Many of those who I learned from who people, people with faults who were not perfect people, but I feel I had great examples to learn from.

Naturally over the years from college, I must have saved every book I had, totally over 100 books at least, some academics, some literature, some factual such as maps or books based on certain subjects like marine life, oceanography, I grew to respect and love books, because deep down there are countries that may not have the same selection of books and availability as we do. You may say well that is a strange statement, but certain countries really do try to limit what you can access, afraid of you becoming informed, so certain countries like China try to limit access to certain types of media and learning materials, definitely anything related to religion like the bible makes it hard to acquire but not impossible to get.

Most who grow up in the United States and in any developed country like in Europe reading is required in learning, which good reason. Reading has many benefits including the following, which are from this website, but found : https://www.lifehack.org/articles/lifestyle/10-benefits-reading-why-you-should-read-everyday.html

Mental Stimulation

Studies have shown that staying mentally stimulated can slow the progress of (or possibly even prevent) Alzheimer's and Dementia,[1] since keeping your brain active and engaged prevents it from losing power.

Stress Reduction

No matter how much stress you have at work, in your personal relationships, or countless other issues faced in daily life, it all just slips away when you lose yourself in a great story. A well-written novel can transport you to other realms, while an engaging article will distract you and keep you in the present moment, letting tensions drain away and allowing you to relax.

Knowledge

Everything you read fills your head with new bits of information, and you never know when it might come in handy. The more knowledge you have, the better-equipped you are to tackle any challenge you'll ever fac

Vocabulary expansion

The more you read, the more words you gain exposure to, and they'll inevitably make their way into your everyday vocabulary.

Being articulate and well-spoken is of great help in any profession, and knowing that you can speak to higher-ups with self-confidence can be an enormous boost to your self-esteem. It could even aid in your career, as those who are well-read, well-spoken, and knowledgeable on a variety of topics tend to get promotions more quickly (and more often) than those with smaller vocabularies and lack of awareness of literature, scientific breakthroughs, and global events.

Reading books is also vital for learning new languages, as non-native speakers gain exposure to words used in context, which will ameliorate their own speaking and writing fluency

Memory Improvement

When you read a book, you have to remember an assortment of characters, their backgrounds, ambitions, history, and nuances, as well as the various arcs and sub-plots that weave their way through every story. That's a fair bit to remember, but brains are marvellous things and can remember these things with relative ease.

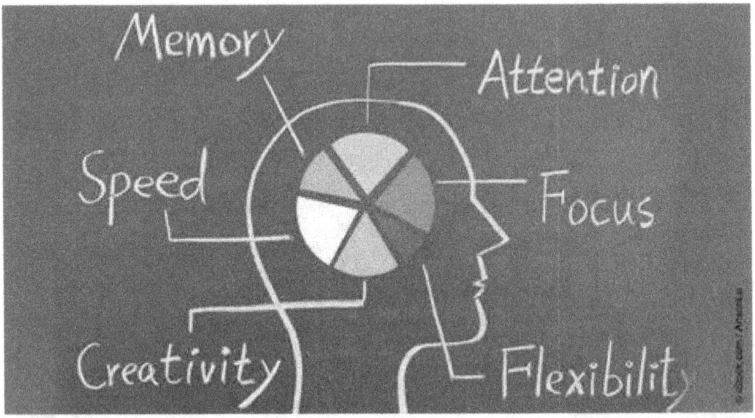

Amazingly enough, every new memory you create forges new synapses (brain pathways)[3] and strengthens existing ones, which assists in short-term memory recall as well as stabilizing moods.[4] How cool is that?

Stronger Analytical Skills

Have you ever read an amazing mystery novel, and solved the mystery yourself before finishing the book? If so, you were able to put critical and analytical thinking to work by taking note of all the details provided and sorting them out to determine "whodunnit".

That same ability to analyze details also comes in handy when it comes to critiquing the plot; determining whether it was a well-written piece, if the characters were properly developed, if the storyline ran smoothly, etc.

Improved Focus and Concentration

Have you ever read an amazing mystery novel, and solved the mystery yourself before finishing the book? If so, you were able to put critical and analytical thinking to work by taking note of all the details provided and sorting them out to determine "whodunnit".

In our internet-crazed world, attention is drawn in a million different directions at once as we multi-task through every day.

In a single 5-minute span, the average person will divide their time between working on a task, checking email, chatting with a couple of people (via gchat, skype, etc.), keeping an eye on twitter, monitoring their smartphone, and interacting with co-workers. This type of ADD-like behaviour causes stress levels to rise, and lowers our productivity.

When you read a book, all of your attention is focused on the story—the rest of the world just falls away, and you can immerse yourself in every fine detail you're absorbing.

Try reading for 15-20 minutes before work (i.e. on your morning commute, if you take public transit), and you'll be surprised at how much more focused you are once you get to the office.

Additional information: if you find staying focus hard and re trying to improve your focus, it's possible **you've been doing it wrong**.

Better Writing skills

This goes hand-in-hand with the expansion of your vocabulary:

Exposure to published, well-written work has a noted effect on one's own writing, as observing the cadence, fluidity, and writing styles of other authors will invariably influence your own work.

In the same way that musicians influence one another and painters use techniques established by previous masters, so do writers learn how to craft prose by reading the works of others.

Tranquility

In addition to the relaxation that accompanies reading a good book, it's possible that the subject you read about can bring about immense inner peace and tranquility.

Reading spiritual texts can lower blood pressure and bring about an immense sense of calm, while reading self-help books has been shown to help people suffering from certain mood disorders and mild mental illnesses.

Why should you care

As someone who works to write and perfect my skills reading is critical to my writing skills, as this is away I can learn new styles of writing , techniques and at the same time it sparks creativity . So you may be saying to your self, I already know this, but are you doing it, is the question. In today's social media quick read world, information now, now, now how many pick up a good book and just ready, put down the remote control and lose yourself in a book. If we all did that we would all be better people, and seeing the incredible worlds writers are creating , while TV can have the opposite affect of affecting our brains desensitizing us to what is important and will continue to be important in reading and while your at it attempt to write, write a story, a poem, your memoir, you will soon see the benefits.

The Health affects

Reading and writing even has proven to have therapeutic effects that can actually help you. You may say to yourself, well I don't have much time to read, I have a family, I have a life, but you will see even short periods of time reading and writing improves mental clarity and can even make you more creative, even if your not a creative person. I encourage to start small, but read a book, I know magazines can have valuable information, but a book any book will open your mind to keep reading in more depth literature, making you more informed, instead of getting your information from a Television source, why not get it first hand, right at the source.

Keep reading and writing, your writing skills need it, as that is our source next to time that gives us the skills to be great!

| 35 |

Inspiration for Great Writing

June 29, 2019

Writing takes a lot of inspiration and time to get down to a story, an image, an idea that I love and your audience will love. When it comes to my writing I don't always get the opportunity to work in silence, which I know is the best way. I work full time, have a wife and daughter. I guess could write late at time or early in the morning, but I haven't gotten to that discipline yet.

When I do write Music is a great way I get inspired, I have found that for some reason Opera works for me, just being able to hear about the tones, sounds , as if a story is playing out as I listen. Most who write know that there is a zone that you get into and once you get started its hard to stop afraid to lose that idea or train of thought because the story is playing out as you write.

Then interruptions come and the story becomes lost, the idea, pivotal points that you wanted to share. I believe when you write, the story is alive at that point, if its a short story you write in an hour or a book who the story continues until you finish, those characters, situations and lives live. Right now I am in the middle of my first book, approximately about 313 pages of fiction. Being that is my first real attempt at a book, I truly hope the story is be good, realistically if I said great I may be setting myself up for failure.

I know that my first real attempt may not be very good, I am not an English major, so once I get to editing I know there will be a lot I will need to change, update or just take out completely. When I write, I write, leaving the idea of being to confined to a story , but allowing inspiration to take over me, because I feel if you get to stuck on one particular premise in writing you limit yourself to sticking to that story and not allowing it to grow and manifest into something better.

I know there are plenty of writers that will stick to a game plan, brain-storming, creating plots before hand, making sure every detail is covered. I hear authors like R.L. Stein are very meticulous about the stories and books he writes. I guess If I was as successful as R.L stein with the amount of fame , wealth and prestige as him, I would have the ability to have a plan. I am not a full time writer, but that would be great if I could. If the heavens open up and allow me to do that, wonderful, but at this point I would settle to finish my book, make into a readable enjoyable piece and move on to the next book and build and create stories and an identity to be a great writer.

I encourage those who want to write start small, write something with a 100 words, than 200 and go on from there and if you feel inspired, keep writing. Many will say what do I write about, write about anything that gives you passion, it could be anything. I continue to be inspired daily, even when it's difficult, I believe life imitates art and the stories in you someone will want to hear, go for it.

| 36 |

The Paranormal in Writing

July 2, 2019

The realm of the paranormal is an area I find most interesting and in today's culture there is no lack of film and writings taking place today. I think that is so important to continue to discover what that world entails. Many will say leave the dead alone and in most part of agree. I believe there is a spiritual realm that exists, but you will find many who only wish to make a quick buck or get a quick thrill and not take the subject seriously.

I believe in writing its fantastic that we can imagine what goes on around us, who is walking about and the stories of those looking to pass on. I have had a few experiences in my life times of dealing with spirits especially living in my last family home which I grew up in for most of my life. I didn't really start to be sensitive to that around me until I was older, but it's real.

My family and I would experience knocks on the door, typically three, walking in the kitchen and one of the most frightening time a violent bang on the door and lastly a time I heard a voice speak, which I thought it was my wife but they were sound asleep. As a child I always had a interest in the paranormal, that could be partly because my father allowed me to watch scary movies at such a young age, which I don't recommend.

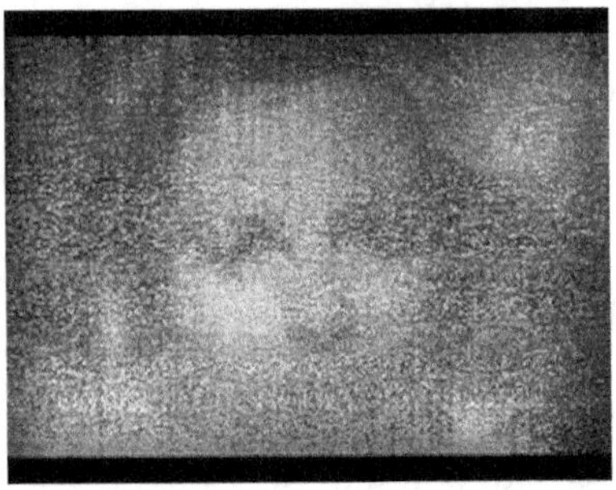

In writing there can definitely be beautiful stories to be told, the story of a love, the passing of one that doesn't wish to leave but continues to love from the grave and beyond, never really leaving that person. For many they probably would not want that, but for some maybe, especially imagine having someone in your life for decades like a parent or spouse and you wanting them to be near all the time. I thought I would want that when my mother passed and at first I thought I would sense her, but really had to rely on my belief that I would want my mother to pass on to the next life and not be stuck.

Over the years when it came to paranormal love stories, we revert to great movies like Ghost to show there are those we leave behind that may still need something. Personally I don't know if I would want to haunt my wife and daughter or anyone for that matter, but it goes to show you the strong will of our spirits to keep going even after death.

Personally I have watched some of the reality shows like Ghost Adventures, trying to reach out to those who wish to stay and haunt, I am a bit of skeptic in those situations because I know many times it's for entertainment value, but there are true cases of those who wish not to leave, because maybe they died angry full of hate or sadness.

I truly would love to write about the love of someone living in the spirit world trying to help those who are living, continuing their love story. I am very interested in those stories that pass centuries and decades of that spirit still continuing to haunt a certain place for whatever reason. It just goes to show you our individual spirits are strong, that we as people do everything we can to leave our footprint here on earth, but once gone are unfortunately forgotten which is is natural.

I find the history who where spirits dwell even more fascinating, asking myself the question, why don't they move on, what is keeping them here, what hurt or pain did they experience in their life. For those who write paranormal stories, I would love to read it.

| 37 |

The Beginning of my Writing Journey but Not Really

June 27, 2019

I would like to think of myself as a writer, someone who has always been a writer and a lover of books. For my lifetime I have written but nothing published. Now will be my time to write and push myself to be the writer I want to be. The writing outlet for me lets me be creative, create new worlds, new scenarios and allow me to create the narrative. My hope is that my writing will be enjoyed by those who read it.

Starting a blog was one of first steps to doing that, but in the process I am writing my first novel which is currently untitled, but that's ok, I believe we shouldn't commit to a title until you are well and finished with your work, because it will change, manifest, grow and take a life of it's own.

I hope to use this opportunity to share with you my Journey in Life as well, my struggles to finish my first book, but show you that their are many writers out there with the hopes of being discovered but just having the joy of someone reading your working and hopefully loving it. As the great writer Stephen King once wrote in his memoirs there will be people who will criticize your work and that is being part of a writers life. Not to set myself for failure but I know my writing may not be great at first and I am O.K. with that, i am growing when I write.

Writing is my outlet as a human being, because I know words matter, and in this day in age we need words to inspire not tear us down or apart. Some of favorite Authors that draw inspiration from is Don Winslow, Stephen King and J.R.R Tolkien and of course the classics like Jules Verne and Herman Melville and H.G. Wells.

My other love is film and some T.V. but I have come to see from what Stephen King has said Television ruins creativity so I try to limit my exposure, even though there is great writing in T.V. I have to be sure not to focus on that or I will end up not writing. I am a classic Action junkie when it comes to films. My book and future books will probably draw inspiration from those films, but I know I need to be creative and not rely on Hollywood to give me Ideas, I need to be the one giving them ideas, so everyone one day can enjoy my work.

I have heard writing can be a selfish art, which it can be because you must dedicate your time to it not matter what. I have a six year old and wife, so devotion to them is so important and by no means who I want to be a neglectful father and husband and lost my family to writing.

I look forward to those out there to read my blogs, respond and have a conversation, I am reachable. Thank you for going on this journey with me!

| 38 |

The End of My Teaching for Now

June 29, 2019

Teaching has always been a passion of mine from a early age, going to college, looking up to my professors I still remember. Thinking how do you get that job, I must do that, but I knew in most cases I needed a higher degree like a Masters or Ph.D but went as far as my Master's in Business Admin. Sadly this week I was notified that my Teaching Career will come to a halt, that's if I choose not to apply at other schools.

Mt. Sierra College is where I have been at for the past nine years, teaching everything from Business to Finance to Economics and general ed. I loved every moment of it, from my first day, when I had no idea how to create a course and teach a class to know, where I hope to have perfected a teaching style that allow my students to learn and use that know they gain in a positive way.

I have seen many graduates come and go in my years, many I see are successful and like anything else someone who are getting there. There is a lot of blame for our school closely, primarily it was that those in charge were not fiscally responsible with the school. I am not saying we blew it on usefulness things, I believe it all went to the students. Until a few years ago, we were at another location down the street which I loved, but then we went to bigger and better things which is nice, change owners a few times and those who originally started the school are long gone, getting their investment while the students, faculty and staff are the ones who lost in the end.

There are many opinions out there like we ripped students off, our prices were too high, just go to Junior College its cheaper. The reality is that many who makes those comments have no clue. Junior colleges although cheaper take longer to graduate and finish due to the large amounts of students who go to those colleges. We are a small private college which allows us to have smaller class sizes and in effect and get students to graduate sooner. Are we exorbitant in our prices? absolutely NOT we are in line with what the Market is offering. Other colleges are worst offenders such as UEI and Corinthian colleges , which I worked for at one point.

We offered students a bachelors degrees which many want, Like any business or organization there is a market for us, unfortunately a few years ago things really started to change when ownership changed hands and employees used Mt.Sierra as a place to wait for their next opportunity. We lost many over the years and before you know only a few including myself remained loyal to the school.

These years at Mt. Sierra were the best and the Worst, because this was a time when I was starting my family and it was Great experience and having two incomes to help out, but the days were long, working from 6pm to 10pm sometimes working Monday to Thursday and some Saturdays away from family, but supporting them.

The people I came across are incredible professionals who were devoted to education and who I can truly say taught me so many skills I probably would not have learn else where. It's heart breaking when you see people who comment on the state of the school and know knowing. Of course they are entitled to their opinion doesn't make it right.

Even in the last few days I have seen commentators say how we took advantage of students, stole from them, charge them too much and why didn't they just go to a Junior College or State college. Yet those who make those are comments are ignorant to the fact that not everyone has the time to go to a Junior College that may not be very flexible sharing a classroom with 40-100 students and the professor who care less about your achievement. Our classroom sizes were small many times 10 students or less and max 20 students. Those students made a choice to go there and continued to go there, because they knew we cared about them.

The other factor is Junior colleges tend to take more than time because of class room overcrowding with the influx of foreign students taking spots, spots personally I feel should go to residents firsts. I have been a student a student and continue to learn on my own til this day, that will never stop me, and I only tried to be an example for my students.

I think ultimately we have to remember a college especially a private one is a business and is susceptible to failure in many different ways, this was just a prime example of what can happen.

I hope in time I can teach again, it will never be Mt. Sierra but maybe something close or better.

https://www.nbclosangeles.com/news/local/Mt-Sierra-College-Closes-Before-Graduation-511940572.html

| 39 |

A Writer's Life: The Struggle, To Never Give Up

August 1, 2019

As a writer, something I will call myself simply because of not only my love for writing but my love for reading and knowledge. For those following my blog, you will see and be a part of my Weekly features of writings from my childhood past. Reflecting on my life as a writer, I stopped for many years, but over time I never really stopped as I tended to write about business, leadership, efficiency things that in all honesty are not the most exciting topics to read.

I guess I stopped writing fiction for the same reason many of us stop doing something lack of time, lack of interest, not motivated, stress, probably a list of of reasons one stops things. I guess one of the reasons I have stopped many things is time, the start of a family, the stress of trying to keep things together at times. Being a father and provider is by far one of the hardest roles anyone can have, which this role is a lifetime role and not for the faint of heart.

Tough Times Shape You

Going through young adulthood was tough enough as it is, especially my twenties were horrible to me as a struggle to find my place especially after college. I didn't get much help sad to say, it had a lot to do with the people or the lack thereof people in my life throughout those years. I was particularly shy, quiet and an introvert and tack on the depression, anxiety and always the sense that I was not good enough in anything I did. It didn't help growing up with a grandfather who told me how worthless I was each day until the day I moved out. Growing up like that completely destroyed my motivation for any attempt at bettering my life.

Even going to college(s), yes you read that right, I went to a few, but graduated one college, but I was searching for something. I was searching for a better life, but what many don't explain to you early in life is that most of what you want to accomplish takes time and there rarely is a quick fix to getting that great position or making a great money, which many of us equate to being successful, because who doesn't love money, we could rent an apartment, buy great clothes, buy a great car, get in to a relationship and spoil that person with good things. You can see from what I wrote I still equate money to happiness, even though the old adage that "Money doesn't buy happiness" and for the most part it doesn't, how many times do we see the wealthy take their lives, even though they live the dream of what many wish for including me.

I am Just not Good Enough

I guess a good part of my life even today is that I look at others success as a barometer my success and failures constantly evaluating those around me, asking myself the question, why don't have what they have, I am intelligent, hardworking, wise in my own right, I have what it takes to succeed but never really getting the chance. Again I am still an introvert so many people tend to equate those people as not leadership material, for those who read this may not agree because some of you may be introverts and are leaders, most likely because my only did you work hard, but someone saw how special introverts can be once you give them a chance to shine.

Again I am observer, a judger of situations in my life always trying to piece together why I am treated a certain way, Why others treat those in my life better whether it's a co-worker, a friend, a family member, always observing. If you were ever to meet me I hope I come across pleasant and kind, but somewhat awkward in the way I constantly observe people, but ultimately it's my way of evaluating you and your character, something I find incredibly important. For example over the course of being married, there have been many people who I have come into our life who I immediately could see major character flaws that ultimately destroyed my feelings keeping them in my life.

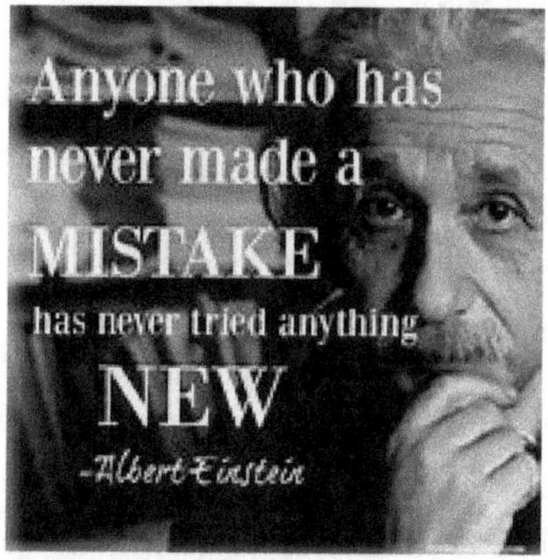

Everyone's Failure and Success

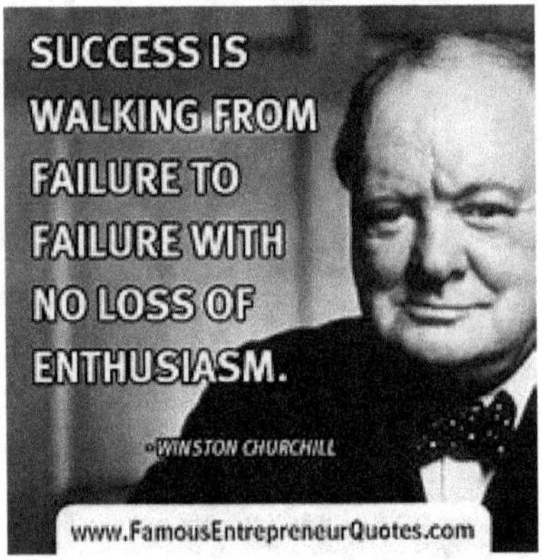

Why am I saying all of this you ask, why do you care, you live your life and I live mine simple as that right? Well yes and no, we are here to learn from each other, grow with each other as human beings, and although we live many times in a complete upside-down world, we must always evaluate ourselves, perfecting ourselves the best way we can, but learning, growing, learning some more, removing those habits that make us flawed. Some flaws are perfectly fine, but others destroy us from being the true potential we can become.

I know deep down I have so much more to be in this life, as a Writer I write the story I want to live in and hope those who one day read my books live through my books to, knowing someone out there knows how they feel and can relate.

<u>Coping In Your Own Way</u>

Living this life I have had to learn to cope with the hard times like many, I do that in a few different ways, one is writing which again I can write characters into existence and create a story out of thin air, something hopefully unique, I honestly feel we all have this ability but many just don't have the interest and discipline to sit down and write a piece of literature, a story, a poem, I take great brainpower to think in that manner, when many times our minds are wrapped up in watching TV or being on social media.

The other way I cope is reading getting lost in a great book, something I know took the writer time, energy, sleepless nights struggles, pain both physical and financial at times, blood wrapped in sweat and tears in words.

Movies are another Love, certain movies have really gotten me through some tough times in my life, one of those would be Rocky, each and everyone one of those Rocky movies in some fashion helped me cope with feeling worthless, that is the power of a great character. For many you may say well its Rocky, an old character that has been around for decades, there are better characters than him and I ask you really are there more poignant characters than Rocky. Here is a character that was dirt poor, breaking fingers, winning fights that meant nothing just to survive finally getting rags to riches to rags story again, hard to beat that. Ultimately his strength continues on in every obstacle almost being beaten each time but getting up and surviving.

<u>The Power of Music and Film Inspire Me</u>

Lastly, Music gets me through those days of feeling inadequate, obliviously music is very powerful, but I have always loved very traditional music like Classical, Opera, Show Tunes, eighty's and ninety's pop and anything that will make me feel like there is a better day tomorrow. I think for all those major successes and failures in my life, music, movies, and writing has been there for me. To this day, I have to get in my car, turn on a certain tune each time which ultimately creates my mood for the day, making me feel invisible or quite the opposite on those days I have the hardest times getting through it.

You may read this and if you have gotten to the end, what was the point of this, did I waste my time reading this and the answer is NO! this was a reflection that if you get up each day and struggle to do the right thing to make it, go to work, support yourself and or your family and life is tough, NOT to give up, tomorrow is a better day even if it may not look that way. I have a wife and daughter I love and support, and will do whatever it takes until my last breath to support them, there is NOTHING I won't do for them to survive. One of those ways is writing, hoping to turn my writing into something others will read and enjoy very soon hopefully, as I continue to work on my WIP (Work In Progress), my novel. So stay with me, get to know me because for those who stick by my side I shall not forget you.

Thank you for listening to me rant and rave this time, stay tuned for my weekly feature this weekend, story to TBA. Cheers and Peace!

| 40 |

Creating Worlds with Words: Writing & Expression

August 8, 2019

As a writer I like to think that I have a lot to pull from in my life to make great literature, well at least one day I do. I never thought of myself as a writer, but many be I should have because I have always thought about it since a child. I always felt words have meaning, words are powerful and they can either build up or breakdown a person. With words, without you knowing me I can build a connection with you and that is the power of words and reading.

It Starts with Reading

Naturally I love to read, diving into a book, looking for adventures, the author's personal touch, knowing that that put their sweat into that book probably getting up early or staying up late to finish their masterpiece. By reading an author's work, you are giving respect to the time it took the author to write it. Currently I am writing my untitled and un-chaptered book coming in 116 thousand characters, and the story is still not finished.

Something within me has always wanted to write a book, something exciting, fun, something the reader will not want to put down. On the other hand I too want the book I write to have twist and turns enticing me not to put it down either, allowing me to forget any troubles I have in my life at the moment and live through my characters.

In my opinion although there are so many great books out there, I think society doesn't read as much as the once before, now with social media and computers, many seem to devote them time to other things, that may not benefit them. For those who read my blogs, I recommend you read Reading: The tools you need in better writing are in a good book!. https://adventuresinwriting675191505.wordpress.com/2019/07/11/reading-the-tools-you-need-in-better-writing-are-an-a-good-book/

Yes I know the title is long but I happen to love long titles with descriptions. Reading has incredible benefits that many may not realize that could possibly solve some of the issues that people have like relaxing for one.

When Society Stops Reading

I am not sure why but it seems to me society may be as bright as they once were when they read a book, simply because we rely heavily on information at our fingertips, like our

IPhone or Tablet to feed us information. These forms of technology are not necessarily bad, technology is actually a good thing to have and it seems to be getting better each year.

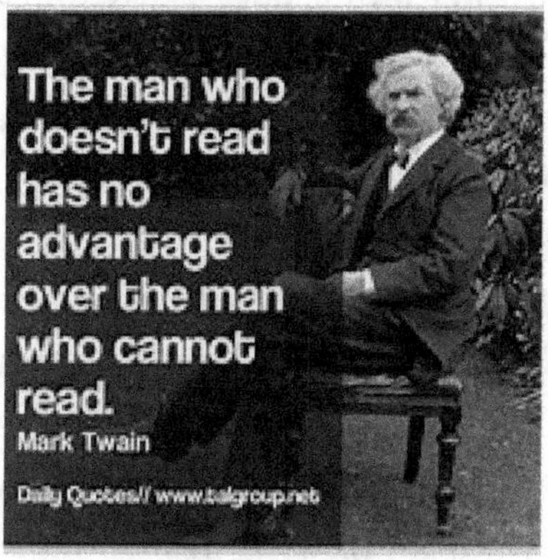

I find using technology and apps very efficient for getting a quick fix on information, as well as have a kindle to read, which I personally love because you have the ability to download books, read them, highlight them, book mark them and so many other things.

Based on this article I was researching here are some reasons people may not read anymore: https://www.thoughtco.com/why-people-dont-read-738494

- Not Enough Time
- Not Enough Money
- Not Enough Experience
- Too Tired
- Too Hard
- Multimedia Experience
- Not a Habit

All of these list of items I could probably write pages and pages on how these are just excuses to do something better in the eyes of the reader but I will stick with a couple of these as I appear to be getting off topic which I do a lot

1. Not enough Time – How much time does it take to read, well realistically you don't need much time and throughout our day there are plenty of chances to read like your Lunch time, turning off the TV and read instead, get up a little earlier, go to bed a little later, tell your friends you rather stay home. Tons of reason to read, but what many don't realize is that once they start to read it's hard to stop, because your brain is growing with the knowledge you are gaining from reading. Some may argue, what knowledge can I get from reading, how about better speech, strong vocabulary and so much more.
2. Too hard- Reading can be hard, but that's ok, it just means that our minds are not being used to the full capacity like they are meant too. I remember in High School I forced myself to read Moby Dick by Herman Melville, one of the most difficult books I have encountered but I love it, I loved books that challenged me to learn new words, words I didn't know existed until I read those hard to read books and in the end I was a better young man for it.
3. It's not a habit – Make it habit, taking thirty minutes each day to read, just a measly thirty minutes and then make it an hour , start with every day, pick a book you want to read or a certain genre you feel you will like and read. That's how simple it is, read all kinds of different

books, no books are off topic, even kid's book but those may be too easy to read, but just read.

I will stop at those points, because you get the point to reading, it's something most of us are engrained with from a young age, many of my childhood books are still around today, that my young daughter is reading, that is the power or reading it leaves a lasting memory.

Bringing Reading and Writing Together

So once you start reading, getting to writing, you will see and learn different styles of writing and eventually adapting your own style. Some styles very traditional, some styles are a little strange in the sense that the author uses words to detail a character or scene or plot in completely different way we never thought you could. Writing allows you to experiment and there is nothing wrong with that, there are obliviously rules to writing, but what you write is all on you.

"Words are sacred. They deserve respect. If you get the right ones, in the right order, you can nudge the world a little."

Tom Stoppard

I deeply regret not focusing on my writing years ago, I mean I imagine where my writing career would be if I focused on my writing twenty years ago, but I try not to think about that because then I will Not focus on my current book, which at the moment is Not perfect, but once I get to editing I will go back and update and upgrade this version to a better version I hope.

Writing is a love of mine and I am thankful each day I can express myself with all of you, knowing I am not being judged but hopefully loved for my expression. The point of this piece was really a reminder to all of us that although writing is fantastic and brings many of us joy we must always be Reader Advocates encouraging those around us to read.

Continuing with My Love of Writing

I guess what also spurred this piece is that I see so much hate on the web, social media, Television and many of those who spew hate , probably never pick up a book. So you may ask how I come to that conclusion that is because when you read, you find beauty in words and you see the importance of words and the affect they have over people and society. That is why when I write and we write, we should write with purpose to bring people together and not divide.

The power of writing and words are who I am, although I am sorry to say like anyone one of us we don't always use our writing and words to uplift people especially in professional settings where we fire off an e-mail, or troll someone on social media, or speak to our loved ones, that is why words matter, so make them good ones.

| 41 |

Are You a Scrooge or a Cratchit?

December 23, 2021

The holidays can be filled with joy, good food, family and stress not necessarily in that order, so you can imagine why the holidays are dreaded at times. One of my favorite pastimes is movies and boy are there a ton of them from comedies, dramas to horror and all in between. Many of the films today and yesterday do have some sort of message about being kinder, having patience in all the chaos. Some of the central figures I look at include the grinch, Scrooge and even Bob Cratchit. There are of course others that we can look at but I am reminded of my favorite story A Christmas Carol by Charles Dickens.

One of the most common themes during these times is being kind to one another, being more giving and remembering what is important. From the films and books Bob Crachit was an abused, underpaid clerk of Ebenezer Scrooge, symbolizing the poor working conditions, long hours and low pay during the Victorian era.

Bob Cratchit Was a Good Man But Flawed

There have been many versions of Bob Cratchit all different and similar at the same time reflecting Bob as a hardworking family man with a wife Mrs. Cratchit, Tiny Tim, Martha, Belinda, Peter. Often times Bob is displayed as poor, working class trying to survive and never making enough to pay for Tiny Tim's medical needs, but would it surprise you to know that Bob was possibly a spendthrift or shopaholic which is why he suffered financial hardships.

Bob Cratchit a member of the British middle class lives a respectable life working in a coat and tie on living in a four-bedroom house and appears to live in much better conditions then most. Earning more than an ample wage is told to be earning fifteen shillings a week. The British pound was divided into twenty shillings and each shilling was divided into twelve pennies or pence. SO, lets do the math as Bob Cratchit earns 15 shillings or180 pence each week about the wage of a metropolitan police officer and well above the truly needy.

Martha is apprenticed to a milliner and earns an additional income and Peter, their eldest son is about to obtain a job earning five shillings and six pence weekly. He, too, is to be a man of business.

So why is the Cratchits family so poor?

The reason that best could explain this is that Bob Cratchit is a spendthrift or a Shopaholic. The shopaholic being on of the eight different personality types in Bert Whiteheads book "Facing Financial Dysfunction." Cratchit is on the opposite end of the spectrum from Ebenezer Scrooge. Whereas Scrooge combines greed with a propensity to save, Bob Cratchit combines fear with a propensity to spend.

What is a SpendThrift?

Spendthrifts are some of the most pleasant people to be around. They are socially outgoing and often demonstrate their own friendliness by buying things for other people.

Bob raised in poverty and buying gave him great pleasure in life which equated to almost like a high helping Bob establish social status. For Bob living within a budget and saving money would be like setting out to deprive yourself and suffer. Living for the pleasure of the moment by eating out, buying clothes and doesn't realize the purpose of budgeting and saving.

This story brings this close to home for me because although don't think of myself as a spendthrift maybe I am after all. I too grew up in poverty, although we did have a roof over our head, clothes and food mom dad had no wealth always appearing to struggle. Living in the poorest of neighborhoods often cheap due to the demographics living in South Central Los Angeles.

My Own Lessons Learned

Growing up I was not really taught the importance of a budget or saving but taught to be giving to others at the expense of hurting myself at times feeling that I was investing in people instead of helping myself. From the outside we appeared to have it all. As I got older, I would buy nice clothes, eat out often and working to live in better neighborhood often expensive. At times I did leave beyond my means because of the despair I felt living in poor neighborhoods, looking around while others appeared to prosper.

Thinking of Bob Cratchit and his family they are typical spendthrifts when it comes to clothing. On Christmas day, Bob Cratchit confers on his son Peter a shirt in honor of his apprenticeship. It was common in the day for the RICH to go through the parks to show off their finery. And Peter is amazed to find himself gallantly attired that he be too anxious to show off his fashionable new linen in the park.

While Bob fears in poverty, he also resents wealth. He is caught in the consumerism of the rising Victorian social and professional class. It is the propensity to spend that is the true cause of the Cratchits lack of means.

What does this story and backstory tell us about us and society today, it tells us to be warned? Scrooge has earned the financial means to help the Cratchit family, but the spirits don't always give us a reformed scrooge to bail us out of financial problems. Sometimes they want us to become reformed Cratchits! Perhaps that's why the spirits visited Ebenezer? It was easier to make a frugal man generous then to make a spendthrift father financial responsibility.

As we look at this holiday seasons and lessons learned from Film, TV and books we can see there is a message here. Yes we can be kind and generous but not at the expense of our own financial security and if others feel we are not generous enough that is not our problem its theirs.

In the new year lets start on the right foot looking a examples of Bob Cratchit and Scrooge to how two different examples can hurt or hep us. Living like Bob often bankrupting us and especially relevant during these times thinking of the time Bob Cratchit bought the Christmas goose, not really saying how much that goose cost but estimated to be around 400 pence (1.5 pounds). At this moment, the Cratchit family goose is costing the family a years supply of medical attention for the entire family.

Lastly one of the saddest parts of the Cratchits is Tiny Tim, because of their choices, Tiny Tim is suffering unable to get the help he needs. Now mind you it could be the lack of medicine or care at that time, but regardless when Scrooge is reborn he often helps the Cratchit family and Tiny Tim is ok, but couldn't that have been done by Bob Cratchit if he had been more fiscally responsible, the answer is YES.

Looking at these two examples, each having their good and bad traits we can all learn from, being Scrooge is not the answer, but neither is being the Bob Cratchits of the world.

In the new year we all have a fresh start even from being a Bob Cratchit or Scrooge, we can all be better for good and learn from these central figures.

Chapter 37- Merry Christmas! How Scrooge Teaches us Valuable Lessons on Kindness and Love

December 25, 2020

Merry Christmas to all!

Thank you so much for all of those who take the time to read my blog and are part of my life I truly do Love you all. I know this year has been particularly difficult with COVID, politics and the incredible times we are facing.

This year I have tried to be incredibly real with all of you concerning my thoughts, feelings and what is going on in my world as like any human I work to grow. For many who read my blogs you may or may not believe in my positions whether its in politics, my thoughts on societal changes taking place or just in general, but I try to be genuine and true to all.

Over time my views do and will change because I am constantly looking to change in a good way, something I encourage all of us to try to do. All to often people get stuck in one position in life and stay there unwilling to grow. I am not staying change or principles or values but we should all try to have an option mind and the acceptance of other thoughts and opinions something I think in today's society we greatly lack.

During this time of year its especially important to look at what is important, having watched Charles Dickens a Christmas Carol, a story that all too often we all take for granted as just being a film or book we can watch or read at Christmas, but the message can be appreciate all days in our life. We truly live in a time of greed and oppression of people, some of you out there may feel like there is no such thing in society and I would ask you to look deeper in those who are suffering today.

Ebenezer Scrooge a man of business who started out in a life of solitude and loneliness never truly felt loved hence the reason I think he rejected Love and stuck to the cold hard world of money and prestige. The story is so important to look at what happens when it set aside people in our life and focus on wealth instead of what is important. I get that we all need to live a life, we all need to eat, we all need to survive and most all want to prosper in life, but its tough.

Not everyone is born with a silver spoon in their mouth, many have to slowly work their way in life to create a life. Some in this life have incredible fortune in their life, lots of money, big house, nice care, supportive family and support system to make sure they succeed. While others struggle to make it, pinching pennies with little or no support system alone in this dark cold world failing to succeed in a world that says you are not good enough unless you have this or do this, I have lived this life. Yes I have my wife and daughter, my sister, father, brother in law who support me, but deep within side me I ask for more.

Back to Scrooge, a man who was in the perfect position to live a comfortable life in his wealth and not worry about where his next meal would come from or where he would live. While others were truly suffering like today. Interesting how Scrooge mentioned workhouses and prisons which he fully supported. Obliviously we know what prisons are , but workhouses or poor houses existed which where placed that supported those who could not survive on their own. Imagine if you will these were the places people went to work, not that there was anything wrong with that, but these were considered dismal horrible places eventually turning to place to care for the elderly and resembling almost a prison environment, but again maybe it could be better then being homeless. Remembering when Scrooge was approached for a donation telling those :

The coldness in his voice, the heartlessness so reminiscent of today and the coldness in people today. I will say that I know that's Not everyone, many do care for sick and unfortunate like the homeless but there is very little help compared to the size of our societies today, we need more. It's so oblivious when you've made it life why should you have to give back, thinking only what how no one helped you succeed but in reality, you were helped, GOD provided for you, giving you the mind and body, you have to today along with the gifts in your life something many forget. But again, Scrooge eventually say that through the three ghosts of Christmas Past, Present and Future.

I love that Dickens focused on this in his book because its something we should all see in hopes of redeeming ourselves and our souls to be better. Now you may think well I am good person and maybe you are but you can always be better.

Scrooge was redeemed by seeing his life from his past, but the biggest impacts were the present and future being able to see his impact on Bob Crachit , his family and Tiny Tim forgetting the impact people make in those lives we touch whether we think so or not. Ultimately Scrooge was even able to see his own death in a way and those people who truly despised and hated him, something again we should all see because many live-in illusions we are well loved, and we are not.

The ending is by far the best part of this incredible story as Scrooge corrects his ways immediately. He doesn't say well maybe I will fix me tomorrow; no he said I will fix myself NOW and he did. First order of business being more giving and treating those in his life as he should have always treated them with love and respect even paying them fairly. Being a miser and pay all too often people accept a modern day miser and feel well I deserve this and we do not, we accept misers and shouldn't.

Scrooge I believe once had a large heart especially when he worked for Fezziwig, he seemed so happy and cheerful even having love in his life but along the way went astray. Something that happens to all of us, going astray, darker, cold and heartless until we wake up but look at what it took for Scrooge to wake up, what will it take for you and I to wake up to be kinder, softer and more loving.

Scrooge continues to be watched in my home every year and different versions, but my favorite by far is the 1954 version with Alastair Sims what a perfect Scrooge, but I am also partial to Reginald Owens and Michael Caine in Muppets Christmas Carol. I know this season we tend to stay indoors a lot even more so today watching our favorite classics, all seem to have message of the hardships of holidays, but ultimately coming to almost the same conclusion to be kinder, love more, look to what is important in life so why can't people just do it. People make the choice not to because frankly people love living in the dark, being mean, cold towards others feeling there is no reward to being kind, but there is a reward our soul is rewarded.

So make Christmas 2020 a time to remember what is important, LOVE, KINDNESS and Peace on Earth each of us have the ability to do these things if we just try making the world less hateful, bitter. Ultimately, I will say this the reason for season as always is to remember Jesus was born to die on this day and his birth is the reason for the season, a ultimate sacrifice to all of us, but the ultimate love for all of us, so lets try to love more like Christ. Regardless if you don't believe in CHRIST, we can all be much kinder to each other.

PART V-FAMILY

| 42 |

This is Me, A Portrait of Me

September 14, 2019

For those who have gotten to know you know I love films and what really inspired this blog was the film "The Greatest Showman" about Barnum Bailey and the circus of entertainers and so called freaks. This story along with the music really touched home to me because of the characters who were often mistreated and thought so poorly of.

I will say many of entertainers although they were ridiculed they knew they were doing something with their life and did not have a lot of choices at the time and if research life in the Circus you will see many of characters in the film resemble true real life people who struggled to survive.

One particular song called "This is Me" inspired me because of the mistreatment and how they realized that they were Not going to be afraid and live their life. Something I have tried to do and wish I had a film like this in my younger years.

https://youtu.be/wEJd2RyGm8Q

I often think about what defines me as a person and who I am, thinking on last days on earth what do I hope to be remembered for. For those out there, some of you don't know me, my thoughts, my feelings towards issues and how I live my life. We as people have many different layers to who we are, I believe we as people are complex, even on the outside we may seem simple.

Growing up I had a complex childhood which is where It began to form my complexities as a human being, rarely do we grow up in a carefree environment, but if you did that's wonderful, I didn't have that privilege. Many of you have read parts of who I am, here I am just going to be more defined. Some of which I say you may not like, but respect that I respect you, no judgement from me and hope you feel the same towards me.

I am a follower of Jesus Christ

First and foremost, I am a Christian man, but you may see that some of writings are NOT Christian based, you never hear me speak about Jesus or the Bible and those who read this may feel like I am denying my faith and I am NOT. I just chose to not talk about my faith, religion and even politics because I have found those topics to be controversial.

Yes, I said it Jesus who which I love and adore can be a hard person to talk about because, the moment you start, people shut down. I am believer in people getting to know me first and then displaying my faith. I am not a perfect Christian, because there are NO perfect Christians.

Even the word Christian is no longer accurate because many people throw that term around a lot. I see it the media, news and really everywhere, a true Christian is a follower of Jesus and practices what he Practices which is Love Thy Neighbor, Devote your Life to Christ, be Christ Like and knowing that Jesus died for our sins.

I know there is so much more to speak about, but often times many people associate Christianity with Hate because those who called themselves Christian Hated people and did pretty horrible things to their fellow man and women.

But I digress, Christianity I guess has been always apart of my life, first going to a catholic church and then becoming a believe in 2008 and that's when my life started to turn around for the better, I was a real mess before that. I has never into drugs or alcohol, but destructive to have I treated myself with Hate at times. Being told I was worthless by my grandfather from a young age until really my adult years.

My mother was my main rock at times, my defender from his abusive ways, but the same time she took a bullet for me and my sister at times because we lived with him. But anyways Christianity is apart of me, going to church, listening to the word of God and trying to bring those principles in my life each day.

I am a Father and Husband

I was Married October 2, 2010 and my Daughter Mikaylah Born January 2013, both the loves of my life, two who have changed my life forever and forever grateful to have in my life. Aside from them I have my father, Sister and Brother in Law, who I love too and that's pretty much it. I devote most of time to keeping my family going, surviving trying to help us be better people.

Being Married has probably been the biggest challenge only because I was never really in relationships prior to meeting my wife and I also didn't live on my own. I wish I had at least learned to be a little more independent after college, but much of my twenties I was suffering through deep depression, so I lived at home with my father, and then my mother and grandfather until I got married. I won't lie being married is one of the hardest roles I have ever faced next to being a father, being the sole provider and try to give them everything we need and want at times.

Financially I have struggled the most since what many don't tell you when you get married and have a child is how expensive it will be and how it can be hard to keep things together.

My wife stayed home for the most part and took care of our daughter which did make it harder, but our daughter is better for it I think because we didn't put her in childcare and pay that high cost.

I am not a perfect husband or father, I have had to struggle with managing my emotions at times due to high stress I was under usually working two Jobs, one full time and One part time at the College and One time working as a Lyft driver.

I have basically tried to do whatever it took to provide and as a father and husband am willing to do anything for them, working three jobs if I have too and actually attempted to do that.

At the end of the day, I am the one who has to live with if I am a good father and husband, even though I am human, I make mistakes and I know there things I do today I am trying to work on, but I feel I have been a good provider, we are not rich, times we struggle, but we survive.

I am a writer

As many of you are already aware, I write, I write fiction, I write what interests me and what I think will interest readers. I feel I have always been a writer from age 10, but just stopped for many years. Writing now is where I intend to take myself professionally if doors open for me and If I good enough for mainstream, but it's to say with all the competition out there today. Writing has allowed me to really take all of my thoughts and put them in a format where I can share those with everyone.

I am a writer.

That is who and what I am. **I will write, even on the hard days. I won't make excuses.** ***I won't doubt my own abilities.*** I will be humble and know that I can always improve. *My goal will always be to create something beautiful, for myself and for my readers.* I will always remember that this is what I love and what I want to be doing. **I will put in the work and make the time.**

I am a writer.

Currently I just finished my first draft of my book, still need to edit it, have beta readers and finally try to query it for an agent, if not I will try other routes. Writing is an ongoing process for me as I fine tune my skills. I am an avid reader which does help in my writing skills, as this another part of who I am constantly wanting to learn.

What I hope to accomplish in my writing is to continue to build my blog of great content, working with NeedtoLive Blog to get those blogs out to students and really try to be a role model writer that people can come to for advice, one day.

I have a Political Side to Me

The political side I don't necessary like to characterize but I guess I am closest to a democrat, but truly I don't know, because I have never really followed politics. I do get angry with the world of politics both for republicans and democrats, who both seem to get their act together as they fight and bicker and really don't represent the values I value. I value the following:

Treating people humanely, especially immigrants because my wife is Salvadorian and not caging people like animals. I believe if you are going imprison people, they should not be treated like cold blood murders, these are trying to have a better life for themselves and family.

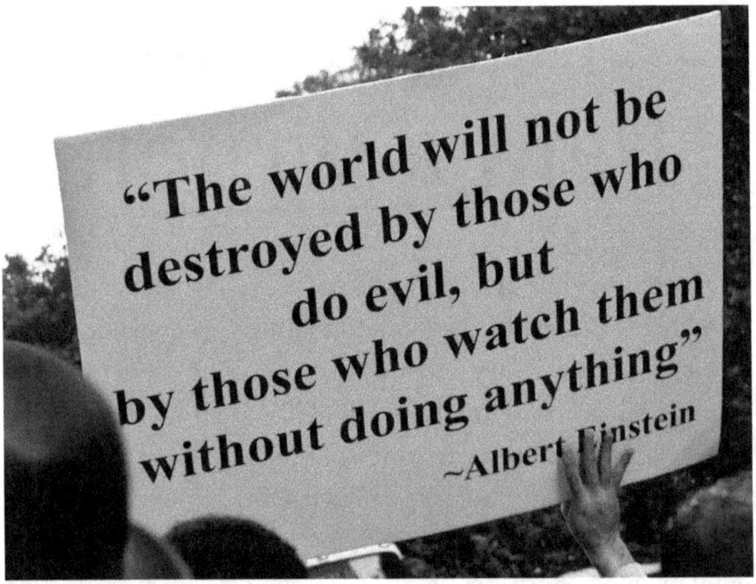

Being that my wife is a Naturalized citizen, it's sad to see the horrors of people who are fleeing violence and survival for a better life, something any one of us who do. I hate the argument, oh well if they came here legally it would better. Well yeah, but unfortunately with the Visa lottery, many of those struggling who never get here, because truly that system is crooked for those fleeing poverty and violence.

I see every day we are not the only country dealing with this issue especially in Europe, they struggle with the same issue of people trying to survive.

Another part wants to help the less fortunate like the homeless and especially homeless veterans who I feel have been left behind when they served our country but our forgotten. I find that many needs helps and it should not begrudged those who are just looking to better their lives, I hear to often the argument why I should I help others, I pay my taxes that's enough. Its enough until those same people need help and expect to be helped when they coldly didn't want to help those in need.

I seems like the things I mentioned are too much to ask especially treating people with dignity when they struggle, something all of us want and need. No person is perfect, yet we as people like to shove our unrighteousness down people's throats. Stop the hate, accept people for whoever they are and where they come from and live you life, but that seems too hard to for many, as others have to meddle in those peoples life we don't understand.

Put our differences aside for a moment and come to solutions that help build people up for better instead of trying too often to tear people down. I know we all have our wants to the perfect Political system, but it will never be perfect but we can try to get pretty close if we work together.

Work together like we were taught in school, even though we have different views, cultures, beliefs, we were able to make a decision together which seems unlikely in today's political climate where NOTHING get done and people are truly suffering.

Politics has become very divisive in this country as many no longer really look at facts but what is being told to him by the media or online, without proper research. That is why I fail to believe everything unless I research it myself. In today's culture it has become us versus them and them are fellow human beings.

Since rejoining Twitter, which I had account many years ago but cancelled it due to the hate that was spreading online, I could not take that anyone. It doesn't seem to have changed much as the Hate has magnified to great proportions and people are no long accountable to what they say, as if free speech gives people the freedom to spread hate and lies.

I am a generation who didn't have computers and the internet until mid nineties so I lived happily without. I am more concerned for my daughter who will grow up with tech even more so.

I do believe we live in a great country, not perfect, but still fairly new in our democracy compared to other countries who have centuries on us, but we will not get anything done until we work together, stop the hate and bitterness and really work for what the people of the United States and do their job. I may not understand what goes on in the world of politics, but it appears inaction is what happens the most.

Where Am I going?

Each year is like a new journey for me and I get older, wiser and more handsome (jk). I have seen myself grow angrier at times over the fact that I wish I had greater professional success earlier in my life, but unfortunately it didn't work out that way. I hope I have a long life ahead at least to one day retire and live a life of leisure. I hope to write many books in my life time and it would be a dream to write professionally, but we shall see where my writing takes me. I believe I am doing more than most with my blog(s) and my novel which hope to be done by next year some time and than turn it into a blockbuster movie.

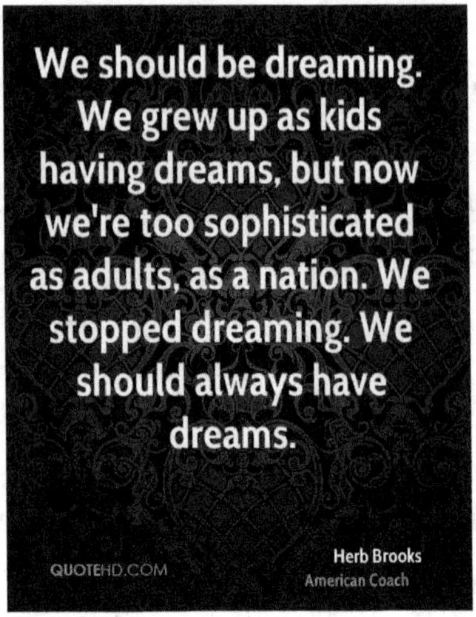

Ultimately I want to love more, love people more even when they are unlovable and that is really hard but a must as a follower of Christ. As a follower the most disheartening thing I see is people who say they are followers of Jesus turn a blind eye to people who are being treated so poorly. I am sorry but you can not say you a follower and accept those things, accept what a government official says or people in Congress.

I tend to get off topic at times, but I look to raise my family, make them better people each and continue being a provider as long as I can. Deep down I am tired, I feel like I have working a lot for the last few years. I feel like the moment Bilbo Baggans is speaking with Gandalf the grey about how tired he is like bread scrapped to much, looking for an adventure and off he goes.

I am going on my adventure now, please continue to join me, get to know me and thank you as always.

| 43 |

Goodbye Thirties, Hello Forties

December 2, 2019

Today is my 40th birthday. Wow where has the time gone, I feel like I was just turning 10 years old although I don't remember much from that time. I do remember my 20's and 30's and even some of my teens, many rough years I will say.

Thirty's were a particularly important decade in my life, this was the time I met my wife and had our daughter, but although it was very beautiful because I finally had a family of my own, it was also some of the hardest times due to trying figure out what it meant to be a good husband and then father.

I certainly have failed along the way sometimes major failures trying to keep the finances together, keep the family going why my Wife stayed home and cared for our daughter but in all it was worth the sacrifice. I would do anything for them .

Over this decade I have really tried to grow professionally helping our family financially prosper even that has been a major struggle, I have had my success and failures in that area too. I feel I am wiser now then those years, maybe by 50 I can call myself wise.

I have calmed down somewhat but within me is still a fire to work hard, make money, provide for my family and continue to myself better. I am more intune to my abilities as a professional and my worth to a certain degree even though I do beat myself up over my failures and those mistakes that have set me back.

My twenties where very difficult, as those where the years I really tried to push myself to strive for greatness which I think pushed me over the edge at times causing my mental break at times. I still reflect on those times because those were important years for me to grow and learn from major mistakes.

I know most of us have a struggle in our teens and twenties but sometimes I feel I cant get over a hump of feel satisfied with my life and what I have. Its not that I want more and more although that is nice, I just want to feel secure in what I have like I am not going to lose it, difficult when right now I am not working , looking for work and trying to have a healthy state of mind knowing that it will be ok, but my mind always reverts to the negative.

Like most of us I still struggle to keep the finances going for a family, but I am confident we will make it because when your willing to do anything for your family anything is possible that I believe, I will do anything.

Deep down by now I should have stopped caring what people think of me, but i still care because we rely on people to help us get where we need to be. But ultimately it is GOD who has control in my life, where I will be placed in this life whether in a great job or on the street, preferably in a great job who provides for me and my family.

I have no idea what the next 10 , 20 , 30 years will bring, I pray that it will bring prosperity but life is full of surprise's so who knows what it will bring. I hope like anyone else to have financial prosperity, good health and be happy, but I know happy is a state of mind.

I do know at this point in my life I am definitely more self reflective of my life, my successes, my failures, where I want to go, something I wasn't always too sure about in my Twenties, I guess some people find themselves later in life, I am still searching to a certain degree, but I try to enjoy life because as we get older, time ticks a way one less day on this earth, I imagine someone who is in their 60's, 70's and 80's really must feel like yeah I am more than half way done with life.

Everyone feels differently about getting older, some dread it, some look forward to it, I am in between because deep down I don't feel I have accomplish all I want to, but there is still time. As I focus on my writing praying one day I become a published author whether being an Indie author or traditional that I am looking forward too.

Thank you to everyone who follows my journey and looking forward a new year of life, only god knows how long he will give me in this life.

| 44 |

Merry Christmas and The Meaning To Me.

December 25, 2019

Ah Christmas once again! the time of year we are all called to be kinder for our fellow man and women and of course to remember the reason for the season the birth of Christ. As a Christian I must remember in the hustle and bustle of busy time that there is a reason I need to be joyous.

I know not everyone celebrates the birth of Jesus, as we live in a diverse world but I respect whatever you celebrate even it means a time to appreciate what one has in your life even if by the worlds standards you have little. If you have life, health and hopefully a place to live then you have much to be thankful for. If you have life but no place to live remember you are loved and pray in time your situation will improve.

Living in Los Angeles area Homeless is at a crisis for many who live on the streets, in their cars , fellow man , women and children who may be your co-workers and friends who may be homeless that you have no idea what struggles they go through, that is where be kind comes from.

Christmas for many is not celebrated as the birth of Jesus but many feel its a time to give, party, live in the moment, spend money on gifts, eat to your hearts content. My view is Christmas is not about gifts or what one gets because deep down those gifts have no real value and the so often the feel of happiness lasts only a moment and then those things are stuffed in a drawer, thrown in the trash or just forgotten about.

Christmas to me is a very hard holiday to begin with due to my mother passing away four years ago Dec 9th. My mother who didn't have much money did her best to make sure my sister and I had a decent Christmas with gifts and good food. The company was not always great because of my grandfather I will refer to as the Devil. For much of my youth holidays were filled with arguing over the sacrifice of living with him and him caring for us, opposite of what a grandfather is in very sense.

Sad I think I blocked out most of my Christmases not even remember what I have gotten in those years, I guess that's a lot to do with my depression over the years and just not feeling like celebrating and honestly for much of my young twenties I was single and felt alone.

I do remember fond memories of seeing my grandmother for holidays who loved us dearly, but she passed at a young age of 55, too young and my mother was 56.

I have always found Christmas to be a holiday that I Know is important next to Easter and as Christian I must remember during this time of year it can have both a positive and negative affect on people especially the need to purchase gifts. As a family man and with a young daughter I enjoy making sure these years are important not to repeat history of sad holidays. I don't overboard with gifts like many parents do and that is because I buy my daughter things throughout the years and her birthday is over a week after Christmas.

These times can get very hard with all the responsibilities of bills, rent , food and the necessities but I am believer that these years with my wife and daughter I can never recover or make up so might as well make the best of it. Why be a scrooge even though I want to at times and it seems that those who are scrooges in life seem to have all the possessions they could dream of.

I do wish I could relive some of my favorite Christmas films like "A Christmas Carol" and "It's a Wonderful Life and even "The family Man" films that all the characters to see the past , present and future and even get a glimpse of a different life if one didn't exist or if one made different choices.

I would go back in time and maybe would life be like, as a man who has suffered with depression in the past sometimes I regretted living and felt that others would be better off without me. But if that was to happen my daughter would never exist and I would not be married.

Christmas tends to make many of us sentimental or hate the holidays due to our history, as there are others who have had horrible holidays with family, many who suffer through depression and even abuse something I know something about but others have more extreme examples.

I wanted these days to be remembered with Joy, but although I have my family I have struggled these many years especially with employment and money which wipes away good memories at times, even on the year my mother passed was one of the worst year to date.

Each year I tried to replace no memories or bad/sad memories with good memories. 2019 is my 40th Christmas on this earth, a milestone in itself and one I hope to remember in a positive way except this year I am unemployed looking for work but I will try not let that dampen my spirit.

The point of this is to remember the reason and even though we struggle in this life lets try to be happy especially with those in our life and remember that our life days are numbered, for we don't know when our last day will be one this earth so lets make our days great!

Merry Christmas, Happy Holidays to everyone, have peace and joy! on to the new year!

| 45 |

Happy New Year, Self Reflection and New Beginnings

December 31, 2019

The New Year is almost here 2020, Wow! What a year 2019 has been in a good and bad way, but I guess not every day, month or year can be perfect, believe me I have had a lot worse. As someone who is a self-reflector of 2019, I can say that I have definitely grew a lot at least I think I have learned. This year I have the honor of working for a good company that allowed me to learn skills that no one can take from me and then unfortunately I lost that job.

Life Events That Change You!

This company I was with since February 2018 until November 2019 and I can say it was a year and a half of hard work, struggles, growth and learning, but in the end, it didn't turn out the way I hoped. I definitely learned some personal lessons about wising up in the workforce who to trust and how to adjust my learning style in learning new skills.

Since November I have been unemployed which has been hell because I don't like staying home searching for work that was a painful part of this test and trial. I did get to spend more time with my family which was nice and trying to remain positive in this hardship was not easy. At times I did take my frustration out on my family over this difficult time.

I actually lost two Positions this year and the second one was with Mt. Sierra College where I taught for over eight years due to the school closing due to financial reason a total unexpected change as I can honestly say many of those I worked with were my friends who I had known for years going back as far as 2010. I still miss the school as it happened in June.

In addition to learning new skills on the job I made other strides to self-improvement one which included take courses online in Python and web design to give me stronger understanding in coding, web design and understanding XML which is the language I was using at my recent employer. I can honestly say that learning to code was fun, but I just need to put into practice which is something I have difficultly doing because although I followed step by step approaches to coding it will honestly take me wanting to build or create something to put those skills to the test.

My Writing Journey Re-started

The other major step I took was to my writing this year which I am so proud of both in my Blog which many of you are now reading to my First Book which I am right in the middle of editing as we speak hopefully finishing it in 2020. The creation of the book in addition to working towards creating a platform on Twitter and Facebook has been fun as well meeting writers like myself who have the drive and passion to create works of art.

The End of an Era

There were also a lot of other personal changes this year one being the selling of my fathers home in South Los Angeles which I can say was my childhood home but not my only home. This home had both good and bad memories intertwined as this was the house I lived with my father and grandfather from the age of 19 to about 26 and then with my family, wife and daughter from 2014 until 2018. This house in my eyes had a horrible energy that brought me a lot of pain as I personally believe spirits dwelled there and it affected my mental health, but due to the fact I was going to major hardships financially and work related it had no choice but to run to that house.

Major Changes also included my sister moving closer to where I live now so we have her closer to not only spend time with us but be a support if we need anything along with father too and her Husband.

New Blessings for 2020

The new Year is about to start even greater as I have landed a position that starts January 13th, so YAY! I am excited for this opportunity and its even close to home which is even better. I am thankful during this time to GOD who has never left my side even thought it felt quiet at times as he was working in my life, my Wife and Daughter for her support, my sister of course, father, her husband and the very few friends who prayed for me and talked me down some ledges over my hardship at times. Losing one's job is never easy as it was not by choice. I was pretty upset when this happens as it was unexpected, and it was a good income and benefits.

The other Major announcement is I also landed a Part time Sub teaching role for another school which a position that has potential to additional income and opportunities, but this position will be on call so not every day, but hopefully in time I can provide my worth and be asked to teach regularly.

The sting of losing two positions this year not by choice still bothers me immensely but I am trying to believe this all has a purpose for my life which I will see soon. I am grateful and thankful for allowed the opportunity to work and know its getting more difficult as I get older, so each position I genuinely look for positions where I can have long term growth and stability for me and my family.

New year to restart and do overs encouraged

The new year is a fresh start to start over, but it also means growing older as I just celebrated my 40th Birthday in December a reminder how fast time flies as I feel like I just graduated college a few years ago but it was actually many many years ago. 2020 is the year I hope to learn new skills in a different industry, build on a strong relationship with GOD, be kinder to my family, pay down some debt that I have, Lose weight by being disciplined in the Gym and continue my writing, reading new books and just growing myself in the new year.

New Perspectives due to Hardships

During this time of not working has given me new perspective on things like finances, what's important in my life, what I want in the new year and so much more I probably haven't thought of. I am very thankful for my followers which is YOU! My followers on Twitter who listen to be rant and rave about nonsense sometimes or many times.

God giveth , God Take a way for reasons only he knows about for his purpose alone and who am I to question him but to only ask what am I too learn from this experience, this trial and test.

Make it a Great One!

Here's to 2020, may it be exciting in a good way, prosperous and to new growth! Wishing all of you the same in the new year, be safe, happy and only try to be you. I encourage you to reflect on 2019, how you were grew, your hardships, failures, successes and how you can make the new year better. Some of you may not be thinking about this right now, but I encourage you to remember what is important in your life, is it Family, your career, money, whatever it may be we can strive for better in the new year and no one can stop you.

| 46 |

Happy Easter From My Family to Yours!

April 13, 2020

Happy Easter everyone on this somber time in our lives as we celebrate at home. What a strange time this is as it's hard not to think about last Easter and previous Easter's. It's quite amazing how the times change so quickly. As a Christian I need to remember that GOD is in control of everything that happens in this world and our lives.

I am thankful that my company is doing ok and has not initiated any layoffs, but still that could change too as my organization although quite large is in the real estate industry. I am also a fairly new employee only been there a few months, so I am somewhat nervous about major changes taking place.

I just need to have faith and know that everything will work out, stay in doors and be safe and this will pass in time. Many tend to over hype the situation like we are in a long term battle with COVID-19 but not true. What we need is to be patient and soon enough we will be back to business as usual.

But once again remembering the reason for Easter is to remember and appreciate what Jesus did for us as the cross which is Died for ALL of our sins. Easter does hold personal importance to me other then the death of Christ but in remembrance of those Easter's when my mother was alive as kids we would dress up, have a Easter dinner, which I feel like I could smell to this day.

Wishing everyone a special Easter with those family we can spend time at this time, appreciating our precious time filled with Love. For those who are alone at this time, cut yourself some slack, take care of your mental health. I am particularly concerned about those who suffer with mental health, those families who are stuck at home with an abuser who this situation only makes worse being with those type of people. I Should know I have lived with them they are horrible people.

Sorry for the long pause in writing, I am still here, trying to get back into blogging regularly but at the moment I going through my own changes of working from home with my daughter who is seven, my wife and my mother in law so its kind of stressful time.

| 47 |

Happy Father's Day!

June 21, 2020

Father's day is here, a day I find to be special in its own right but on the other hand not very important. I am very thankful for being a father and trying to be a good dad. I know it's not easy being a dad in today's culture because so many fathers have ruin fatherhood for some many of their kids lives leaving a bad taste in their month.

Growing up my father was in my life, although my parents were divorced we would see him every other weekend and to this day is still in our life. I am sorry to say I didn't have too many male role models in my life. My father tried, but he was always working and when we were together was too tired at times which left me and my sister to our devices.

My grandfathers who were also in my life but only one I can say truly played a real grandfather who was my father's father and his name was Moses. My grandfather a WWII vet, tough a nails Christian, hard worker and fought to his last breath.

One the other end of the spectrum my other grandfather who I will refer as to the "Devil" was a self love, narcissistic evil Som of a Bitch who made life a living hell most of my life who resembled nothing of father and grandfather.

Once I became a father I knew I had to change all of that and although I am far from perfect I only hope I can give my daughter a better father and hope one day she sees me as a good day. My father refers to be a DA DA or Daddy, Papa whatever mood she is in to address me.

My daughter Mikaylah is the love of my life next to wife and of course GOD and my sister, father and brother in law. As father I have tried to give my father a good life but I have failed at times especially trying to move up the professional latter of sucess. As she only 7 at this time I don't know if she realizes if she has a good life yet, but one day she will realize like I did.

Growing up I didn't truly realize that my family didn't have a lot of money, but did have roof over our head, clothes and food in our bellies, so I guess we were ok. Plus an abundance of toys, toys and more toys courtesty of my mother and father.

This is a day that my life changed forever on January 2013 is when my daughter was born, never going back to living alife alone although I have been married since 2010. My daughter who has given me pure joy and love and an expensive lesson is raising a child, but Its all worth it.

Father's day for some may not a be a day that many wish to celebrate as there are many many fathers who have not been around or ruin their childhood in some way. If that is the case for you I am very very sorry, becasue fatherhood is meant to be about love, guidance, patience and treating that child like a precious gift which kids are.

I guess we never really know what one will truly become in life if your father provided a good upbringing as I have seen that fathers do have an impact over the development of children when they grow up. I am in no way saying Mother's don't they do of course, but this is about dad's today. I know many mom's who have to play the father figure too and I know that is a hard role especially when raising a young man.

If you are a father and feel you are failing, be kinder to yourself and know you are important to your child's life and if you are not your child's life then try to be in their life if possible. I say if possible because many fathers dont have the best relationships with the mother of their children or have court orders or live a 1000 miles away, but its always possible.

My only hope is when my father is older and on her own she will know I tried my hardest to raise her in a good way, even though I feel I work alot too which is provide for her.

The sad truth is fathers are some times made to be jokes especially in Movies and Television, something I don't always agree with but I am not offended, such shows as The Simpsons. The bumbling Homer Simpson who reminds me of my father in a way.

I think many fathers today don't fully get the respect we deserve and that is becaues so many fathers have screwed up fatherhood, especially those who leave to live the single life not appreciating fatherhood and making some kids go through sufferage to survive.

No father is perfect and we all know that, some fathers are poor, some deal with drug abuse, gambling, porn addictions, tons of vices that fathers struggle with. But there are truly horrific fathers who beat their kids and wives, verbally abuse and physically abuse their kids, that is NOT love.

So if you are father in your kids lives apprecaite that and lets try to be better dad's to our kids, love them more, apprecaite them for who they our and know we have a short time to spend with our kids before they grow and leave us for their own life.

As a father my hope is to leave a legacy in some way not just money, but my words and writing and even my Pod cast. so one day we can hear my thoughts, see my words and know that I put something down for her. Honestly my father and grandparents I didn't know much about them which I know its pretty sad that Is why I am trying to change that for my dauther now.

It would be great to get my book published one day and have that as part our legacy especially for my daughter to have in rememberance of me and what I attempted to do in this life, because I love her so much!

One this day wishing all the fathers a great food filled day with lots and lots of ties , cards and sweet memories. Cheers to all you out there, Happy Pop's day!

| 48 |

Happy Fourth Of July!

July 4, 2020

As an American I should take great honor in this holiday, but along the way I feel I lost the meaning of this day as so many tend to do. This day is usually filled with families and friends gathering around a BBQ, watching fire works and drinking a few brews. That is not me, yes we have had our occasional BBQ on the forth, pigged out and sat around watching TV or movies.

For those who know my blogs I love the movies and as you can see this is from the blockbuster film Independence Day with Will Smith and V for Vendetta. Although we are not under attack from aliens, although I would take that over this pandemic we still are in dire needs to peace in our nation , of unity and now destruction from those who want to bring the US to its knees. I am reminded of these images of those who wish to destroy the US and remake it into a new Amerika foreign and domestic.

A Whole New Meaning in 2020

But this year should have a whole new meaning to the importance of independence day as we celebrate the declaration of independence. For those reading this are not from the good ole USA, the Declaration of Independence is a pronouncement adapted by the Second Continental of Congress meeting at the

Pennsylvania state house in Philadelphia on July 4th 1776. The declaration explained why the Thirteen colonies at war with the Kingdom of Great Britain regarded themselves as thirteen sovereign states, no longer under British rule. With the Declaration, these new states took a collective first step towards forming the United States of America. The declaration was signed by representatives from New Hampshire, Massachusetts Bay, Connecticut, New York, New Jersey, Pennsylvania, Maryland, Delaware, Virginia, North Carolina, South Carolina and Georgia.

In the United States Independence Day is a national holiday marked by fire works, BBQ's and typically this is day most have off because it is considered a federal holiday.

The fourth of July of course is not without criticism as in 1852, Frederick Douglass gave a speech now called "What to the Slave Is the Fourth of July?" at a time when slavery was still legal in southern states, and free African-American elsewhere still faced discrimination and brutality. Douglass found the celebration of "justice, liberty, prosperity and independence" offensive to enslaved people who had none of those things. The Declaration asserts that all men are created equal.

It's so important to not let the true meaning of this holiday get lost and the importance of it today. Although its nice to think we have come far since then and with out a doubt we have, we still deal with racism and hate in this country that has not been eradicated and probably never will be because others choose to want to treat others as less than equal. In our country we are starting to open our eyes and the people are truly fed up with being put down by a system that can do better for its citizens. No one should have to be in fear of being discriminated against or hate, we should all be able to walk out our door and feel accepted but that's rarely the case.

As we are currently going to a pandemic, murders and violence continue to rise, racism, hate is getting worse and the future looks bleak but lets not lose hope. The thing I look forward to is the generations to come who we hope will lead us into a better century, we can only hope.

I do feel that we as a country are ripe for an awakening which could be good or bad as there are those out there who will look to take advantage using violence and hate to get their way. As a Christian I do believe we also need a spiritual awakening but who knows if that will ever happen, I see Christians hugely divided among each other as man seem to be the worst spreaders of hate and self-righteousness.

Some of you may be asking what does this have to do with Independence Day? It has to do with it because the fourth signified a change for the better , of unity in what would be the future of United States, men and women who loved the country to make it better. Although there are many who wish to make this country out to be better, many equally want to tear this country apart, even those who proclaim to love America.

Let's open our eyes to this fourth and appreciate what we have and let's all as people know we are real danger of losing of freedoms not due to Democrats and Republicans, although they could very well lead to those loss of freedoms, but the citizens of this United States who wish to bring their hate. I guess in the US we are free to hate, but that does not make it right.

I know this 2020 will be completely different as the in fighting has already begun to act as its 1999 or even 2019 but it isn't. We are still in a pandemic, stay home with family, BBQ at home, wear your damn mask and lets move on from pandemic and have a great 2021 Fourth celebrating hopefully the end of pandemic and more freedoms returning to our lives like being outside, shopping again, getting out and living our life as normal as can be.

I Love the US and I know that each day Men and Women are fighting to keep our freedoms alive, but lets remember it can not be done alone it requires its citizens to value the freedoms we have. Many do not truly appreciate what we have. Although we are free, that freedom could one day disappear if we can not keep the republic:

Let's remember we live in republic not ruled by a monarchy, a king, a queen , a prime ministers, not by democratics or Republicans or even an emperior , but we by the people for the people lets keep it that way and remember our independence.

| 49 |

Happy Birthday Mom! You Will Always Be Loved and M

August 30, 2020

Today would have been your 61st birthday and you are incredibly missed each day. This day is truly a blessing and a curse and I am sure I am not the one who feels this way when we think of loved ones who have passed and wish and know they should be here today.

My mother Linda Gutierrez, Born August 30, 1959 , Death December 9th 2015 was an incredible human being who provided love and sacrifice each day in our lives. She was truly the sacrificial mother who did everything in her power to keep me and my sister going. Life was not easy for my mom as a single parent living with a verbally abusive father and my grandfather who made life a living hell each day.

Despite those incredible adversities that we lived in she still focused on my sister and I to bring us to be the people we are today. Both my sister and I have different traits of my mother both physically, mentally, and emotionally. My mother in my opinion was a soft soul, a sensitive soul which I believe had a lot to do with her own upbringing.

Growing up she had a mother, step father, brothers and sisters many of which didn't truly treat her right and it was not just siblings being siblings deep down it was more than that but I will never fully know because she never liked speaking about it.

Growing up my mother went search of her birth father who would soon take her in along with two young children, a decision I feel she deeply regretted but again made a choice to make sure my sister and I always had a roof over our head, food in our tummies but it didn't come without a high price.

I know this may not have anything to do with celebrating her birth but without her birth, her pain, her sacrifice we would not be the people we are today which is good and bad because we all imperfections and flaws that carry on from our parents.

I am forever grateful my mother got the chance to see her only grand child before she passed and I know Mikaylah brought great joy and love to her life from day one. I will forever honor my mother in her life and be sure to pass who my mother was to my daughter, so she knew she has two Grand mothers who love her, one grandparent fortunately lives today and we were blessed enough to have her spend months together.

Again we I know we don't all have good relationships with Mothers and fathers and many of you may not feel the feel to honor their memory for your own reasons, but I choose to keep my mother alive in us, my life and my life taking away what she had taught me in my lifetime.

Love You Mom

| 50 |

Happy 10 year Wedding Anniversary to my Love

October 3, 2020

Today I celebrate an incredible milestone as I celebrate my 10 year wedding anniversary. There is so much to say to commemorate this day. Delia and I married on October 2nd, 2010 in small wedding at my wife's church. A church I attended too but it was her home church. I met my future wife to be in the year of 2008 introduced by a previous friend who I worked with at the time.

God's joining of two souls

Thinking back I can honestly say that I never imagined I would need the love of my life because for most my adult life until meeting my wife I was alone. We came from two different life's she being Salvadorian and I American two very different cultures which took some time to get use to as her first language was Spanish and of course mine English but she spoke English too. Over the years especially in the beginning it was tough, the previous friend I mentioned was someone who initially introduced us but also attempted to divide us and break up our relationship to this day I don't know why but she tried and failed because I knew I wanted to be with her.

The only Women Who Truly Loves Me

I can truly say that Delia is the only women to love me and to give me the time of day despite my flaws. Like any relationship and marriage, it has its highs and lows, good times and bad but we got through it. She has been nothing but supportive of me in our life even though I made some major errors in our financial life and our life together which included leaving jobs, moving to Los Angeles in the Hood so we could save money and recover from some hardships. But I too had been there to support here as she stay home, took care of our daughter while I worked two, three jobs for us to make but it was all worth it.

There are obviously things I would have done differently if I could go back in time primarily saving more money, being kinder to her and our daughter and not letting life get me down. Our life has not been a fairly tail although I tend to look at younger married couples who tend to have everything, I desire a big nice house, money and much more. But I look at my life, my wife and our daughter and this is my life and is was the life GOD created for me.

God is our Center

GOD has been the center of our life and give him the glory in our marriage and even our failures because GOD has not left us. In today's day and age it seems marriage is rarity where its so easy to get divorced and give up on a relationship and to a certain degree that's the freedom we have as a culture to move on and in a way that's a good thing, but we choose to stick together, grow through failures and love each other unconditionally.

I know I am not the same man I was ten years ago and I am constantly evolving sometimes not in good ways and that's not because of my wife and daughter its me because of how life changes a person, I am definitely more cynical now adays, but I look forward to each day with her and watching her grow and our daughter grow into new people each day. I look forward to 10, 20, 30 years or more that's if we live that long who knows only GOD knows our end date but until then I will devote my life to GOD, Her and our daughter Mikaylah.

For those our that may find this post too sappy my apologies, but I only wished to remember this day, remember the day my life changed forever and even remember the people who shared in this day like my mother who is no longer here anymore, quite frankly all those people who came to our wedding are no longer in our life, amazing how time changes people and relationship as our life has been whittled down to just myself, wife , daughter and of course my father, sister and brother in law are in my life, but other then that no one else.

Thank you for sharing in this day and here is our wife's favorite song that truly signifies our love, so many choices but this is the one we most remember.

| 51 |

Happy Halloween! Have a Spooktacular Day

October 26, 2020

A time when it feels like we are already in a nightmare situation with Life imitating art and even a premise in my novel that I have been writing for two years now which I just finish editing my 1st draft. My book which I wrote well before COVID-19 details a pandemic taking over the world, but one in which is virus is completely manufactured by the United States government in their attempt to rule over the world where they are the only ones who hold the keys to curing the world. There is so much more of course, but in these scary times can one really enjoy Halloween, Thanksgiving, Christmas and then the New Year, hard to say.

As a Christian we are taught that we shouldn't really celebrate Halloween as it has evil significance in what is stands for. Prior to becoming a Christian, I was not really a Halloween celebrator but of course growing up I went treat or treating, wore a costume the whole nine yards it was fun. I remember as a child I dressed up as Freddy Krueger, Michael Myers, Jason, E.T., Killer Clown.

I have always loved horror movies which now as a Christian goes against my beliefs but I can't help but to love Horror movies especially watching the marathons during this time watching Halloween about five zillion times, but yet I never get tired of watching them. Some of other favorites include the Exorcist, the Insidious Series, Saw Series, Nightmare on Elm Streets series and whatever else TV wants to throw my way I will enjoy.

Why Christians Don't Celebrate Halloween

1. October 31st has long been known as "The Festival of the Dead." The Celtic tribes and their priests the Druids celebrated this day as a marker for the change from life to death.

2. Halloween today is performed usually by adherents of witchcraft who use the night for their rituals. Witches celebrate Halloween as the "Feast of Samhain," the first feast of

the witchcraft year. Being a festival of the dead, Halloween is a time when witches attempt to communicate with the dead through various forms of divination.

3. Christians should not be involved with occultist practice or divination. Note God's command against divination in Deuteronomy 18.

4. Occultists believe Halloween is a time of transition between life and death. Some occult practitioners practiced divination and believed you could learn the secrets of life and wisdom by Lying on a grave and listening to the messages from the long-departed.

5. Occultists also taught that spirits and ghosts left the grave during this night and would seek out warmth in their previous homes. Villagers, fearful of the possibility of being visited by the ghosts of past occupants, would dress up in costumes to scare the spirits on their way. They would also leave food and other treats at their door to appease the spirits so they would not destroy their homes or crops but instead move on down the road. That is the real reason why kids dress up in costumes today and go door-to-door seeking treats.

6. Occultists also would try to scare away the spirits by carving a scary face into a pumpkin. This horrible visage would hopefully move the spirit on to another home or village and spare that home from destruction. Sometimes the villagers would light a candle and place it within the pumpkin and use it as a lantern (hence the name, Jack-o-Lantern). This is the origin of carving pumpkins at Halloween.

7. In some witchcraft covens, the closing ritual includes eating an apple or engaging in fertility rites. In the Bible (Genesis

3), eating a piece of fruit brought sin and death into the world. In witchcraft, eating an apple is symbolic of bringing life. The practice of bobbing for apples brings together two pagan traditions: divination and the fertility ritual.

8. Schools are removing any religious significance from Christmas (often called winter break) and Easter (spring break). Isn't it ironic that most public schools still celebrate Halloween even though it has occultist origins?

9. Participating in Halloween gives sanction to a holiday that promotes witches, divination, haunted houses, and other occultic practices.

10. Christians should avoid Halloween and develop creative alternatives. Churches can hold a Fall Fun Festival and/or celebrate Reformation Day (also October 31). They should not endorse or promote Halloween.

Many churches today do provide some form of activities to non-believers where many will wear costumes, but these events are not meant to pass judgment but to spread the gospel to non-believers in a loving way which I encourage, but ultimately we all have to make our own decisions if we choose to celebrate.

I have seen many Christians still celebrate with candy, costumes and I always wonder how they justify participating. Many say its all in good fun, they still believe in JESUS, they will ask for forgiveness and many other excuses. I am not perfect there is no such thing as the perfect Christian regardless if you think they are.

But Halloween to me has a special significance as a time when I was in school would dress up, have our miniature parades where we would be walking around in our costumes, get candy. After a certain point I got to old for trick or treating and although adults still do it I felt I no longer wanted to go door to door so my mother would take my sister and I to Mcdonald's for our Happy Meals.

This year I anticipated Halloween will not be canceled but many should be cautious, but in most cases kids are wearing masks as part of the costumes and in any case it appears Kids affected with COVID has no spiked like adults but still strange days in what each of us have to endure.

The other parts of Halloween I always enjoyed was decorating my house inside and out, it must be something my mother passed down to me because she always loved decorating for holidays. There was one time I decorated the house and hung a fake dummy from a tree which many passerby's thought it was a real person, but if that was seen today surely I would be told to take it down.

I guess the main interest in Halloween has always been the spirits especially what may or may not happen on this day. I encourage you to listen to my Halloween Pod on some of the creepy event dealing with spirits in my life, something I feel is attracted to me and my family.

Remembering this year and Halloween my only wish is for everyone to be safe, enjoy the day! With hopes by this time next year we will be enjoying the year, the holidays with a whole new light.

Have a ghoulish day!

| 52 |

Being Thankful Even When its Tough to do so!

November 22, 2020

Tis the season to be thankful as we round out 2020, I find this time of year difficult for so many reasons but at the same time remembering to be thankful. Coming up on the five-year anniversary of my mother's passing who was only 56 at time as my life has never been the same since her passing. She truly was the only who held the family together giving me a purpose to celebrate holidays.

I am Thankful for...

Now don't get me wrong I have my wife and daughter which in a sense provides me that purpose but for anyone who knows Mothers are irreplaceable regardless how old we are especially during the holidays. Yes we have other family like my Father, Sister, Wife and Daughter, Brother in Law to spend those holidays and I am thankful for them being there.

I try not to think about my mother's passing to much as It really brings me down in the sense but remembering those things I should be thankful for. Being thankful for my wife and daughter who I love, my sister, father and brother in law being close to me, a roof over my head, Two jobs and stability. For many years I have lived an unstable life due to my lingering career and the lack of accompanying money and although I am NOT a millionaire I have enough to be content. Of course life is not perfect and frankly not sure if anyone's life is perfect I doubt it. But at this point in my life it can be hard to thankful even when we look around and should be.

The State of Our Nation in Trouble

I guess the biggest part of my unhappiness at this point is the state of our country, watching our country crumble as many in our country wish to destroy each other with hate and racism. I will say that its not just the trumpers, or the Dems or Republicans its really across the board which is quite sad and disappointing, thinking just why cant people just respect and be civil to one another and then I remember that we live in a fallen world. Our world ripe for the people to take advantage to truly destroy democracy as we see it. I never understand how one can think it helps to burn the place down helps society, its selfish, but who are we kidding we live in a selfish world, a hateful country built on racism that will never go away.

Many could say well not everyone is a racist, not everyone hates there are good people in our country and world and I truly believe that, but it appears we have more filled with hate then those who truly just wan to love. The people I feel I am most disappointed with are the Christians, the evangelicals who I am apart of that group being the main agitators of bring their biases , prejudices and hate in the open when they preach the name of Jesus. I have to remember even if one says I love Jesus, they are still human and even though they are too afraid to look in the mirror to see their projected hate, they are haters who spread lies and deceit to those around them truly Sheep in wolves clothing.

Many of you who read my blogs probably feel I am way to hard on Christians when I call myself a Christ Believer. I believe in righteousness, doing the right thing, being loving and kind which I have tried to do although many people in the world are just unlovable. I know Jesus definitely loves the unlovable as he died for them too just like you and me, but I know I have a long way to go to love to unlovable people.

It's Not Us Versus Them!

Thinking of one of favorite films Rocky IV , so reminiscent of what is happening today with US Versus them, them being Trumpers who claim to stand up for good, for doing what is right, but rarely have seen in the last four years. Don't get me wrong the Left are not much better at times acting terribly despite saying they stand for true justice in America while they commit terrible acts too, this is why its so hard to be thankful at times.

Some of you may be saying what does what your saying have anything to do with being thankful and how it relates is that what is going on in our country well ultimately it's about seeing the good in our country and frankly I don't see it right now. Yes I can I just focus on those in my life and I do, but our thankfulness in this life has so many areas that we need to be right. I know that many in the world today are truly suffering living in true poverty.

Especially in our country due to the Pandemic, many are out of work, on the verge of a losing everything in a country that says hey your important but reality we know we are alone here, survival of the fittest, White Versus Black, Rich Versus Poor, Haves and Have Not's has anything really changes in the over 200 years our country has existed since the first Thanksgiving.

I truly believe if your poor in this country others will make you feel criminal for being poor, a leach off society which is what society tells those just trying to make it. I ask you can those people who are called leaches be thankful when society has deemed them unfit to live here or just to live in general. Again my point being be Thankful for lack of means still allows us to look on the brighter side of things, but when I look at my thankfulness I claw for those things I need to be thankful for.

Being Thankful Despite the Bleakness

For 2020 lets all try to be thankful even though its hard with all the death, destruction in our country that is taking place. I know for those families who have lost family due to COVID may find it hard to be thankful this time of year, but there is always something. Hug those people in your life if you can, tell those in your life family and friends you love them, look around and even when it seems pretty bleak we can remember tomorrow is another day to be thankful for the air we breath and life itself because we have more opportunities to have redo's to better ourselves, our lives and our families lives that is something to be thankful for.

For many who read this, this may not all make sense to you, but if it does then we truly see eye to eye by making it our life's mission to be thankful even when its hard because we will not allow this country, this world to bring us down and destroy our spirit.

Give Thanks and Enjoy the Day!

Have a great thanksgiving, make sure you pig out with all of your favorites. Personally, I love turkey, Mash, Sweet Potatoes, you know all the carbs and lets not forget the deserts oh yeah!

| 53 |

The Real Reason We Should

November 26, 2020

Happy Thanksgiving! Today is a day we should appreciate even if you may not be in America but all over the world by being thankful. I understand that this may be hard to do especially in today's time, but we MUST try.

Why We Give Thanks

Today we have LIFE and it sad to say that many today are dying, have died and can no longer appreciate Life and giving thanks. This day is for those who have lost their lives, not only those who have died from COVID-19, but from others sicknesses and suicides due to having to deal with these unprecedented times. Surely many people in our country and the world are going hungry on the verge of homeliness and poverty I know it may be hard for those individuals to be thankful, but many are because they have LIFE.

I truly people humanity is a lot tougher than we give ourselves credit for. One thing I am truly thankful among many things Is GOD in my life and that he has been there in my life through thick and thin never leaving me behind even when I felt he would and should leave me. JESUS is the center of my life, my Rock giving me the means to seeing the brightness in another day ahead. I have not been the perfect Christian and I ask myself who is.

I have sinned, have acted and thought in ways that were unchristian. I have struggled this year with my faith, no necessarily in my lack of faith in GOD but more so into practicing my faith and not letting the world and its cruelty get into my life.

I have been angry especially with the world of politics being told as a Christian who I should support and if I don't then why call myself a Christian. I have taken that anger and frustration and projected it online in social media being a troll at times.

Looking in the mirror I had to leave social media behind which was difficult but necessary in my life. I am working to refocus on what is important such as my family, my writing and my relationship with GOD.

Giving Thanks to GOD

As a Christian we are to see Thanksgiving differently then others as this day is NOT just about stuffing my face, but about giving thanks, being grateful for my life which I still have a problem with at times because frankly I still look at others lives who I perceive to be better and I say to myself where did I fall short, I know I know we shouldn't compare ourselves to others but it is difficult when I look at my life and yes I have blessings my wife, daughter, a roof over my head and even some money, Jobs of course so yes from many I am blessed and I say I am.

The problem for me is wanting more blessings , but I guess that can seem selfish at times and I admit It can be but I will do better to be more grateful for what I have now.

Its so important to be grateful to GOD and give thanks because studies have shown when we reflect thankfulness, we experience fewer heart issues, fewer aches and pains and of course affects our outlook on life.

As a Christian this is what GOD says about being thankful:

Enter his gates with thanksgiving; go into his courts with praise. Give thanks to him and praise his name. For the Lord is good. His unfailing love continues forever, and his faithfulness continues to each generation, Psalm 100:4-5 NLT.

God is truly on our side especially when we are in crisis and trouble which it appears much of world is at this time, we are to call in the name of the Lord. I know when things are good like when we have money in the bank, the bills are paid life is good we tend to forget about GOD, lets not do that.

As mentioned I have focused at times on materialistic things in a way to weigh whether I should be more or less thankful but know I need to be more thankful especially in these times and should really work to remember:

"Don't love money; be satisfied with what you have. For God has said, 'I will never fail you. I will never abandon you'"

Remembering what GOD says we must stop always wanting and I know that can be hard, we live in a world of consumerism focused on getting us things we may not need but just want redirecting our focus away from what is truly important like our family, our health and of course our relationship with God Almighty.

For those reading this you may say well I don't believe in GOD, I am an atheist, but truly you do believe in something. A simple metaphor is when you drive your car you put on your seat belt believing the seat belt will save your life in time of crash, again showing you Believe. GOD is no different in believing yes we may not physically see him but he is omnipresent watching over us , caring for us even when we may not want it.

A Day I was Most Thankful

The best example I can remember is a rather tragic event that happened on thanksgiving two years ago, the day I almost LOST my daughter , yes I was afraid she was going to Die. Everything was happy on that day as we were going to celebrate with my sister , future brother in law and father for thanksgiving dinner.

Pull up in front of her crowded apartment building unloading the family when suddenly my then six year old daughter Mikaylah ran to her grandfather who at the time was not truly paying attention but distracted by the dog when a speeding car driving down the street already filled with cars struck my daughter.

As my back was turned I heard the screams of my wife and her mother that our daughter was hit by a car. As I look in agony and fear seeing my daughter lying conscience scared and crying. Running up to her , there was no blood, no broken bones but tossed to the side. Unsure of how she was hit as it appeared she hit the back of head.

Long story short she was ok, with a few scraps and bruises, no concussion, Thank God. What was clear to me was it was as If an Angel had pulled my daughter to safety giving my wife and I a valuable lesson in trust and never fully letting kids have control over their own movement as they are unpredictable.

For a few hours we did spend in the hospital , returning later to share in our thanksgiving dinner, a thanksgiving truly unforgettable remembering the day we almost lost the most precious god given gift we had our daughter.

As you imagine today we must give thanks for our daughter who continues to amaze us with her strength thankful for her in our lives.

God Sustains Us

Remember God sustains us, everything we have is a gift from God. Every breath and every beat in our heart are gifts from God.

Maybe right now, you have a lot of uncertainty in your life, like a job loss, a family member loss, sickness, no money and a slew of other things bringing you down this season. Remember it's a season and it shall pass as well, but you can still give thanks. You can give thanks because God Loves you and this is the time to put aside the anger, the division in your life, the hate and just give thanks to the people in our life who we love, that we find irreplaceable, but also to remember we are one of billions in this world, yet GOD loves you equally not more or less but equal, where else can you truly say that you are loved equally, certainty not in this world, but only by GOD.

If these message was too preachy for you I am sorry but not sorry, because deep down I just want to share the importance of being thankful. God Bless you and remember what Jesus says even if you are not a believer:

> Remember God is good, give thanks because as the bible says He "causes everything to work together for the good of those who love God and are called according to his purpose for them" (Romans 8:28 NLT).

Each year is one less year we have in this life even if you are young and especially if you are old, we all have an end date and only God knows that end date so why not live in thankfulness.

Hopefully you see my heart through this message, wishing you, your loved ones a blessed thanksgiving.

| 54 |

Happy New Year! Here's to a Great 2021

January 1, 2021

Happy New Year! See ya later 2020 good riddance is the sentiment many are feeling this year around the world. While many stayed home this year, something I have always done many did go out, partied like it was 1899. 2020 will truly be unforgettable not only for the pandemic but for personal reason such as the job changes, having my wife and daughter home 24/7 but also a year of politics as we will soon have a new president, president elect Joe Biden and Vice President elect Kamala Harris.

es 2021 hopefully should be better but many will continue to be the same nasty self's not really looking to grow to change but just be more sinister then previously. Some of you may say hey that is a crazy comment and let me had some context if anything I have learned in 2020 with the pandemic is how truly evil people can be and just the amount of hate that current resides in our country, which is scary because it's not like the evil just appeared it was already there festering into a new bred of hate and evil.

Can't we just get along

Quite sad really that we as a society can not just get along and have peace and just do what is right in society. I guess you can say that evilness is nothing new and it is not but as society you would think we would learn by now, but I guess not. I get there is a lot of injustice in the world and many feel well since people are getting away with murder I might as well try to break the rules too and I know it can be attempting but I urge all of us to think again. Even myself I have thought yeah look over here they get away with this maybe I can too, who is going to stop me, who will care but ultimately, I will care as if I can live with myself.

When I look back at 2020, 2019, shoot I will go as far as 1998, the year I turned 18 from a point when many of us realize what it means to grow and be better people do we honestly make the effort to do that or just continue being the same. I know we all grow older and we naturally change some change for the worse. I am certainty not the same man I was at 18, actually even from the time I met my wife in 2008, she was tell you I have changed drastically I am not as sweet or kind as I once was, but may sound mean but the truth is she is right. Struggle and fighting life has changed my character, made me tougher.

Now don't get the wrong impression I don't go home or stay home and beat my wife and child or emotionally abuse them or any kind of abuse, but my words are not as soft as once before and that is because I really innocent prior to meeting my wife, I was softer because in a sense my family mom held me and protected me. Part of my softness for most of my young life and into adulthood was that was verbally beaten down each day since I was about five until I left home by my grandfather who never loved me but treated me as an inconvenience which had great psychological affects in my life and even today affects my self-esteem, but I have gotten a lot better seeing the errors of my ways.

Remembering Past Year Failures

For the last few years, I feel I have had a combination of success and failures which I guess I quite normal, but the last few years with jobs has been rough starting in 2015 so over the last five years. Not to dwell on the past but in 2015 I left a full-time job to try to go to school to be an electrical lineman, which I failed because it was a lot more difficult than I could physically take. Came back home with no job at the time, go hired back at my old employer part time, got another part time job to fill the gap but the hardest time was living in my fathers' home which I grew up in.

My family suffered for years until we moved out and although I am thankful, we could live there rent free but we did take care of my father, but a house that has also caused a great deal of pain in my life, but I was struggling to stay afloat and did what we had to do to survive in south Los Angeles (AKA The Hood). Eventually one of the PT positions turned full time but was there until January 2018 when I was let go, luckily had a position by February which again got let go November 2019, got another position in January 2020, left that position for a better position which is where I am happily today.

What I have seen professionally is that I am in a much better place then I was five years ago, but I equate to divine intervention and I give the credit to GOD, because deep down I don't see myself as that spectacular but as a family man I have worked to be a good father and husband, but there is always room for improvement.

The other important changes in my life have also been my other career, which was teaching, which the biggest jolt happened in June 2019 when the school I taught at for close to nine years closed unexpectedly but I was able to find another teaching position in December 2019, again thank God.

This year I hope to save more money, even go back to school even though I already have a bachelors and master's degree in business but again anything I can do to improve me. Many of you today may not be thinking about being a better you but just surviving to get to the point where you can refocus on improving you and making your life better. We are certainly in a time where millions are on the verge of losing everything, their homes, jobs trying to get back to a way of life they once knew and its my hope that you will get there soon, not to give up.

It is my belief it will get tougher before it gets better especially with COVID, loss of jobs and life but we as society will prevail and hopefully stronger than ever. As a man of faith in GOD, I know times will get harder, society will grow colder, meaner, and harsher but that does not mean we have to turn this way, lets continue to work towards being kinder, gentler towards each other and focusing on making ourselves better we can all work towards that.

A Year to Self Reflect

This new year is a time of self-reflection, a time you can make those resolutions but know that if you fail those resolutions that does not make you a failure, but human just showing you the importance of choosing goals that will stick whatever those goals may be focus, dedicate yourself to achieving your goals and remember the hardest part is getting started but once you do its gravy from there. Lets all work in 2021 to be better. Honestly, I'd like to think I have faith in society to be better, but I don't let's hope I am wrong.

I pray for the new year, pray for those in the world that are hurting, pray for my family to have prosperity and good health and that ultimately that my faith grows stronger and bigger and try to lay off the politics and social media which in my opinion has affected my mental health this year and I'm probably not alone there.

Please to all of you, GOD bless you in the new year, here is to a great 2021.

| 55 |

Happy 8th Birthday to Daughter Mikaylah

January 9th, 2021

Today is my daughter's 8th Birthday, actually it was January 5th but with the hustle and bustle of work and life it's so hard to through a good day during the week. I can truthfully can not imagine my life with out my daughter and my wife of course. eight years ago, my life changed forever and prior to that getting married to my wife and her mother Delia.

Mikaylah being our only child is a blessing and continues to be, although raising kids is a tough role like most parents realize but it pays great dividends. Not sure, why I used a financial analogy because kids even one is expensive but in the long run we remember we are raising a human being who will grow up, leave up and go take on the world. I honestly cannot remember being eight years old, but I hope these years she remembers, and I work to make them memorable for her. At my eight years old, it would 1988, a great year probably , you can see here:

But enough about me, my daughter who has been home school since March has really excelled and I am truly amazed at how well she has adapted to zoom and being online. Although like most parents this not the way we would prefer our kids learn, preferably being in school but she has worked hard to keep going and I have worked to support her anyway I can. Luckily, she has her friends she can speak to every day, playing games, having deep philosophical conversations but ultimately not losing her childhood. It is my hope one day that she reads my blogs she will see how much I love her and cherish her, having almost lost her a few years ago on Thanksgiving. The years continue to fly by and it can foresee one day her graduating high school, go to college, be an adult and see the fruits of our labor as parents. I know parenthood is never perfect and will Not have control over our kids once they come of age. That is why we MUST cherish them, treat them with respect, even at times when they may not.

Like anything else in life, I reflect on this time in my child's life, knowing she is a gift from GOD that I was given to care for and bring up in the Lord and in some sense, I fail like many of us parents do at times, since she didn't come with an instruction manual. She is a good girl with her own great qualities but many of qualities she takes after me like she loves to read and write, her character is her own but very similar to her mothers and grandmothers who have and had hard characters to deal with at times.

But like I was saying I try to member when I was eight but cannot, but for many of you who read my blogs know I didn't have the best childhood. I hope as a parent she will remember these times, but if we can't show her pictures and videos, something many of us didn't really have especially videos of those big events. My daughter will always be my little girl no matter now or until adulthood, Happy Birthday to my baby Mikaylah who is 8th year old. Love You.

| 56 |

Rediscovering Halloween Traditions Through Family

October 31, 2021

Happy Halloween everyone to those who celebrate and to those who don't. Strangely I am someone who doesn't really celebrate this day and its not completely because of my faith. You see growing up I was like most children and even young adults who celebrated by dressing up, going trick or treating and handing out candy. I loved to decorate the home for Halloween which included fake spider webs and a realistic dummy I would hang from our tree in the front yard.

Growing up with all the classic horror films Halloween, Nightmare on Elm Street, Child's play, Hellraiser and Gremlins (Yes this is a horror film) and many others and I can not forget IT.

Movies always being my escape into another reality from my own life as its amazing that I remember more about seeing movies then about my own childhood.

During those years I dressed up, I was a few different characters including Freddy Kreuger, Michael Myers, E.T., Michelangelo the Teenage mutant ninja Turtle, Jason and I was a killer clown, Gizmo from Gremlins and I believe I was He-Man.

As a Christian we are taught not to celebrate this evil holiday as it's a day that gives honor to Satan and what it stands for. A time when Satanist worship their god and in pagan times would sacrifice babies on in honor of Baal. I personally don't just celebrate it for that but maybe Its difficult to fully separate myself from this day because I have a daughter who is eight years old. She personally has never had any real interest in this day herself and that could be because she doesn't see mom and dad celebrate it which is fine. We still want to give her a choice and in years she has said she didn't wish to dress up but loves when she is given candy.

One of my fondest memories of Halloween is that mom would take myself and sister to McDonalds on this day and get us our Happy meals that came with our plastic candy pail coming in a variety of colors and faces.

Mom always made a point to get us out of our own house of hell from the devil in carnet that we live with our grandfather. I guess there was no point in celebrating Halloween because we were living in a hellish situation at times. There were also times when we would spend this day with our father when we would spend time at grandma and grandpas and technically his home too pigging out on Pizza, soda, and candy watching scary movies and playing Nintendo for the whole weekend.

I guess you could say I had a someone average childhood despite parents being divorced we didn't miss out on holidays and those things a child should experience but it was still a sad time for myself as I always had to return back to the hell house.

Halloween does get me excited about what is to come in the coming weeks, one of favorite holidays Thanksgiving.

For those who celebrate today, dress up, hand out candy or just have a relaxing time at home remember these days even if they may seem not very important as I truly to think back on these days in my own childhood, looking at my daughter as she grows up so fast, I want her to remember these days.

Happy Halloween everyone, be safe, wear a mask and if you have a spooky mask where another one, LOL.

| 57 |

Happy Birthday Delia, To My Beautiful Wife

March 21, 2021

Today is my wife's birthday and although I will not mention her age because frankly what women would appreciate their age posted online. I will say that since meeting my wife in 2008, it has been a true blessing. Yes, like any couple we have had our up's and down's, disagreements but nothing we couldn't put past us. Over the years I have grown to love my wife more each day as my love is limitless. She has only given me love, understanding and patience all these years and we have grown as one person. These years do just fly by as we both age together raising our young daughter Mikaylah.

Like most of us we don't like to age as our bodies slowly or rapidly depreciate but I wouldn't have it any other way as we both grow older together. I can truly say that my wife and daughter have saved my life, but of course I give the glory to Lord Jesus for putting us together. Prior to meeting Delia I was alone and miserable and years prior I made choices that could have prevented me from being here today.

I know all birthdays may not be memorable for all us, but as her husband, I always tried to make it special with her traditional bouquet of flowers, a heartly meal, cake and to top it off Love, oh and gifts of course. My wife is not a vain person with the expectation of expensive gifts and vacations but humbly only wanting the necessities food, shelter, and of course a nice hair style at the local stylist and she is happy. I know I lucked out with her and thank GOD each day I have her in my life.

Happy Birthday to my Love, my partner and the woman I thank God each day for putting her in my life. I know life is precious and none us know the day or hour of our passing, but until then I will love, appreciate my wife each day.

I love you my love and here is to many more years to come with peace and prosperity to you and your life.

| 58 |

Happy Resurrection Day!

April 3, 2021

This weekend is particularly important to my faith as a Christian man. Celebrating Easter has always been apart of my life but didn't always have the meaning it has today. Like many growing up Easter for kids meant the Easter bunny, eggs and mom's cooking. It wasn't until I got older when I gave my life to Christ and Easter had a whole new meaning.

I still like the fact that Easter incorporates bunnies, chocolate, spring. The Christian side of me knows that's not what Easter is about that's just plain consumerism at its best. Now that I am a father myself my daughter loves that part of Easter, but I have to remind her what Easter is truly about.

For those of you who may not know what Christians celebrate during this time we do call it Easter or Resurrection day, but most prefer to call this day Happy Resurrection day. This is day we celebrate the death of Christ's death and rising from the dead. Christ or Jesus Christ born of a virgin and dying for all of our sins of the world.

Now I know that many may not believe that a man could die and come back from the dead, but Its true because he was part man part God and that was his sole purpose born to die you would say taking on all of our sins. To this day due to Christ's sacrifice, we no longer have to fear death or going to hell because of Christ. He dead a painful excruciating death at the hands of Rome and those who hated Jesus for what he stood for. Today is no different with those who don't believe, who hate Jesus for what he stands for, but Jesus died for all of us even those we feel don't deserve his forgiveness.

This year has been particularly difficult since the last time I physically attended a church was right before the pandemic started and I am sure many will fill the pews this easter. Although I know the threat of COVID still exist its not as critical as it once was now that we have a vaccine.

One would even say how can you be a believer if you don't physically attend a church and I say to those that my faith, my relationship is personal like all believers and although GOD calls us to be together God is forgiving and I know in time I will be back with my family as we once did. I do truly miss Easters especially when I used to attend the Sunrise service at the crack of five am service, it was incredible.

Today for Christians around the world is considered thy the most important event in history along with Jesus' birth of course, but Easter is what really made it possible to allow our sins forgiven and have the hope of living in eternally with Christ.

These are my beliefs and I know some may think or feel well I don't believe in GOD, that god doesn't exist, but I know that to be false because I have personally seen God work in my life and be there for me. I know I fail as a Christian many times sometimes daily, but Jesus forgives and forget casting our sins and failures into the deepest ocean.

At times it difficult to describe because to truly experience what Easter means you need to be open to Christ and why he dead. For many media even helps whether its watching a film like the "Passion of the Christ" which I highly recommend although nothing can compare to what Jesus went through in real life it is a beautiful yet gruesome picture of the pain he was inflicted with something that many of would have never been able to endure. If after watching just that film doesn't do it for you, are plenty others made in the golden age of holiday with Charleston Heston in the ten commandments and so many others.

During these difficult times lets take a step back and remember what is truly important to me Its Jesus Christ and his death that gave us a way to live in eternally once we die. For others this is a time to spend with family, have a picnic or eat a good meal but ultimately at the end of the day you give this day your full remembrance and not just think of it as another candy food fille day. It's a day to appreciate life regardless of how tough it has been and I am sure this year has been tough but there is end one day. I choose to think that one day when my time comes to remember where I am going and who made it possible Jesus because he died for us, all of us.

Have a wonderful Easter and or Resurrection Sunday anyway you spend it.

God Bless,

| 59 |

Happy Mother's Day

May 9, 2021

Happy Mother's Day to all the mothers out there, today is your day although you deserve every day to honor the sacrifice to do for us and our children each day. Dad's we will get our day next month so don't fret. For some this day is not a good day because of maybe your own inability to have children and for that I am sorry I can only imagine the pain you go through since motherhood is so appreciated but unappreciated at times.

For many out there maybe you didn't have the ideal Mother, maybe your mom was pretty crappy and for that I am truly sorry, motherhood is meant to be a beautiful thing between a son and daughter of love, compassion and patience in addition to much more.

My Mother

My Mother Linda who passed away in December 2015 will always be remembered for the love and sacrifice she gave to myself and sister. I can say my mother did not have an easy life even from the time she gave birth to me and my sister as it was a constant struggle just to survive, money was tight and encouragement was anemic from dad and her family with little or no support for her new role.

I think of all of the hard times she went through just to put food on the table, to clothe us and encourage us but he was difficult, she tried her best. Growing up I didn't fully appreciate what she did for us, I guess you could say I was blind to her efforts as I was going through my own hardships and mistreating by people in my life. Getting older I was able to see what she did for us. Even in her final years she got very ill and eventually passed, I tried to be there for her and maybe I failed her in those final years trying to raise my own family with a new born and wife , but I know she knew I loved her and she loved me. One thing I am elated about is she gave her heart to the LORD Jesus so I know I will see her again one day and I feel she is always there for me watching from above with Lord Jesus.

Mother and Wife to our Daughter

The 2nd special mother in my life is my wife and mother to our daughter Mikaylah. Delia who has also made great sacrifices from the beginning as she stayed and cared for daughter from birth until she went to school as I worked for us. Putting her own career and job aside knowing it has not been easy as we have struggled as family to keep things going financially, but deep down I am thankful for her being there always and thankful she could spend those years with our daughter which I find incredibly important despite our hardships.

Each day Delia grows as a mother who I pray one day Mikaylah will see how special her mother is although I feel she does at the young age of eight she may not always see it. Delia is an incredible mom and wife in my eyes who loves us so much and shows it every day. She works so hard in her job even though deep down she may not always like her job or feel appreciated in her job.

I work to make sure she feels valued and appreciated but I know I fail in that area in times. I am thankful to have a wife and mother of my child who will grow up with both loving parents. I thank God each day I have and had great examples of Mothers in my life. Wishing my wife Delia an incredible mothers day where she can enjoy a day of flowers, gifts and food to show our appreciation, but every mom should be appreciated every day not just one day a year.

Happy mothers day and God Bless to all!

| 60 |

Happy Father's Day

June 19, 2021

Happy Father's day to all the dads, fathers, pops , grand dads and whatever else you call your dad in honor of him. This weekend in the United States particularly we celebrate fathers although in my opinion fathers do get a bad rap at times simply because fathers screw up the family at times. As a father myself I know I am far from perfect and being a father is no easy task especially if you have a daughter who many times look up to dad as a role model. I only have a daughter so I wouldn't know what It means to have a son. But growing up I did have my own father who is still living and in good health.

I have written about my father in my blogs and even in my podcast have spoken about fatherhood, but each year there are new memories and new things I learn as a father. I look back on life and my father who I love but know he was far from perfect as he has caused me and my sister a lot of anguish at times but at the end of the day, he is still my father and I must appreciate he still being in our life and alive when so many fathers are not today.

My father whose name is Moses born on September 9th, 1956 grew up in Los Angeles with his father Moses Sr., Mother Isabel , Sisters Elizabeth and Rachel. Up until a few years ago live in his father's, my grandfathers' home and of course many of who have read my blogs know about that house which I believe had evil entities that live or current still live in that house. But anyways back to fatherhood. Mom and dad divorced when I was five and sister three, having to move in and live with an actual Devil of a grandfather named Raul who was a grandfather in name only as he displayed no love for myself, sister and mother making our lives a living hell for most of my childhood and into adulthood. I do not have the best representation of fathers in my life, except my grandfather Moses Sr. but even at the beginning of my life he did not believe I was his grandchild and refused to believe it until he realized the family resemblance.

Growing up I would see my father every two weeks for court order visitation where we would go to my grandfathers house for the weekend where my dad would sit back relax while my sister and I feasted on Pizza, Soda, candy, sweets, watch TV late and really do whatever we wanted. A child's dream where we would also go to Chuck E. Cheese and Toys R' Us on the weekend to get our favorite toy. The weekend with Grandma and Grandpa was our getaway to a normal childhood before we had to go back to the devils house and submit to his will of making us do labor in the house, while he verbally abused my sister, myself and mother. Growing up basically we would be considered low income living in Bell Gardens or as I refer to that city as Bell Garbage and Huntington Park.

Sad to say I don't remember much about my childhood as I feel I blocked out those memories because they were really painful to remember. As I think of my own daughter, I work each day to give her a normal childhood of happiness and peace so that one day she will have fond memories of her dad and mom who love her.

As a father I made my life's mission to not have my daughter grow up in that shithole of Los Angeles , more specifically Bell Garbage, South Gate, Huntington Park, Compton, Watts and the list goes on but I failed at that a few years ago when I moved my family to Los Angeles for financial reason, a decision that has affected me to this day.

My father who did help me get through some darks times in my life, but at the same time wasn't always the most supportive as a father would be saying I love you enough, a hug or even a kind word that just was never him I guess. Growing up I didn't have a lot of kind words from fathers, grandfathers or many so when others do praise me or give me props, I feel like I do not deserve those. Today my father lives with my sister and her husband near by to us which allows me to see my father whenever I like or he can see his granddaughter too. Sad to say I don't know much about my father, his life growing up with Grandma , grandpa and his sisters he has pretty much refused to even talk about his childhood which leads me to believe it may not have been that great.

As a father to my daughter Mikaylah she is the greatest gift in my life that God has blessed me and I am so thankful each day I get to spend the day and days with her watching her grow in the last 8 years. The years have not been easy raising our daughter as fatherhood is no joke as I have struggled with the financials of fatherhood, diapers, formula, food you name it I went through it. I am blessed to say my daughter has never really gotten sick or had any injuries as she has always been healthy aside from a cold and few fevers but nothing major.

My daughter and I are very much the same and different as she is almost my physical copy and many of her interests like Art, reading and writing she loves as well. But of course like any child she is a lot like her mother too with her hard character at times and stubbornness. I looked forward to see her grow each day and every year and day I see the changes in her growing from a baby, toddler, little girl and eventually a tween and teen and finally an adult. I pray God gives me the good health and life to be around her all her life.

As a father we have to remember fatherhood is a blessing, but many fathers choose not to take the responsibility seriously and abandon their kids. I do believe fathers make a difference in this world especially to daughters. I still ponder what makes even bad fathers so important to daughters, thinking of my mother who had a shitty father yet still went searching for him late in her life bringing the Devil into my sister and I's life causing reprehensible harm to us. The man is now dead and I try to move on but the damage he did to myself and sister is unforgettable as he was no father and grandfather just a devil incarnate. Anyways back to good fathering may this day be filled with Joy and peace, pigging out on your favorite meal as mine is Bar-b-que and giving dad a gift to show your love for him.

This day I am thankful to spend with my daughter and as a father I work to grow to be better, stronger for her and days to come because I know she will need me. Everything I do I do for her and our life together.

God bless all the pops out there and have a blessed day, this is your day and we honor you!

| 61 |

Happy Independence Day! 2021

July 4th, 2021

Today is a day that many can appreciate but many do not as we sometimes forget the meaning of this day, I am guilty of this as well. Many will think of this day as a holiday that many have off to fire up the old Bar-B-Que, invite friends and family over and pig out, drink up and maybe light up some sparklers. But lets try to remember that today. Today represents the day the continental congress signed and finally approved the text that Thomas Jefferson wrote in June 1776 and that was signed on July 2nd, 1776.

The fourth of July was the date chosen by those who signed it so that people would remember it. The Declaration of Independence is a treasured document that is still displayed in the National archives in Washington D.C. and one of the most important documents in the country.

What Today Represents

The 4th of July represents the birth of a nation, the United States of America, that got their independence from the British and is therefore a day to celebrate the creation of a country.

The Declaration of Independence didn't have the symbolism it has nowadays during its first years of life. It was not until the 19th century. When the new political parties were born that the Declaration was promoted by the Democratic-Republicans as an important piece of American history.

It was not until 1870 that congress declared the 4th of July a national holiday to commemorate the birth of this American nation.

We Have Come a Long Way but Have Ways to Go

As an American I can appreciate that our country has come a long way from the birth as a nation, but we are still a young country regardless and have a lot of work to do. As a country I am thankful I live here as there are many countries who don't share our beliefs and put so much effort in making our country better. Many will disparage our country for our western beliefs but those are beliefs and I still believe we are one of the strongest countries in the world fighting for the rights of others. Thankful that freedom exists in our country, something not every country has.

Many countries today attempt to mimic our systems because they see the incredible benefits but again, we do have a lot of work to do and many will disagree that we still live in the past as we haven't not moved the needle far enough. We have to remember that we are run by man and man/women will always fail, they are not GOD. I truly believe GOD has blessed our country because we are still a Christ believing country, but the moment we turn our back on GOD then truly are country will suffer those consequences.

We are a Nation under GOD

As a believer in Christ, I know this personally that if I was turn my back on Christ, he would still love me , but it would hurt GOD. Our country is loved by Christ, but we are ultimately still hurting him by our lifestyles, which is afforded to us by the freedom of our country. I am not saying we should not have freedoms, we should but have to remember the importance of that and not take it for granted because one day our freedoms may not be here.

May we all remember the importance of our forefathers who worked to create a system, a foundation because many countries do not , but rule by unfairness and an iron fist. Let's all have a blessed Independence day, enjoy the day.

Be Safe, God Bless.

| 62 |

Happy Wedding Anniversary 11 Years of Love

October 10, 2021

October 2nd marks 11 years of marriage to my beautiful wife Delia. I honestly can not imagine my life without her and thankful for her love and devotion to our marriage each day. I know no marriage is perfect and I am far from perfect to be the greatest spouse. I have changed over the years since first meeting her.

Having a family is no easy task but puts a lot of pressure on anyone to be sure everyone eats, has a place to sleep and at the end of the day there is still love in the marriage and family. To often the marriages survive don't outweigh the ones that are breaking up. We certainty live in a world of temptations, thinking there is a better man or woman out there for us making the decision to forgo our vows for better or worse, richer or poorer, through good times and bad. For my life GOD has been and will always be the center of our life and love.

Each day I look at myself, how I can be better; a better husband, father, son, brother and I know I fall short at times, sometimes spectacularly. I am in a constant state of comparison to better fathers, brothers and sons out there and I make it known to my wife there are better guys out there, but she still loves me the way I am. I know I have changed over the years; I am less soft to my attitude and tone at times compared to when we first met I was sweeter, gentler and more reserved.

Although I don't know why marriages don't last today, but much of the time I suspect there is strain of finances, personal and loss of faith.

Over the years I have seen my wife change so much into an incredible woman, who was always incredible but who only gets better, stronger and filled with more love than before especially since the birth of our daughter Mikaylah. I look forward to each day knowing she is there, remembering a time in my youth, that no women appeared to want me, desire me or feel I was worth their time, which I found quite hurtful.

For many who have been married or are married maybe you look back not at what you could have had but appreciate what you have now and how that those out there were never meant to fill that void in your life and that at times we find that person and that times we don't. Yes, It hurts remembering all the times I really looked for that special someone, although many will say you shouldn't try to search for someone that they will come naturally, I find that a bunch of hooey at times although I understand it has happened, because it happened to me through a co-worker who introduced me to my future wife.

Each year we all get another year older, wiser hopefully and more in tuned to knowing each other better, because knowing each other is a lifelong process all to often people forget that in marriage. I think all to often people forget people are imperfect, some have more imperfections than others and many tend to change how to they feel about a person because of those imperfections.

My love continues to grow for my wife and of course our daughter looking forward to each day of marriage no matter how hard are days are but looking to see the beauty of a strong marriage built on love and appreciation. I know deep down my wife deserves better, a better looking, stronger, better provider of a husband thinking the grass is greener for her out there for her because I know there are better men then me, I see it myself. Some may say well you don't know that a lot of men appear better, better looking, better job, more money, better everything that doesn't mean that can love, care for a wife and daughter like I do. I do work each day to give my heart, mind and body to my family to make sure I do everything in my power to provide for them.

Here's to another year of marriage, of love and growing old together.

| 63 |

Have a Hap-Hap Happiest Christmas!

December 23, 2021

Have the hap hap Happiest Christmas since Bing Crosby tap-danced with Danny F*cking Kay. As I wanted to start this off with one of the most classic Christmas moments in movie history. I love this time of year for the most part as this is a time that we should all spread a little cheer, be kinder towards our fellow man and women and child, but all too often we are not.

What I love most about this holiday season is the food, movie fest and the music bringing me back to current memories and past memories of times when Christmas was both special and frustrating and sometimes filled with despair.

Why is there so much pressure during this time of year? Could it be that each of us feel that we MUST purchase that special gift because this time of year is full of commercialism, going to debt, spend, spend, spend into the new year.

I know, I know what else is new as I live in the United States where this is almost traditional to spend into oblivion, but maybe I am being over dramatic since many of you may say I am not required to buy anything for anyone, I can be a total scrooge if I want to be, but I honestly that is not in my nature.

Growing up mom loved Christmas, decorating the home, fresh baked goods, home cooking, presents and all around trying to make the time special although It was difficult living with the devil incarnate who is currently tapping dancing in hell as we speak, which I know is not very nice.

As like Christmas Vacation its anything but smooth at times as you have seen with family bringing a degree of stress for just being your family. My family is relatively small with my Wife, Daughter, Sister, father and brother-in-law, their two dogs and a cat. I do of course have an uncle who lives out of state, cousins and distant family members, but my immediate family is those I see often.

Since my mother passed away in 2015, the holidays have not been the same, she was the glue during those times and what has made it particularly difficult is the financial struggles I had over the years which made those times difficult but tried my best to make it special especially cooking my Prime Rib. Holidays have been quite special during the years since getting married in 2010 and having my daughter in 2013 reliving the moments through her childhood and bringing joy to this time for her, personally I think I have succeeded in that department. I have over the years worked to introduce my traditions and movie favorites to my eight going on nine-year-old, some film choices still too mature for her but some that I enjoyed she hasn't really enjoyed like the Christmas classic Gremlins.

Some of the moments I enjoy as a child was getting toys of course for Christmas, like Teenage mutant ninja turtles, having a Teddy ruxsbin that I could dress up as Santa and he would tell stories. I remember having two Christmases with Mom and dad, spending time with my grandpa and Grandmas where we would eat, drink and be merry along with all the gifts, it was special. As I got older my memories fade as to those Christmases although I am sure they were special.

Some of the more special moments were those times in our local church as I remember the reason for this season, which is our belief in Jesus and his birth, born to die as I say for our sins.

As you can see this time of year has true significance for many reasons, deep down I am conflicted at the times we live in and past, present and future Christmases as I look forward to seeing my daughter grow up but know in time these holidays will change in hopes they only get better but who knows.

I do know I continue to get older, and the years tend to pass me by that one day I will be an old man in age as those years I once remember can be forgotten, but I guess that is why we have pictures to remember these times.

During these times lets think about those in our life, the love ones we have to share these times as there may be a time they may not be here as life is unpredictable and at the end of the day what we have is those people in our life.

Have a Merry Christmas, be merry, be joyful, be kind make it a good one!

| 64 |

Being Thankful When It's Difficult!

November 13, 2021

Twenty-Twenty has been one heck of year as much of the world is entrenched with COVID-19, many on the verge of poverty and homelessness. I know It seems pretty bleak as someone who lives in the United States it was been particularly difficult with lockdowns, with the family home and home-schooling. I obviously shouldn't complain compared to last November when I lost my job I was in a much worse place. This year has had some major blessings with finding a job in January and then finding an even better one in July but I must remember all of those who are suffering as we speak, many getting sick, dying , losing their homes and livelihoods. Having the opportunity to work from school has been one of the biggest joys and struggles of adjustments to make. Along with my seven-year-old homeschooling and me working while not being in an office for the first time ever.

But one of the hardest situations I have struggled with until now is the state of our country , being that we are in an election year seeing our country essentially tear each other apart as if we are two different species of people. Whether you are in America, United Kingdom or anywhere else on the globe treating each other so poorly is not something anyone should see. Yes we all have our beliefs, our values but we are also all human beings who really need to be thankful for the lives we live. I truly believe we live in a country that lives better in the terms on wealth yet many are so unthankful to realize what is important.

Being that's its Thanksgiving next week I really do reflect on thankfulness regularly and not just when we get close to the holiday and at this time it's a good reminder that we should be thankful, here are some tips to help get us there:

- Every day, say aloud three good things that happened - This can be turned into an activity you can share with your family, around the dinner table expressing gratitude aloud when your alone.
- Keep a gratitude journal - Write down the small things from your day that mattered to you, in those few minutes of quiet time, on your drive to work fitting in those moments when you can write down what you are grateful for.
- Say thanks to your partner - Couples who express gratitude toward one another set up a powerful feedback loop of intimacy and trust, where both partners feel as if their needs are being met.

- Cool a hot temper with a quick gratitude inventory - Take a moment to do a quick inventory of five things you are thankful for in the moment, it could be health, family, a great memory giving you a chance to lose the temper and put things in perspective.
- Thank yourself - Gratitude doesn't always need to be focused on what other people have done for you! make sure you give yourself a thank you for the healthy habits you cultivated in your life.
- Savor the good moments - Stop and smell the roses as the old saying goes. remember the good moments in your life, the memories and the joys we all have them even the little moments
- Check for silver linings - Even the most difficult life challenges come with some benefit - you just have to look to find them. When things grow hard, ask yourself: What is good here?
- Look outward, not inward - Empathy for others can trigger a sense of gratitude, and people who have an outward focus tend to experience stronger beliefs
- Change your perspective - If you struggle to come up with something to feel grateful for, put yourself in the shoes of someone who is experiencing misfortunes greater than your own.
- My post is not meant to be political in anyway but just a reflection that the world is looking at us and probably thinking, America what is going with you? I get it and I can't help to feel sad and disappointed about our di-

rection as people, a country and realize we have a lot of work to do.

- I am thankful I get the chance to have a roof over my head, clothes on my back, two jobs, a car, some money, a beautiful wife and daughter that I adore and hopefully adore me back (Haha). At the end of day, the people in our life is what is important not things although I get things like a big home, money, a nice car do make life a whole lot sweeter and more comfortable but I believe money and wealth will not buy you happiness because if that was true why do so many rich and famous take their lives.
- Back to my point, what are you thankful for? Are you thankful for good health, your family, your education whatever it may be remember why your thankful? Each morning is so important to just thank the stars that you have something to be thankful for, many today don't feel they can. Many today are having lost complete hope as they look around. I remember those days in my life when the outside appeared, I had everything, and one would say I have nothing to be unhappy or unthankful for.
- As my family and I celebrate Thanksgiving reflecting on the year, my life and years of thanks remembering that I could be in far worse place in my life and have been, but we must give thanks. Many of you who may read this may think I have nothing to be thankful for, I lost my job, I am sick, no money, negative, negative, negative. I get it , its tough to see the good in your life, remembering even life itself is a gift and we should thankful,

as someone who has suffered with manic depression and who at one point lost sight of my life and giving thanks remembering life is short and we must live it to the fullest appreciating it regardless of the ups and downs it is worth appreciating and being thankful.

- This year certainly has been tough, the word tough many be an understatement, but this is the time of year to tell those in your life you are thankful for them, you love them and show it in a social distancing kind of way.
- I know not everyone will share my sentiment of thankfulness as many will reflect on what is wrong with the world and their lives spreading hate and dissatisfaction online and to those around them and I say Stop. Stop being unthankful, stop hating and remember it's not us versus them, we are one all human and should treat each other as such, regardless if you agree with ones beliefs and values or not just be kind, be thankful and remember what is in important in your life.
- Again if this message came off preachy I apologize, my heart and intentions are good and felt it in my heart to remember what is important and so should you! Wishing all those who celebrate Thanksgiving a peaceful holiday and if you don't celebrate, you can still be thankful every day of the year.

AFTERWORD

I can truly say that having this blog gave me focus in a way I didn't have before as it reignited my love of writing, putting my thoughts, my emotions into words. Starting of the blog also forced to reach for a long goal I never thought was possible which was to be a novelist as since 2019 I began to write my first book the POX, which was self published in 2023 after years of editing, years of pain which is detailed in my blogs from my happiness to my sadness to my pain, ultimately leading to my poor state of mental health. My blog began and has become my therapy even today.

Blogs can be a look in time for many, depending on what a person makes their blog about as you can make a blog about anything food, mental health, cars, gardening and the list goes on, but for myself, I made this blog my journal, my ability to share my thoughts with the world, although my voice is not widespread. I do have followers, but I doubt they hang on my every word, which is one of the reasons I write books.

Deciding to turn my blogs into a book for the world to read if they choose, but really its meant to be a stamp in time for what I was going through at that specific time, that day and my state of mind. Often its going through it, but there are moments of happiness, joy, celebration, milestones, but man blogs are filled with my depression, my self loathing, my pain, maybe not physical but mental anguish.

My blog can be bit of a roller coaster at times, but my other hope is that my family, my daughter, my wife can have something that displays who am, how I think, my thought process and my internal war. Choosing not to share my blogs with my young daughter as if she was to read them they may frighten her and she may not fully understand, but will one day when she is older. My wife on the other hand does read my blogs, they give her insight to my pain, my heart ache and my depression, which concerns her gravely, when I speak of death and suicide, which I often speak of, but try to assure her I am okay, but the damage is done. Goes to show you the effects that go on inside of each of us can affect those we care about and love if they were just to read our thoughts, they each get a glimpse into each of us. But I have found that many don't like to write, journal finding it a useless task, but I found it enlightening and it can bring enlightenment to you if we just did it more.

I hope each who read my blogs enjoy, but at the same time empathize and allow you to self-reflect on your own life, your own joy and pain and maybe push yourself to write, another theme of my writing is just to write, a simple pen and paper will do, but have found word press to be incredible for my writing journey and this blog was the result. Those who read are coming along my writing journey and appreciate you for that.

WORKS

Short Stories

- Gutierrez, Joseph., **Short Stories From a Child's Mind – Animal Friends Edition**, Pub. May 12th, 2024, ISBN: 9798869320803, 68 pgs.
- Gutierrez, Joseph. , **Short Stories From a Child's Mind – Swashbuckler & Gunslinger Edition**, Pub. June 18th, 2024, ISBN: 9798869332608, 84 pgs.
- Gutierrez, Joseph. , **Short Stories From a Child's Mind – The Monster's Edition**, Pub. July 8th , 2024, ISBN: 9798869341525, 40 pgs.
- Gutierrez, Joseph., **Short Stories from a Child's Mind – A Collection**, Pub. Aug 30th, 2025, ISBN: 9798348540555, 180 pgs.

Non-Fiction

- Gutierrez, Joseph., **The Forgotten Son- Chapter 2**, Pub. Oct 31st, 2025: 9798348532901, 282 Pgs.
- Gutierrez, Joseph., **The Forgotten Son- Chapter 1**, Pub. June 15th, 2025: 9798348523930, 204 Pgs.
- Gutierrez, Joseph., **The Forgotten Son**, Pub. February 7th, 2025: 9798348211059, 840 Pgs.

<u>**Novels**</u>

- Meyer, Joe R., **The Pox**, Pub. June 18, 2023, ISBN: 9781088235973, **First Edition (Out of Print)**
- Meyer, Joe R., **The Pox**, Pub. January 18th, 2025, **Second Edition**, ISBN: 9798330560424, 420 pgs.
- Meyer, Joe R., **The Menagerie Locket**, Pub. March 17th, 2024, ISBN: 9798869186348, 254 pgs.
- Meyer, Joe R., **Pounds of Flesh**, Pub. October 2nd, 2024, ISBN: 9798330371617, 246 pgs.

www.ingramcontent.com/pod-product-compliance
Lightning Source LLC
LaVergne TN
LVHW052220200926
848481LV00001B/168

* 9 7 9 8 3 4 8 5 7 5 4 7 2 *